NN-Y-2

LOUISA, DUCHESS OF ABERCORN, IN HER NINETY-FIRST YEAR,
WITH HER GRANDSON'S GRANDSON, LORD DUNGLASS

THE DAYS BEFORE YESTERDAY

2.

BY

LORD FREDERIC HAMILTON

AUTHOR OF
"THE VANISHED POMPS OF YESTERDAY," "NINE HOLIDAY ADVENTURES
OF MR. P. J. DAVENANT,' ETC., ETC.

HODDER AND STOUGHTON
LIMITED   LONDON

TO

MY BROTHER

ERNEST

FOREWORD

THE Public has given so kindly a reception to *The Vanished Pomps of Yesterday* (a reception which took its author wholly by surprise), that I have extracted some further reminiscences from the lumber-room of recollections. Those who expect startling revelations, or stale whiffs of forgotten scandals in these pages, will, I fear, be disappointed, for the book contains neither. It is merely a record of everyday events, covering different ground to those recounted in the former book, which may, or may not, prove of interest. I must tender my apologies for the insistent recurrence of the first person singular; in a book of this description this is difficult to avoid.

London, 1920.

CONTENTS

V

CONTENTS

CHAPTER IV

CHAPTER V

CHAPTER VI

CHAPTER VII

CONTENTS

vii

CONTENTS

CHAPTER I

I WAS born the thirteenth child of a family of
fourteen, on the thirteenth day of the month, and
I have for many years resided at No. 13 in a certain
street in Westminster. In spite of the popular
prejudice attached to this numeral, I am not
conscious of having derived any particular ill-
fortune from my accidental association with it.

Owing to my sequence in the family procession,
I found myself on my entry into the world already
equipped with seven sisters and four surviving
brothers. I was also in the unusual position of
being born an uncle, finding myself furnished with
four ready-made nephews — the present Lord
Durham, his two brothers Mr. Frederick Lambton
and Admiral-of-the-Fleet Sir Hedworth Meux,
and the late Lord Lichfield.

Looking down the long vista of sixty years with
eyes that have already lost their keen vision, the

B

most vivid impression that remains of my early childhood is the nightly ordeal of the journey down "The Passage of Many Terrors" in our Irish home. It had been decreed that, as I had reached the mature age of six, I was quite old enough to come downstairs in the evening by myself without the escort of a maid, but no one seemed to realise what this entailed on the small boy immediately concerned. The house had evidently been built by some malevolent architect with the sole object of terrifying little boys. Never, surely, had such a prodigious length of twisting, winding passages and such a superfluity of staircases been crammed into one building, and as in the early "sixties" electric light had not been thought of, and there was no gas in the house, these endless passages were only sparingly lit with dim colza-oil lamps. From his nursery the little boy had to make his way alone through a passage and up some steps. These were brightly lit, and concealed no terrors. The staircase that had to be negotiated was also reassuringly bright, but at its base came the "Terrible Passage." It was interminably long, and only lit by an oil lamp at its far end. Almost at once a long corridor running at right angles to the main one, and plunged in total darkness, had to be crossed. This was an awful place, for under a marble slab in its dim recesses a stuffed crocodile reposed. Of course in the day-time the crocodile *pretended* to be very dead, but every one knew that as soon as it grew dark, the crocodile came to life again, and padded noiselessly about the passage on its scaly paws seeking for its prey, with its great cruel jaws snapping, its fierce teeth gleaming, and its horny tail lashing savagely from side to side. It was also a matter of common knowledge that the favourite article of diet of crocodiles was a little boy with bare legs in a white suit.

Even should one be fortunate enough to escape the crocodile's jaws, there were countless other terrors awaiting the traveller down this awe-inspiring passage. A little farther on there was a dark lobby, with cupboards surrounding it. Any one examining these cupboards by daylight would have found that they contained innocuous cricket-bats and stumps, croquet-mallets and balls, and sets of bowls. But as soon as the shades of night fell, these harmless sporting accessories were changed by some mysterious and malign agency into grizzly bears, and grizzly bears are notoriously the fiercest of their species. It was advisable to walk very quickly, but quietly, past the lair of the grizzlies, for they would have gobbled up a little boy in one second. Immediately after the bears' den came the culminating terror of all—the haunt of the wicked little hunchbacks. These malignant little beings inhabited an arched and recessed cross-passage. It was their horrible habit to creep noiselessly behind their victims, tip . . . tip . . . tip-toeing silently but swiftly behind their prey, and then . . . with a sudden spring they threw themselves on to little boys' backs, and getting their arms round their necks, they remorselessly throttled the life out of them. In the early "sixties" there was a perfect epidemic of so-called "garrotting" in London. Harmless citizens proceeding peaceably homeward through unfrequented streets or down suburban roads at night were suddenly seized from behind by nefarious hands, and found arms pressed under their chins against their windpipe, with a second hand drawing their heads back until they collapsed insensible, and could be despoiled leisurely of any valuables they might happen to have about them. Those familiar with John Leech's *Punch Albums* will recollect how many of his drawings turned on this outbreak of garrotting. The little boy had heard his elders talking about this garrotting, and had somehow mixed it up with a story about hunchbacks and the fascinating local tales about "the wee people," but the terror was a very real one for all that. The hunchbacks baffled, there only remained a dark archway to pass, but this archway led to the "Robbers' Passage." A peculiarly bloodthirsty gang of malefactors had their fastnesses along this passage, but the dread of being in the immediate neighbourhood of such a band of desperadoes was considerably modified by the increasing light, as the solitary oil-lamp of the passage was approached. Under the comforting beams of this lamp the little boy would pause until his heart began to thump less wildly after his deadly perils, and he would turn the handle of the door and walk into the great hall as demurely as though he had merely traversed an ordinary everyday passage in broad daylight. It was very reassuring to see the big hall blazing with light, with the logs roaring on the open hearth, and grown-ups writing, reading, and talking unconcernedly, as though unconscious of the awful dangers lurking within a few yards of them. In that friendly atmosphere, what with toys and picture-books, the fearful experiences of the "Passage of Many Terrors" soon faded away, and the return journey upstairs would be free from alarms, for Catherine, the nursery-maid, would come to fetch the little boy when his bedtime arrived.

Catherine was fat, freckled, and French. She was also of a very stolid disposition. She stumped unconcernedly along the "Passage of Terrors," and any reference to its hidden dangers of robbers, hunchbacks, bears, and crocodiles only provoked the remark, "Quel tas de bêtises!" In order to reassure the little boy, Catherine took him to view the stuffed crocodile reposing inertly under its marble slab. Of course, before a grown-up the crocodile would pretend to be dead and stuffed, but . . . the little boy knew better. It occurred gleefully to him, too, that the plump French damsel might prove more satisfactory as a repast to a hungry saurian than a skinny little boy with thin legs. In the cheerful nursery, with its fragrant peat fire (we called it "turf"), the terrors of the evening were quickly forgotten, only to be renewed with tenfold activity next evening, as the moment for making the dreaded journey again approached.

The little boy had had the *Pilgrim's Progress* read to him on Sundays. He envied "Christian," who not only usually enjoyed the benefit of some reassuring companion, such as "Mr. Interpreter," or "Mr. Greatheart," to help him on his road, but had also been expressly told, "Keep in the midst of the path, and no harm shall come to thee." This was distinctly comforting, and Christian enjoyed another conspicuous advantage. All the lions he encountered in the course of his journey were chained up, and could not reach him provided he adhered to the Narrow Way. The little boy thought seriously of tying a rolled-up table-cloth to his back to represent Christian's pack; in his white suit, he might perhaps then pass for a pilgrim, and the strip of carpet down the centre of the passage would make an admirable Narrow Way, but it all depended on whether the crocodile, bears, and hunchbacks knew, and would observe the rules of the game. It was most improbable that the crocodile had ever had the *Pilgrim's Progress* read to him in his youth, and he might not understand that the carpet representing the Narrow Way was inviolable territory. Again, the bears might make their spring before they realised that, strictly speaking, they ought to consider themselves chained up. The ferocious little hunchbacks were clearly past praying for; nothing would give them a sense of the most elementary decency.

On the whole, the safest plan seemed to be, on reaching the foot of the stairs, to keep an eye on the distant lamp and to run to it as fast as short legs and small feet could carry one. Once safe under its friendly beams, panting breath could be recovered, and the necessary stolid look assumed before entering the hall.

There was another voyage, rich in its promise of ultimate rewards, but so perilous that it would only be undertaken under escort. That was to the housekeeper's room through a maze of basement passages. On the road two fiercely-gleaming roaring pits of fire had to be encountered. Grown-ups said this was the furnace that heated the house, but the little boy had his own ideas on the subject. Every Sunday his nurse used to read to him out of a little devotional book, much in vogue in the "sixties," called *The Peep of Day*, a book with the most terrifying pictures. One Sunday evening, so it is said, the little boy's mother came into the nursery to find him listening in rapt attention to what his nurse was reading him.

"Emery is reading to me out of a good book," explained the small boy quite superfluously.

"And do you like it, dear?"

"Very much indeed."

"What is Emery reading to you about? Is it about Heaven?"

"No, it's about 'ell," gleefully responded the little boy, who had not yet found all his "h's."

Those glowing furnace-bars; those roaring

flames . . . there could be no doubt whatever about it. A hymn spoke of "Gates of Hell" . . . of course they just called it the heating furnace to avoid frightening him. The little boy became acutely conscious of his misdeeds. He had taken . . . no, stolen an apple from the nursery pantry and had eaten it. Against all orders he had played with the taps in the sink. The burden of his iniquities pressed heavily on him; remembering the encouraging warnings Mrs. Fairchild, of *The Fairchild Family*, gave her offspring as to their certain ultimate destiny when they happened to break any domestic rule, he simply dared not pass those fiery apertures alone. With his hand in that of his friend Joseph, the footman, it was quite another matter. Out of gratitude, he addressed Joseph as "Mr. Greatheart," but Joseph, probably unfamiliar with the *Pilgrim's Progress*, replied that his name was Smith.

The interminable labyrinth of passages threaded, the warm, comfortable housekeeper's room, with its red curtains, oak presses and a delicious smell of spice pervading it, was a real haven of rest. To this very day, nearly sixty years afterwards, it still looks just the same, and keeps its old fragrant spicy odour. Common politeness dictated a brief period of conversation, until Mrs. Pithers, the housekeeper, should take up her wicker key-basket and select a key (the second press on the left). From that inexhaustible treasure-house dates and figs would appear, also dried apricots and those little discs of crystallised apple-paste which, impaled upon straws, and coloured green, red and yellow, were in those days manufactured for the special delectation of greedy little boys. What a happy woman Mrs. Pithers must have been with such a prodigal wealth of delicious products always at her command! It was comforting, too, to converse with Mrs. Pithers, for though this intrepid woman was alarmed neither by bears, hunchbacks nor crocodiles, she was terribly frightened by what she termed "cows," and regulated her daily walks so as to avoid any portion of the park where cattle were grazing. Here the little boy experienced a delightful sense of masculine superiority. He was not the least afraid of cattle, or of other things in daylight and the open air; of course at night in dark passages infested with bears and little hunchbacks . . . Well, it was obviously different. And yet that woman who was afraid of "cows" could walk without a tremor, or a little shiver down the spine, past the very "Gates of Hell," where they roared and blazed in the dark passage.

Our English home had brightly-lit passages, and was consequently practically free from bears and robbers. Still, we all preferred the Ulster home in spite of its obvious perils. Here were a chain of lakes, wide silvery expanses of gleaming water reflecting the woods and hills. Here were great tracts of woodlands where countless little burns chattered and tinkled in their rocky beds as they hurried down to the lakes, laughing as they tumbled in miniature cascades over rocky ledges into swirling pools, in their mad haste to reach the placid waters below. Here were purple heather-clad hills, with their bigger brethren rising mistily blue in the distance, and great wine-coloured tracts of bog (we called them "flows") interspersed with glistening bands of water, where the turf had been cut which hung over the village in a thin haze of fragrant blue smoke.

The woods in the English place were beautifully kept, but they were uninteresting, for there were no rocks or great stones in them. An English brook was a dull, prosaic, lifeless stream, rolling its clay-stained waters stolidly along, with never a dimple of laughter on its surface, or a joyous little gurgle of surprise at finding that it was suddenly called upon to take a headlong leap of ten feet. The English brooks were so silent, too, compared to our noisy Ulster burns, whose short lives were one clamorous turmoil of protest against the many obstacles with which nature had barred their progress to the sea; here swirling over a miniature crag, there babbling noisily among a labyrinth of stones. They ultimately became merged in a foaming roaring salmon river expanding into amber-coloured pools, or breaking into white rapids; a river which retained to the last its lordly independence and reached the sea still free, refusing to be harnessed or confined by man. Our English brook, after its uneventful childhood, made its stolid matter-of-fact way into an equally dull little river which crawled inertly along to its destiny somewhere down by the docks. I know so many people whose whole lives are like that of that particular English brook.

We lived then in London at Chesterfield House, South Audley Street, which covered three times the amount of ground it does at present, for at the back it had a very large garden, on which Chesterfield Gardens are now built. In addition to this it had two wings at right angles to it, one now occupied by Lord Leconfield's house, the other by Nos. 1 and 2, South Audley Street. The left-hand wing was used as our stables and contained a well which enjoyed an immense local reputation in Mayfair. Never was such drinking-water! My father allowed any one in the neighbourhood to fetch their drinking-water from our well, and one of my earliest recollections is watching the long daily procession of men-servants in the curious yellow-jean jackets of the "sixties," each with two large cans in his hands, fetching the day's supply of our matchless water. No inhabitants of Curzon Street, Great Stanhope Street, or South Audley Street would dream of touching any water but that from the famous Chesterfield House spring. In 1867 there was a serious outbreak of Asiatic cholera in London, and my father determined to have the water of the celebrated spring analysed. There were loud protests at this:—what, analyse the finest drinking-water in England! My father, however, persisted, and the result of the analysis was that our incomparable drinking-water was found to contain thirty per cent. of organic matter. The analyst reported that fifteen per cent. of the water must be pure sewage. My father had the spring sealed and bricked up at once, but it is a marvel that we had not poisoned every single inhabitant of the Mayfair district years before.

In the early "sixties" the barbarous practice of sending wretched little "climbing boys" up chimneys to sweep them still prevailed. In common with most other children of that day, I was perfectly terrified when the chimney-sweep arrived with his attendant coal-black imps, for the usual threat of foolish nurses to their charges when they proved refractory was, "If you are not good I shall give you to the sweep, and then you will have to climb up the chimney." When the dust-sheets laid on the floors announced the advent of the sweeps, I used, if possible, to hide until they had left the house. I cannot understand how public opinion tolerated for so long the abominable cruelty of forcing little boys to clamber up flues. These unhappy brats were made to creep into the chimneys from the grates, and then to wriggle their way up by digging their bare toes into the interstices of the bricks, and by working their elbows and knees alternately; stifled in the pitch-darkness of the narrow flue by foul air, suffocated by the showers of soot that fell on them, perhaps losing their way in the black maze of chimneys, and liable at any moment, should they lose their footing,

12

to come crashing down twenty feet, either to be killed outright in the dark or to lie with a broken limb until they were extricated—should, indeed, it be possible to rescue them at all. These unfortunate children, too, were certain to get abrasions on their bare feet and on their elbows and knees from the rough edges of the bricks. The soot working into these abrasions gave them a peculiar form of sore. Think of the terrible brutality to which a nervous child must have been subjected before he could be induced to undertake so hateful a journey for the first time. Should the boy hesitate to ascend, many of the master-sweeps had no compunction in giving him what was termed a "tickler"—that is, in lighting some straw in the grate below him. The poor little urchin had perforce to scramble up his chimney then, to avoid being roasted alive.

All honour to the seventh Earl of Shaftesbury, the philanthropist, who as Lord Ashley never rested in the House of Commons until he got a measure placed on the Statute Book making the employment of climbing-boys illegal.

It will be remembered that little Tom, the hero of Charles Kingsley's delightful *Water-Babies*, was a climbing-sweep. In spite of all my care, I occasionally met some of these little fellows in the passages, inky-black with soot from the soles of their bare feet to the crowns of their heads, except for the whites of their eyes. They could not have been above eight or nine years old. I looked on them as awful warnings, for of course they would not have occupied their present position had they not been little boys who had habitually disobeyed the orders of their nurses.

Even the wretched little climbing-boys had their gala-day on the 1st of May, when they had a holiday and a feast under the terms of Mrs. Montagu's will.

The story of Mrs. Montagu is well known. The large house standing in a garden at the corner of Portman Square and Gloucester Place, now owned by Lord Portman, was built for Mrs. Montagu by James Wyatt at the end of the eighteenth century, and the adjoining Montagu Street and Montagu Square derive their names from her. Somehow Mrs. Montagu's only son got kidnapped, and all attempts to recover the child failed. Time went on, and he was regarded as dead. On a certain 1st of May the sweeps arrived to clean Mrs. Montagu's chimneys, and a climbing-boy was sent up to his horrible task. Like Tom in the *Water-Babies*, he lost his way in the network of flues and emerged in a different room to the one he had started from. Something in the aspect of the room struck a half-familiar, half-forgotten chord in his brain. He turned the handle of the door of the next room and found a lady seated there. Then he remembered. Filthy and soot-stained as he was, the little sweep flung himself into the arms of the beautiful lady with a cry of "Mother!" Mrs. Montagu had found her lost son.

In gratitude for the recovery of her son, Mrs. Montagu entertained every climbing-boy in London at dinner on the anniversary of her son's return, and arranged that they should all have a holiday on that day. At her death she left a legacy to continue the treat.

Such, at least, is the story as I have always heard it.

At the Sweeps' Carnival, there was always a grown-up man figuring as "Jack-in-the-green." Encased in an immense frame of wicker-work covered with laurels and artificial flowers, from the midst of which his face and arms protruded with a comical effect, "Jack-in-the-green" capered slowly about in the midst of the street, surrounded by some twenty little climbing-boys, who danced joyously round him with black faces, their soot-stained clothes decorated with tags of bright ribbon, and making a deafening clamour with their dustpans and brushes as they sang some popular ditty. They then collected money from the passers-by, making usually quite a good haul. There were dozens of these "Jacks-in-the-green" to be seen then on Mayday in the London streets, each one with his attendant band of little black familiars. I summoned up enough courage once to ask a small inky-black urchin whether he had disobeyed his nurse very often in order to be condemned to sweep chimneys. He gaped at me uncomprehendingly, with a grin ; but being a cheerful little soul assured me that, on the whole, he rather enjoyed climbing up chimneys.

It was my father and mother's custom in London to receive any of their friends at luncheon without a formal invitation, and a constant procession of people availed themselves of this privilege. At six years of age I was promoted to lunch in the dining-room with my parents, and I always kept my ears open. I had then one brother in the House of Commons, and we being a politically inclined family, most of the notabilities of the Tory party put in occasional appearances at Chesterfield House at luncheon-time. There was Mr. Disraeli, for whom my father had an immense admiration, although he had not yet occupied the post of Prime Minister. Mr. Disraeli's curiously impassive face, with its entire absence of colouring, rather frightened me. It looked like a mask. He had, too, a most singular voice, with a very impressive style of utterance. After 1868, by which time my three elder brothers were all in the House of Commons, and Disraeli himself was Prime Minister, he was a more frequent visitor at our house.

In 1865 my uncle Lord John Russell, my mother's brother, was Prime Minister. My uncle, who had been born as far back as 1792, was a very tiny man, who always wore one of the old-fashioned, high black-satin stocks right up to his chin. I liked him, for he was always full of fun and small jokes, but in that rigorously Tory household he was looked on with scant favour. It was his second term of office as Prime Minister, for he had been First Lord of the Treasury from 1846 to 1852; he had also sat in the House of Commons for forty-seven years. My father was rather inclined to ridicule his brother-in-law's small stature, and absolutely detested his political opinions, declaring that he united all the ineradicable faults of the Whigs in his diminutive person. Listening, as a child will do, to the conversation of his elders, I derived the most grotesquely false ideas as to the Whigs and their traditional policy. I gathered that, with their tongues in their cheeks, they advocated measures in which they did not themselves believe, should they think that by so doing they would be able to enhance their popularity and maintain themselves in office: that, in order to extricate themselves from some present difficulty, they were always prepared to mortgage the future recklessly, quite regardless of the ultimate consequences: that whilst professing the most liberal principles, they were absurdly exclusive in their private lives, not consorting with all and sundry as we poor Tories did: that convictions mattered less than office: that in fact nothing much mattered, provided that the government of the country remained permanently in the hands of a little oligarchy of Whig families, and that every office of profit under the Crown was, as a matter of course, allotted to some member of those favoured families. In proof of the latter statement, I learnt that the first act of my uncle Lord John, as Prime Minister, had been to appoint

c 17

one of his brothers Serjeant-at-Arms of the House of Commons, and to offer to another of his brothers, the Rev. Lord Wriothesley Russell, the vacant Bishopric of Oxford. Much to the credit of my clergyman-uncle, he declined the Bishopric, saying that he had neither the eloquence nor the administrative ability necessary for so high an office in the Church, and that he preferred to remain a plain country parson in his little parish, of which, at the time of his death, he had been Rector for fifty-six years. All of which only goes to show what absurdly erroneous ideas a child, anxious to learn, may pick up from listening to the conversation of his elders, even when one of those elders happened to be Mr. Disraeli himself.

Another ex-Prime Minister who was often at our house was the fourth Earl of Aberdeen, who had held office many times, and had been Prime Minister during the Crimean War. He must have been a very old man then, for he was born in 1784. I have no very distinct recollection of him. Oddly enough, Lord Aberdeen was both my great-uncle and my step-grandfather, for his first wife had been my grandfather's sister, and after her death, he married my grandfather's widow, his two wives thus being sisters-in-law. Judging by their portraits by Lawrence, which hung round our dining-room, my great-grandfather, old Lord Abercorn's sons and daughters must have been of singular and quite unusual personal beauty. Not one of the five attained the age of twenty-nine, all of them succumbing early to consumption. Lord Aberdeen had a most unfortunate skin and complexion, and in addition he was deeply pitted with small-pox. As a result his face looked exactly like a slice of brown bread, and "Old Brown Bread" he was always called by my elder brothers and sisters, who had but little love for him, for he disliked young people, and always made the most disagreeable remarks he could think of to them. I remember once being taken to see him at Argyll House, Regent Street, on the site of which the "Palladium" now stands. I recollect perfectly the ugly, gloomy house, and its uglier and gloomier garden, but I have no remembrance of "Old Brown Bread" himself, or of what he said to me, which, considering his notorious dislike to children, is perhaps quite as well.

Of a very different type was another constant and always welcome visitor to our house, Sir Edwin Landseer, the painter. He was one of my father and mother's oldest friends, and had been an equally close friend of my grandparents, the Duke and Duchess of Bedford. He had painted three portraits of my father, and five of my mother. Two of the latter had been engraved, and, under the titles of "Cottage Industry" and "The Mask," had a very large sale in mid-Victorian days. His large picture of my two eldest sisters, which hung over our dining-room chimney-piece, had also been engraved, and was a great favourite, under the title of "The

Abercorn Children." Landseer was a most delightful person, and the best company that can be
imagined. My father and mother were quite devoted to him, and both of them always addressed
him as " Lanny." My mother going to call on him
at his St. John's Wood house, found " Lanny " in
the garden, working from a ladder on a gigantic
mass of clay. Turning the corner, she was somewhat alarmed at finding a full-grown lion stretched
out on the lawn. Landseer had been commissioned
by the Government to model the four lions for the
base of Nelson's pillar in Trafalgar Square. He
had made some studies in the Zoological Gardens,
but as he always preferred working from the live
model, he arranged that an elderly and peculiarly
docile lion should be brought to his house from the
Zoo in a furniture van attended by two keepers.
Should any one wish to know what that particular
lion looked like, they have only to glance at the
base of the Nelson pillar. On paying an afternoon
call, it is so unusual to find a live lion included
amongst the guests, that my mother's perturbation
at finding herself in such close proximity to a huge
loose carnivore is, perhaps, pardonable. Landseer
is, of course, no longer in fashion as a painter. I
quite own that at times his colour is unpleasing,
owing to the bluish tint overlaying it; but surely
no one will question his draughtsmanship? And
has there ever been a finer animal-painter? Perhaps
he was really a black-and-white man. My family
possess some three hundred drawings of his: some

in pen and ink, some in wash, some in pencil. I personally prefer his very delicate pencil work, over which he sometimes threw a light wash of colour. No one, seeing some of his pen and ink work, can deny that he was a master of line. A dozen scratches, and the whole picture is there! He painted a charming portrait of my grandmother on panel, all in blacks and greys except for the flesh tints. Landseer preferred painting on panel, and he never would allow his pictures to be varnished. His wishes have been obeyed in that respect ; none of the Landseers my family possess have ever been varnished.

He was certainly an unconventional guest in a country house. My father had rented a deer-forest on a long lease from Cluny Macpherson, and had built a large house there, on Loch Laggan. As that was before the days of railways, the interior of the house at Ardverikie was necessarily very plain, and the rooms were merely whitewashed. Landseer complained that the glare of the whitewash in the dining-room hurt his eyes, and without saying a word to any one, he one day produced his colours, mounted a pair of steps, and proceeded to rough-in a design in charcoal on the white walls. He worked away until he had completely covered the walls with frescoes in colour. The originals of some of his best-known engravings, "The Sanctuary," "The Challenge," "The Monarch of the Glen," made their first appearance on the walls of the dining-room at Ardverikie. The house was unfortunately destroyed by fire some years later, and Landseer's frescoes perished with it.

At another time, my father leased for two years a large house in the Midlands. The dining-hall of this house was hung with hideously wooden full-length portraits of the family owning it. Landseer declared that these monstrous pictures took away his appetite, so without any permission he one day mounted a ladder, put in high-lights with white chalk over the oils, made the dull eyes sparkle, and gave some semblance of life to these forlorn effigies. Pleased with his success, he then brightened up the flesh tints with red chalk, and put some drawing into the faces. To complete his work, he rubbed blacks into the backgrounds with charcoal. The result was so excellent that we let it remain. At the conclusion of my father's tenancy, the family to whom the place belonged were perfectly furious at the disrespect with which their cherished portraits had been treated, for it was a traditional article of faith with them that they were priceless works of art.

Towards the end of his life Landseer became hopelessly insane and, during his periods of violence, a dangerous homicidal maniac. Such an affection, however, had my father and mother for the friend of their young days, that they still had him to stay with us in Kent for long periods. He had necessarily to bring a large retinue with him: his own trained mental attendant; Dr. Tuke, a very celebrated Alienist in his day; and, above all, Mrs.

Pritchard. The case of Mrs. Pritchard is such an instance of devoted friendship as to be worth recording. She was an elderly widow of small means, Landseer's neighbour in St John's Wood; a little dried-up, shrivelled old woman. The two became firm allies, and when Landseer's reason became hopelessly deranged, Mrs. Pritchard devoted her whole life to looking after her afflicted friend. In spite of her scanty means, she refused to accept any salary, and Landseer was like wax in her hands. In his most violent moods when the keeper and Dr. Tuke both failed to quiet him, Mrs. Pritchard had only to hold up her finger and he became calm at once. Either his clouded reason or some remnant of his old sense of fun led him to talk of Mrs. Pritchard as his "pocket Venus." To people staying with us (who, I think, were a little alarmed at finding themselves in the company of a lunatic, however closely watched he might be), he would say, "In two minutes you will see the loveliest of her sex. A little dainty creature, perfect in feature, perfect in shape, who might have stepped bodily out of the frame of a Greuze. A perfect dream of loveliness." They were considerably astonished when a little wizened woman, with a face like a withered apple, entered the room. He was fond, too, of descanting on Mrs. Pritchard's wonderfully virtuous temperament, notwithstanding her amazing charms. Visitors probably reflected that, given her appearance, the path of duty must have been rendered very easy to her.

Landseer painted his last Academy picture, "The Baptismal Font," whilst staying with us. It is a perfectly meaningless composition, representing a number of sheep huddled round a font, for whatever allegorical significance he originally meant to give it eluded the poor clouded brain. As he always painted from the live model, he sent down to the Home Farm for two sheep, which he wanted driven upstairs into his bedroom, to the furious indignation of the housekeeper, who declared, with a certain amount of reason, that it was impossible to keep a house well if live sheep were to be allowed in the best bedrooms. So Landseer, his easel and colours and his sheep were all transferred to the garden.

On another occasion there was some talk about a savage bull. Landseer, muttering "Bulls! bulls! bulls!" snatched up an album of my sister's, and finding a blank page in it, made an exquisite little drawing of a charging bull. The disordered brain repeating "Bulls! bulls! bulls!" he then drew a bulldog, a pair of bullfinches surrounded by bulrushes, and a hooked bull trout fighting furiously for freedom. That page has been cut out and framed for fifty years.

CHAPTER II

EVERY one familiar with John Leech's *Pictures
from Punch* must have an excellent idea of the
outward appearance of the " swells " of the " sixties."

As a child I had an immense admiration for
these gorgeous beings, though, between ourselves,
they must have been abominably loud dressers.
They affected all the year round sealskin waist-
coats, with the festoons of a long watch-chain
meandering over them, above which they exhibited
a huge expanse of black or blue satin, secured by
two scarf-pins of the same design, linked together,
like Siamese twins, by a little chain.

A reference to Leech's drawings will show the
flamboyant checked " pegtop " trousers in which
they delighted. Their principal adornment lay in

their immense "Dundreary" whiskers, usually at least eight inches long. In a high wind these immensely long whiskers blew back over their owners' shoulders in the most comical fashion, and they must have been horribly inconvenient. I determined early in life to affect, when grown-up, longer whiskers than any one else—if possible down to my waist; but alas for human aspirations! By the time that I had emerged from my chrysalis stage, Dundreary whiskers had ceased to be the fashion; added to which unkind Nature had given me a hairless face.

My uncle, old Lord Claud Hamilton, known in our family as "The Dowager," adhered, to the day of his death, to the William IV. style of dress. He wore an old-fashioned black-satin stock right up to his chin, with white "gills" above, and was invariably seen in a blue coat with brass buttons, and a buff waistcoat. My uncle was one of the handsomest men in England, and had sat for nearly forty years in Parliament. He had one curious faculty. He could talk fluently and well on almost any topic at indefinite length, a very useful gift in the House of Commons of those days. On one occasion when it was necessary "to talk a Bill out," he got up without any preparation whatever, and addressed the House in flowing periods for four hours and twenty minutes. His speech held the record for length for many years, but it was completely eclipsed in the early "eighties" by the late Mr. Biggar, who spoke (if my memory serves me right) for nearly six hours on one occasion. Biggar, however, merely read interminable extracts from Blue Books, whereas my uncle indulged in four hours of genuine rhetorical declamation. My uncle derived his nickname from the fact that in our family the second son is invariably christened Claud, so I had already a brother of that name. There happen to be three Lord Claud Hamiltons living now, of three successive generations.

I shall never forget my bitter disappointment the first time I was taken, at a very early age, to see Queen Victoria. I had pictured to myself a dazzling apparition arrayed in sumptuous robes, seated on a golden throne; a glittering crown on her head, a sceptre in one hand, an orb grasped in the other. I had fancied Her Majesty seated thus, motionless during the greater part of the twenty-four hours, simply "reigning." I could have cried with disappointment when a middle-aged lady, simply dressed in widow's "weeds" and wearing a widow's cap, rose from an ordinary arm-chair to receive us. I duly made my bow, but having a sort of idea that it had to be indefinitely repeated, went on nodding like a porcelain Chinese mandarin, until ordered to stop.

Between ourselves, I behaved far better than a brother of mine once did under similar circumstances. Many years before I was born, my father lent his Scotch house to Queen Victoria and the

Prince Consort for ten days. This entailed my two eldest sisters and two eldest brothers vacating their nurseries in favour of the Royal children, and their being transferred to the farm, where they had very cramped quarters indeed. My second brother deeply resented being turned out of his comfortable nursery, and refused to be placated. On the day after the Queen's arrival, my mother took her four eldest children to present them to Her Majesty, my sisters dressed in their best clothes, my brothers being in kilts. They were duly instructed as to how they were to behave, and upon being presented, my two sisters made their curtsies, and my eldest brother made his best bow. "And this, your Majesty, is my second boy. Make your bow, dear," said my mother; but my brother, his heart still hot within him at being expelled from his nursery, instead of bowing, *stood on his head in his kilt*, and remained like that, an accomplishment of which he was very proud. The Queen was exceedingly angry, so later in the day, upon my brother professing deep penitence, he was taken back to make his apologies, when he did precisely the same thing over again, and was consequently in disgrace during the whole of the Royal visit. In strict confidence, I believe that he would still do it to-day, more than seventy-two years later.

During her stay in my father's house the Queen quite unexpectedly announced that she meant to give a dance. This put my mother in a great difficulty, for my sisters had no proper clothes for a ball, and in those pre-railway days it would have taken at least ten days to get anything from Edinburgh or Glasgow. My mother had a sudden inspiration. The muslin curtains in the drawing-room! The drawing-room curtains were at once commandeered; the ladies'-maids set to work with a will, and I believe that my sisters looked extremely well dressed in the curtains, looped up with bunches of rowan or mountain-ash berries.

My mother was honoured with Queen Victoria's close friendship and confidence for over fifty years. At the time of her death she had in her possession a numerous collection of letters from the Queen, many of them very long ones. By the express terms of my mother's will, those letters will never be published. Many of them touch on exceedingly private matters relating to the Royal family, others refer to various political problems of the day. I have read all those letters carefully, and I fully endorse my mother's views. She was honoured with the confidence of her Sovereign, and that confidence cannot be betrayed. The letters are in safe custody, and there they will remain. On reading them it is impossible not to be struck with Queen Victoria's amazing shrewdness, and with her unfailing common sense. It so happens that both a brother and a sister of mine, the late Duchess of Buccleuch, were brought into very close contact with Queen Victoria. It was this quality of strong common sense in the Queen which continually impressed them, as well as her very high standard of duty.

My brother George was twice Secretary of State for India. The Queen was fond of suggesting amendments in the wording of dispatches relating to India, whilst not altering their sense. My brother tells me that the alterations suggested by the Queen were invariably in the direction of simplification. The Queen had a knack of stripping away unnecessary verbiage and reducing a sentence to its simplest form, in which its meaning was unmistakably clear.

All Queen Victoria's tastes were simple. She liked simplicity in dress, in food, and in her surroundings. If I may say so without disrespect, I think that Queen Victoria's great hold on her people came from the fact that, in spite of her high station, she had the ideals, the tastes, the likes and dislikes of the average clean-living, clean-minded wife of the average British professional man, together with the strict ideals as to the sanctity of the marriage-tie, the strong sense of duty, and the high moral standard such wives usually possess.

It is, of course, the easy fashion now to sneer at Victorian standards. To my mind they embody all that is clean and sound in the nation. It does not follow that because Victorians revelled in hideous wall-papers and loved ugly furniture, that therefore their points-of-view were mistaken ones. There are things more important than wall-papers. They certainly liked the obvious in painting, in music, and perhaps in literature, but it hardly seems to follow logically from that, that their conceptions of a man's duty to his wife, family, and country were necessarily false ones. They were not afflicted with the perpetual modern restlessness, nor did they spend "their time in nothing else, but either to tell, or to hear some new thing"; still, all their ideas seem to me eminently sweet and wholesome.

In her old age my mother was the last person living who had seen George III. She remembered perfectly seeing the old King, in one of his rare lucid intervals, driving through London, when he was enthusiastically cheered.

She was also the last person alive who had been at Carlton House which was pulled down in 1826. My mother at the age of twelve danced as a solo "The Spanish Shawl dance" before George IV. at the Pavilion, Brighton. The King was so delighted with her dancing that he went up to her and said, "You are a very pretty little girl, and you dance charmingly. Now is there anything I can do for you?" The child answered, "Yes, there is. Your Majesty can bring me some ham sandwiches and a glass of port-wine negus, for I am very hungry," and to do George IV. justice, he promptly brought them. My mother was painted by a French artist doing her "shawl dance," and if it is a faithful likeness, she must have been an extraordinarily pretty child. On another occasion at a children's party at Carlton House, my uncle, General Lord Alexander Russell, a very outspoken little boy, had been warned by his mother, the Duchess of Bedford, that though the King wore a palpable wig, he was to take no notice whatever of it. To my mother's dismay, she heard her little brother go up to the King and say, " I know that your Majesty wears a wig, but I've been told not to say anything about it, so I promise not to tell any one."

Carlton House stood, from all I can learn, at the top of the Duke of York's steps. Several engravings of its beautiful gardens are still to be found. These gardens extended from the present Carlton House Terrace to Pall Mall. Not only the Terrace, but the Carlton, Reform, Travellers', Athenæum, and United Service Clubs now stand on their site. They were separated from Pall Mall by an open colonnade, and the Corinthian pillars from the front of Carlton House were re-erected in 1834 as the portico of the National Gallery in Trafalgar Square.

As a child I had a wild adoration for Queen Alexandra (then, of course, Princess of Wales), whom I thought the most beautiful person I had ever seen in my life, and I dare say that I was not far wrong. When I was taken to Marlborough House, I remembered and treasured up every single word she said to me. I was not present at the child's tea-party at Marlborough House given by the little Princes, including his present Majesty, when *some one* (my loyalty absolutely refuses to let me say who) suggested that as the woven flowers on the carpet looked rather faded, it might be as well to water them. The boys present, including the little Princes, gleefully emptied can after can of water on to the floor in their attempts to revive the carpet, to the immense improvement of the ceiling and furniture of the room underneath.

In the "sixties" Sunday was very strictly observed. In our own Sabbatarian family, our toys and books all disappeared on Saturday night. On Sundays we were only allowed to read *Line upon Line*, *The Peep of Day*, and *The Fairchild Family*. I wonder if any one ever reads this book now. If they haven't, they should. Mr. and Mrs. Fairchild were, I regret to say it, self-righteous prigs of the deepest dye, whilst Lucy, Emily, and Henry their children were all little prodigies of precocious piety. It was a curious *ménage;* Mr. Fairchild having no apparent means of livelihood, and no recreations beyond perpetually reading the Bible under a tree in the garden. Mrs. Fairchild had the peculiar gift of being able to recite a different prayer off by heart applicable to every conceivable emergency; whilst John, their man-servant, was a real "handy-man," for he was not only gardener, but looked after the horse and trap, cleaned out the pigsties, and waited at table. One wonders in what sequence he performed his various duties, but perhaps the Fairchilds had not

D

sensitive noses. Even the possibly odoriferous John had a marvellous collection of texts at his command. It was refreshing after all this to learn that on one occasion all three of the little Fairchilds got very drunk, which, as the eldest of them was only ten, would seem to indicate that, in spite of their aggressive piety, they had their fair dose of original sin still left in them. I liked the book notwithstanding. There was plenty about eating and drinking ; one could always skip the prayers, and there were three or four very brightly written accounts of funerals in it. I was present at a "Fairchild Family" dinner given some twenty years ago in London by Lady Buxton, wife of the present Governor-General of South Africa, at which every one of the guests had to enact one of the characters of the book.

My youngest brother had a great taste for drawing, and was perpetually depicting terrific steeple-chases. From a confuson of ideas natural to a child, he always introduced a church steeple into the corner of his drawings. One Sunday he had drawn a most spirited and hotly-contested "finish" to a steeple-chase. When remonstrated with on the ground that it was not a "Sunday" subject, he pointed to the church steeple and said, "You don't understand. This is Sunday, and those jockeys are all racing to see which of them can get to church first," which strikes me as a peculiarly ready and ingenious explanation for a child of six.

In London we all went on Sundays to the

Scottish Presbyterian Church in Crown Court, just opposite Drury Lane Theatre. Dr. Cumming, the minister of the church at that time, enjoyed an immense reputation amongst his congregation. He was a very eloquent man, but was principally known as always prophesying the imminent end of the world. He had been a little unfortunate in some of the dates he had predicted for the final cataclysm, these dates having slipped by uneventfully without anything whatever happening, but finally definitely fixed on a date in 1867 as the exact date of the Great Catastrophe. His influence with his flock rather diminished when it was found that Dr. Cumming had renewed the lease of his house for twenty-one years, only two months before the date he had fixed with absolute certainty as being the end of all things. All the same, I am certain that he was thoroughly in earnest and perfectly genuine in his convictions. As a child I thought the church—since rebuilt—absolutely beautiful, but it was in reality a great, gaunt, barn-like structure. It was always crammed. We were very old-fashioned, for we sat down to sing, and we stood to pray, and there was no instrument of any sort. The pew in front of us belonged to Lord Aberdeen, and his brother Admiral Gordon, one of the Elders, always sat in it with his high hat on, conversing at the top of his voice until the minister entered, when he removed his hat and kept silence. This was, I believe, intended as a protest against the idea of there being any special sanctity attached to the building itself *quâ* building. Dr. Cumming had recently introduced an anthem, a new departure rather dubiously welcomed by his flock. It was the singular custom of his congregation to leave their pews during the singing of this anthem and to move about in the aisles; whether as a protest against a daring innovation, or merely to stretch their limbs, or to seek better places, I could never make out.

Dr. Cumming invariably preached for over an hour, sometimes for an hour and a half, and yet I never felt bored or wearied by his long discourses, but really looked forward to them. This was because his sermons, instead of consisting of a string of pious platitudes, interspersed with trite ejaculations and irrelevant quotations, were one long chain of closely-reasoned argument. Granted his first premiss, his second point followed logically from it, and so he led his hearers on point by point, all closely argued, to an indisputable conclusion. I suppose that the inexorable logic of it all appealed to the Scottish side of me. His preaching had the same fascination for me that Euclid's propositions exercised later, even on my hopelessly unmathematical mind.

Whatever the weather, we invariably walked home from Drury Lane to South Audley Street, a long trudge for young feet, as my mother had scruples about using the carriages on Sundays.

Neither my father nor my mother ever dined out on a Sunday, nor did they invite people to dinner on that day, for they wished as far as possible to give those in their employment a day of rest. All quite hopelessly Victorian! for, after all, why should people ever think of anybody but themselves?

Dr. Cumming was a great bee-fancier, and a recognised authority on bees. Calling one day on my mother, he brought with him four queen-bees of a new breed, each one encased in a little paper bag. He prided himself on his skill in handling bees, and proudly exhibited those treasures to my mother. He replaced them in their paper bags, and being a very absent-minded man, he slipped the bags into the tail pocket of his clerical frock-coat. Soon after he began one of his long arguments (probably fixing the exact date of the end of the world), and, totally oblivious of the presence of the bees in his tail pocket, he leant against the mantelpiece. The queen-bees naturally resenting the pressure, stung him through the cloth on that portion of his anatomy immediately nearest to their temporary prison. Dr. Cumming yelled with pain, and began skipping all round the room. It so tickled my fancy to see the grim and austere minister, who towered above me in the pulpit every Sunday, executing a sort of solo-Jazz dance up and down the big room, punctuated with loud cries, that I rolled about on the floor with laughter.

The London of the "sixties" was a very dark and dingy place. The streets were sparingly lit with the dimmest of gas-jets set very far apart; the shop-windows made no display of lights, and the general effect was one of intense gloom.

Until I was seven years old, I had never left the United Kingdom. We then all went to Paris for a fortnight, on our way to the Riviera. I well remember leaving London at 7 a.m. on a January morning, in the densest of fogs. So thick was the fog, that the footman had to lead the horses all the way to Charing Cross Station. Ten hours later I found myself in a fairy city of clean white stone houses, literally blazing with light. I had never imagined such a beautiful, attractive place, and indeed the contrast between the dismal London of the "sixties" and this brilliant, glittering town was unbelievable. Paris certainly deserved the title of "La Ville Lumière" in a literal sense. I like the French expression, "une ville ruisselante de lumière," "a city dripping with light." That is an apt description of the Paris of the Second Empire, for it was hardly a manufacturing city then, and the great rim of outlying factories that now besmirch the white stone of its house fronts had not come into existence, the atmosphere being as clear as in the country. A naturally retentive memory is apt to store up perfectly useless items of information. What possible object can there be in my remembering that the engine which hauled us from Calais to Paris in 1865 was built by J. Cail of Paris, on the "Crampton" system; that is, that the axle of the big single driving-wheels did not run under the frame of the engine, but passed through the " cab " immediately under the pressure-gauge ?—nor can any useful purpose be served in recalling that we crossed the Channel in the little steamer *La France*.

In those days people of a certain class in England maintained far closer social relations with people of the corresponding class in France than is the custom now, and this was mutual. Society in both capitals was far smaller. My father and mother had many friends in Paris, and amongst the oldest of them were the Comte and Comtesse de Flahault. General de Flahault had been the personal aide-de-camp and trusted friend of Napoleon I. Some people, indeed, declared that his connection with Napoleon III. was of a far closer nature, for his great friendship with Queen Hortense was a matter of common knowledge. For some reason or another the old General took a fancy to me, and finding that I could talk French fluently, he used to take me to his room, stuff me with chocolate, and tell me about Napoleon's Russian campaign of 1812, in which he had taken part. I was then seven years old, and the old Comte must have been seventy-eight or so, but it is curious that I should have heard from the actual lips of a man who had taken part in it, the account of the battle of Borodino, of the entry of the French troops into Moscow, of the burning of Moscow, and of the awful sufferings the French underwent during their disastrous retreat from Moscow. General de Flahault had

been present at the terrible carnage of the crossing
of the Beresina on November 26, 1812, and had
got both his feet frost-bitten there, whilst his
faithful servant David had died from the effects of
the cold. I wish that I could have been older
then, or have had more historical knowledge, for it
was a unique opportunity for acquiring information.
I wish, too, that I could recall more of what M. de
Flahault told me. I have quite vivid recollections
of the old General himself, of the room in which
we sat, and especially of the chocolates which
formed so agreeable an accompaniment to our
conversations. Still it remains an interesting link
with the Napoleonic era. This is 1920; that was
1812!

I can never hear Tchaikovsky's "1812 Over-
ture" without thinking of General de Flahault.
The present Lord Lansdowne is the Comte de
Flahault's grandson.

Nearly fifty years later another interesting link
with the past was forged. I was dining with
Prince and Princess Christian of Schleswig-Holstein
at Schomberg House. When the ladies left the
room after dinner, H.R.H. was good enough to
ask me to sit next him. Some train of thought
was at work in the Prince's mind, for he suddenly
said, "Do you know that you are sitting next a
man who once took Napoleon I.'s widow, the
Empress Marie Louise, in to dinner?" and the
Prince went on to say that as a youth of seventeen
he had accompanied his father on a visit to the

Emperor of Austria at Schönbrunn. On the occasion of a state dinner, one of the Austrian Archdukes became suddenly indisposed. Sooner than upset all the arrangements, the young Prince of Schleswig-Holstein was given the ex-Empress to lead in to dinner.

I must again repeat that this is 1920. Napoleon married Marie Louise in 1810.

Both my younger brother and I were absolutely fascinated by Paris, its streets and public gardens. As regards myself, something of the glamour of those days still remains; Paris is not quite to me as other towns, and I love its peculiar smell, which a discriminating nose would analyse as one-half wood-smoke, one-quarter roasting coffee, and one-quarter drains. During the eighteen years of the Second Empire, Paris reached a height of material prosperity and of dazzling brilliance which she has never known before or since. The undisputed social capital of Europe, the equally undisputed capital of literature and art, the great pleasure-city of the world, she stood alone and without a rival. " La Ville Lumière ! " My mother remembered the Paris of her youth as a place of tortuous, abominably paved, dimly lit streets, poisoned with atrocious smells; this glittering town of palaces and broad white avenues was mainly the creation of Napoleon III. himself, aided by Baron Georges Haussmann and the engineer Adolphe Alphand, who between them evolved and made the splendid Paris that we know.

We loved the Tuileries gardens, a most attractive place for children in those days. There were swings and merry-go-rounds; there were stalls where hot *brioches* and *gaufres* were to be bought; there were, above all, little marionette theatres where the most fascinating dramas were enacted. Our enjoyment of these performances was rather marred by our anxious nurse, who was always terrified lest there should be "something French" in the little plays; something quite unfitted for the eyes and ears of two staid little Britons. As the worthy woman was a most indifferent French scholar, we were often hurried away quite unnecessarily from the most innocuous performances when our faithful watch-dog scented the approach of "something French." All the shops attracted us, but especially the delightful toy-shops. Here, again, we were seldom allowed to linger, our trusty guardian being obsessed with the idea that the toy-shops might include amongst their wares "something French." She was perfectly right; there *was* often something "very French," but my brother and I had always seen it and noted it before we were moved off from the windows.

I wonder if any "marchands de coco" still survive in Paris. "Coco" had nothing to do with cocoa, but was a most mawkish beverage compounded principally of liquorice and water. The attraction about it lay in the great tank the vendor carried strapped to his back. This tank was

42

covered with red velvet and gold tinsel, and was surmounted with a number of little tinkling silver bells. In addition to that, the "marchand de coco" carried all over him dozens of silver goblets, or, at all events, goblets that looked like silver, in which he handed out his insipid brew. Who would not long to drink out of a silver cup a beverage that flowed out of a red and gold tank, covered with little silver bells, be it never so mawkish?

The gardens of the Luxembourg were, if any-thing, even more attractive than the Tuileries gardens.

Another delightful place for children was the Hippodrome, long since demolished and built over. It was a huge open-air stadium, where, in addition to ordinary circus performances, there were chariot-races and gladiatorial combats. The great attrac-tion of the Hippodrome was that all the performers were driven into the arena in a real little Cinderella gilt coach, complete with four little ponies, a diminutive coachman, and two tiny little footmen.

Talking of Cinderella, I always wonder that no one has pointed out the curious mistake the original translator of this story fell into. If any one will take the trouble to consult Perrault's *Cendrillon* in the original French, he or she will find that Cinderella went to the ball with her feet encased in "des pantoufles de *vair*." Now, *vair* means grey or white fur, ermine or miniver. The word is now obsolete, though it still survives in heraldry. The translator, misled by the similarity of sound between "vair" and "verre," rendered it "glass" instead of "ermine," and Cinderella's glass slippers have become a British tradition. What would "Cinderella" be as a pantomime without the scene where she triumphantly puts on her glass slipper? And yet, a little reflection would show that it would be about as easy to dance in a pair of glass slippers as it would in a pair of fisherman's waders.

I remember well seeing Napoleon III. and the Empress Eugenie driving down the Rue de Rivoli on their return from the races at Longchamp. I and my brother were standing close to the edge of the pavement, and they passed within a few feet of us. They were driving in a char-à-bancs—in French parlance, "attelé à la Daumont"—that is, with four horses, of which the wheelers are driven from the box by a coachman, and the leaders ridden by a postilion. The Emperor and Empress were attended by an escort of mounted *Cent-Gardes*, and over the carriage there was a curious awning of light blue silk, with a heavy gold fringe, probably to shield the occupants from the sun at the races. I thought the Emperor looked very old and tired, but the Empress was still radiantly beautiful. My young brother, even then a bigoted little patriot, obstinately refused to take off his cap. "He isn't *my* Emperor," he kept repeating, "and I won't do it." The shrill cries of "Vive l'Empereur!" seemed to me a very inadequate substitute for the full-throated cheers with which our own Queen was received when she drove through London. I used to hear the Emperor alluded to as " Badinguet" by the hall-porter of our hotel, who was a Royalist, and consequently detested the Bonapartes.

My father had been on very friendly terms with Napoleon III., then Prince Louis Napoleon, during the period of his exile in London in 1838, when he lived in King Street, St. James'. Prince Louis Napoleon acted as my father's "Esquire" at the famous Eglinton Tournament in August 1839. The tournament, over which such a vast amount of trouble and expense had been lavished, was ruined by an incessant downpour of rain, which lasted four days. My father gave me as a boy the " Challenge Shield " with coat of arms, which hung outside his tent at the tournament, and that shield has always accompanied me in my wanderings. It hangs within a few feet of me as I write, as it hung forty-three years ago in my room in Berlin, and later in Petrograd, Lisbon, and Buenos Ayres.

One of the great sights of Paris in the "sixties," whilst it was still gas-lighted, was the "cordon de lumière de la Rue de Rivoli." As every one knows, the Rue de Rivoli is nearly two miles long, and runs perfectly straight, being arcaded throughout its length. In every arch of the arcades there hung then a gas lamp. At night the continuous ribbon of flame from these lamps, stretching in endless vista down the street, was a fascinatingly beautiful sight. Every French provincial who visited Paris was expected to admire the "cordon de lumière de la Rue de Rivoli." Now that electricity has replaced gas, I fancy that the lamps are placed further apart, and so the effect of a continuous quivering band of yellow flame is lost. Equally every French provincial had to admire the "luxe de gaz" of the Place de la Concorde. It certainly blazed with gas, but now with electric arc-lamps there is double the light with less than a tenth of the number of old flickering gas-lamps; another example of quality *v.* quantity.

Most of my father and mother's French friends lived in the Faubourg Saint Germain. Their houses, though no doubt very fine for entertaining, were dark and gloomy in the daytime. Our little friends of my own age seemed all to inhabit dim rooms looking into courtyards, where, however, we were bidden to unbelievably succulent repasts, very different to the plain fare to which we were accustomed at home. Both my brother and myself were, I think, unconscious as to whether we were speaking English or French; we could express ourselves with equal facility in either language. When I first went to school, I could speak French as well as English, and it is a wonderful tribute to the efficient methods of teaching foreign languages practised in our English schools, that at the end of nine years of French lessons both at a preparatory school and at Harrow, I had not forgotten much more than seventy-five per cent. of the French I knew when I went there. In the same way, after learning German at Harrow for two-and-a-half years, my linguistic attainments in that language were limited to two words, *ja* and *nein*. It is true that, for some mysterious reason, German was taught us at Harrow by a Frenchman who had merely a bowing acquaintanceship with the tongue.

In 1865 the fastest train from Paris to the Riviera took twenty-six hours to accomplish the journey, and then was limited to first-class passengers. There were, of course, neither dining-cars nor sleeping cars, no heating, and no toilet accommodation. Eight people were jammed into a first-class compartment, faintly lit by the dim flicker of an oil lamp, and there they remained. I remember that all the French ladies took off their bonnets or hats, and replaced them with thick knitted woollen hoods and capes combined, which they fastened tightly round their heads. They also drew on knitted woollen over-boots; these, I suppose, were remnants of the times, not very far distant then, when all-night journeys had frequently to be made in the *diligence*.

The Riviera of 1865 was not the garish, flamboyant rendezvous of cosmopolitan finance, of ostentatious newly acquired wealth, and of highly decorative ladies which it has since become. Cannes, in particular, was a quiet little place of surpassing beauty, frequented by a few French and English people, most of whom were there on account of some delicate member of their families. We went there solely because my sister, Lady Mount Edgcumbe, had already been attacked by lung-disease, and to prolong her life it was absolutely necessary for her to winter in a warm climate. Lord Brougham, the ex-Lord Chancellor, had virtually created Cannes, as far as English people were concerned, and the few hotels there were still unpretentious and comfortable.

Amongst the French boys of our own age with whom we played daily was Antoine de Morès, eldest son of the Duc de Vallombrosa. Later on in life the Marquis de Morès became a fanatical Anglophobe, and he lost his life leading an army of irregular Arab cavalry against the British forces in the Sudan; murdered, if I remember right, by his own men. Most regretfully do I attribute Antoine de Morès' violent Anglophobia to the very rude things I and my brother were in the habit of saying to him when we quarrelled, which happened on an average about four times a day.

The favourite game of these French boys was something like our " King of the Castle," only that the victor had to plant his flag on the summit of the " Castle." Amongst our young friends were the two sons of the Duc Des Cars, a strong Legitimist, the Vallombrosa boy's family being Bonapartists. So whilst my brother and I natur-ally carried " Union Jacks," young Antoine de Morès had a tricolour, but the two Des Cars boys carried white silk flags, with a microscopic border

of blue and red ribbon running down either side.
One day, as boys will do, we marched through the
town in procession with our flags, when the police
stopped us and seized the young Des Cars' white
banners, the display of the white flag of the
Bourbons being then strictly forbidden in France.
The Des Cars boys' abbé, or priest-tutor, pointed
out to the police the narrow edging of red and blue
on either side, and insisted on it that the flags were
really tricolours, though the proportion in which
the colours were displayed might be an unusual
one. The three colours were undoubtedly there,
so the police released the flags, though I feel sure
that that abbé must have been a Jesuit.

The Comte de Chambord (the Henri V. of the
Legitimists) was virtually offered the throne of
France in either 1874 or 1875, but all the negotiations failed because he obstinately refused to
recognise the Tricolour, and insisted upon retaining
the white flag of his ancestors. Any one with
the smallest knowledge of the psychology of the
French nation must have known that under no
circumstances whatever would they consent to
abandon their adored Tricolour. The Tricolour is
part of themselves: it is a part of their very souls;
it is more than a flag, it is almost a religion. I
wonder that in 1875 it never occurred to any one
to suggest to the Comte de Chambord the ingenious expedient of the Des Cars boys. The
Tricolour would be retained as the national flag,
but the King could have as his personal standard

a white flag bordered with almost invisible bands of blue and red. Technically, it would still be a tricolour, and on the white expanse the golden fleur-de-lys of the Bourbons could be embroidered, or any other device.

Even had the Comte de Chambord ascended the throne, I am convinced that his tenure of it as Henri V. would have been a very brief one, given the temperament of the French nation.

My youngest brother managed to contract typhoid fever at Cannes about this time, and during his convalescence he was moved to an hotel standing on much higher ground than our villa, on account of the fresher air there. A Madame Goldschmidt was staying at this hotel, and she took a great fancy to the little fellow, then about six years old. On two occasions I found Madame Goldschmidt in my brother's room, singing to him in a voice as sweet and spontaneous as a bird's. My brother was a very highly favoured little mortal, for Madame Goldschmidt was no other than the world-famous Jenny Lind, the incomparable songstress who had had all Europe at her feet. She had then retired from the stage for some years, but her voice was as sweet as ever. The nineteenth century was fortunate in having produced two such peerless singers as Adelina Patti and Jenny Lind "the Swedish Nightingale." The present generation are not likely to hear their equals. Both these great singers had that same curious bird-like quality in their voices; they sang without any effort in crystal-clear tones, as larks sing.

In 1865 it was announced that there would be a great regatta at Cannes in the spring of 1866, and that the Emperor Napoleon would give a special prize for the open rowing (not sculling) championship of the Mediterranean. We further learnt that the whole of the French Mediterranean fleet would be at Villefranche at the time, and that picked oarsmen from the fleet would compete for the championship. My father at once determined to win this prize; the idea became a perfect obsession with him, and he determined to have a special boat built. When we returned to England, he went to Oxford and entered into long consultations with a famous boat-builder there. The boat, a four-oar, had to be built on special lines. She must be light and fast, yet capable of withstanding a heavy sea, for off Cannes the Mediterranean can be very lumpy indeed, and it would be obviously inconvenient to have the boat swamped, and her crew all drowned. The boat-builder having mastered the conditions, felt certain that he could turn out the craft required, which my father proposed to stroke himself.

When we returned to Cannes in 1866, the completed boat was sent out by sea, and we saw her released from her casing with immense interest. She was christened in due form, with a bottle of champagne, by our first cousin, the venerable Lady de Ros, and named the *Abercorn*. Lady de Ros was a daughter of the Duke of Richmond, and had been present at the famous ball in Brussels on the eve of Waterloo in 1815; a ball given by her father in honour of her youngest sister.

The crew then went into serious training. Bow was Sir David Erskine, for many years Serjeant-at-Arms of the House of Commons; No. 2, my brother-in-law, Lord Mount Edgcumbe; No. 3, General Sir George Higginson, with my father as stroke. Lord Elphinstone, who had been in the Navy early in life, officiated as coxswain. But my father was then fifty-five years old, and he soon found out that his heart was no longer equal to the strain to which so long and so very arduous a course (three miles), in rough water, would subject it. As soon as he realised that his age might militate against the chance of his crew winning, he resigned his place in the boat in favour of Sir George Higginson, who was replaced as No. 3 by Mr. Meysey-Clive. My father took Lord Elphinstone's place as coxswain, but here, again, his weight told against him. He was over six feet high and proportionately broad, and he brought the boat's stern too low down in the water, so Lord Elphinstone was re-installed, and my father most reluctantly had to content himself with the rôle of a spectator, in view of his age. The crew dieted strictly, ran in the mornings, and went to bed early. They were none of them in their first youth, for Sir George Higginson was then forty; Sir David Erskine was twenty-eight; my brother-in-law, Lord Mount

Edgcumbe, thirty-four; and Lord Elphinstone thirty-eight.

The great day of the race arrived. We met with one signal piece of ill-luck. Our No. 3, Mr. Meysey-Clive, had gone on board the French flagship, and was unable to get ashore again in time, so at the very last minute a young Cambridge rowing-man, the late Mr. Philip Green, volunteered to replace him, though he was not then in training. The French men-of-war produced huge thirty-oared galleys, with two men at each oar. There were also smaller twenty and twelve-oared boats, but not a single "four" but ours. The sea was heavy and lumpy, the course was five kilometres (three miles), and there was a fresh breeze blowing off the land. Our little mahogany Oxford-built boat, lying very low in the water, looked pitiably small beside the great French galleys. It wasn't even David and Goliath, it was as though "Little Tich" stood up to Georges Carpentier. We saw the race from a sailing yacht; my father absolutely beside himself with excitement.

Off they went! The French galleys lumbering along at a great pace, their crews pulling a curiously short stroke, and their coxswains yelling " En avant, mes braves !" with all the strength of their lungs. It must have been very like the boat-race Virgil describes in the fifth book of the *Æneid*. There was the "huge *Chimæra*," the "mighty *Centaur*," and possibly even the "dark-blue *Scylla*," with their modern counterparts of Gyas, Sergestus, and Cloanthus, bawling just as lustily as doubtless those coxswains of old shouted ; no one, however, struck on the rocks, as we are told the unfortunate "*Centaur*" did. Still the little mahogany-built *Abercorn* continued to forge ahead of her unwieldy French competitors. The Frenchmen splashed and spurted nobly, but the little Oxford-built boat increased her lead, her silken "Union Jack" trailing in the water. All the muscles of the French fleet came into play ; the admiral's barge churned the water into creaming foam ; "mes braves" were incited to superhuman exertions ; in spite of it all the *Abercorn* shot past the mark-boat, a winner by a length and a half.

My father was absolutely frantic with delight. We reached the shore long before our crew did, for they had to return to receive the judge's formal award. He ceremoniously decorated our boat's bows with a large laurel-wreath, and so—her stem adorned with laurels, and the large silk "Union Jack" trailing over her stern—the little mahogany Oxford-built boat paddled through the lines of her French competitors. I am sorry to have to record that the French took their defeat in a most unsportsmanlike fashion ; the little *Abercorn* was received all down the line with storms of hoots and hisses. Possibly we, too, might feel annoyed if, say at Portsmouth, in a regatta in which all the crack oarsmen of the British Home Fleet were competing, a French four should suddenly appear from nowhere, and walk off with the big prize of the day. Still, the conditions of the Cannes regatta were clear; this was an open race, open to any nationality, and to any rowing craft of any size or build, though the result was thought a foregone certainty for the French naval crews.

Our crew were terribly exhausted when they landed. They had had a very severe pull, in a heavy sea, and with a strong head-wind against them, and most of them were no longer young; still, after a bath and a change of clothing, and, quite possibly, a brandy-and-soda or two (nobody ever drank whisky in the "sixties"), they pulled themselves together again. It was Lord Mount Edgcumbe who first suggested that as there was an afternoon dance that day at the *Cercle Nautique de la Méditerranée*, they should all adjourn to the club and dance vigorously, just to show what sturdy, hard-bitten dogs they were, to whom a strenuous three-mile pull in a heavy sea was a mere trifle, even though some of them were forty years old. So off we all went to the *cercle*, and I well remember seeing my brother-in-law and Sir George Higginson gyrating wildly and ceaselessly round the ball-room, tired out though they were. Between ourselves, our French friends were immensely impressed with this exhibition of British vigour, and almost forgave our boat for having won the rowing championship of the Mediterranean.

At the Villa Beaulieu where we lived, there were immense rejoicings that night. Of course all our crew dined there, and I was allowed to come down to dinner myself. Toasts were proposed; healths were drunk again and again. Speeches were made, and the terrific cheering must have seriously weakened the rafters and roof of the house. No one grudged my father his immense satisfaction, for after all he had originated the idea of winning the championship of the Mediterranean, and had had the boat built at his sole expense, and it was not his defects as an oarsman but his fifty-five years which had prevented him from stroking his own boat.

Long after I had been sent to bed, I heard the uproar from below continuing, and, in the strictest confidence, I have every reason to believe that they made a real night of it.

Two of that crew are still alive. Gallant old Sir George Higginson was born in 1826, consequently the General is now ninety-four years of age. The splendid old veteran's mental faculties are as acute as ever; he is not afflicted with deafness and he is still upright as a dart, though his eyesight has failed him. It is to Sir George and to Sir David Erskine that I am indebted for the greater portion of the details concerning this boat-race of 1866, and of its preliminaries, for many of these would not have come within the scope of my knowledge at nine years of age.

Sir David Erskine, the other member of the crew still surviving, ex-Serjeant-at-Arms, was a most familiar, respected, and greatly esteemed personality to all those who have sat in the House of Commons during the last forty years. I might perhaps have put it more strongly; for he was invariably courteous, and such a great gentleman. Sir David was born in 1838, consequently he is now eighty-two years old.

One of my brothers has still in his keeping a very large gold medal. One side of it bears the effigy of " Napoleon III., Empereur des Français." The other side testifies that it is the " Premier Prix d'Avirons de la Méditerrannée, 1866." The ugly hybrid word " Championnat " for " Championship " had not then been acclimatised in France.

Shortly after the boat-race, being now nine years old, I went home to England to go to school.

CHAPTER III

UPON returning from school for my first holidays,
I learnt that my father had been appointed Lord-
Lieutenant of Ireland, and that we were in con-
sequence to live now for the greater portion of the
year in Dublin.

We were all a little doubtful as to how we
should like this new departure. Dublin was, of
course, fairly familiar to us from our stays there,
when we travelled to and from the north of Ireland.
Some of the minor customs of the "sixties" seem
so remote now that it may be worth while recalling
them. In common with most Ulster people, we
always stayed at the Bilton Hotel in Dublin, a fine
old Georgian house in Sackville Street. Everything at the Bilton was old, solid, heavy, and

eminently respectable. All the plate was of real
Georgian silver, and all the furniture in the big
gloomy bedrooms was of solid, not veneered,
mahogany. Quite invariably my father was received in the hall, on arrival, by the landlord,
with a silver candlestick in his hand. The landlord then proceeded ceremoniously to "light us
upstairs" to a sitting-room on the first floor,
although the staircase was bright with gas. This
was a survival from the eighteenth century, when
staircases and passages in inns were but dimly
lit; but it was an attention that was expected.
In the same way, when dinner was ready in our
sitting-room, the landlord always brought in the
silver soup-tureen with his own hands, placed it
ceremoniously before my father, and removed the
cover with a great flourish; after which he retired,
and left the rest to the waiter. This was another
traditional attention.

Towards the end of dinner it became my father's
turn to repay these civilities. Though he himself
very rarely touched wine, he would look down the
wine-list until he found a peculiarly expensive port.
This he would order for what was then termed
"the good of the house." When this choice
product of the Bilton bins made its appearance,
wreathed in cobwebs, in a wicker cradle, my father
would send the waiter with a message to the
landlord, "My compliments to Mr. Massingberg,
and will he do me the favour of drinking a glass of
wine with me." So the landlord would reappear,

and sitting down opposite my father, they would solemnly dispose of the port, and let us trust that it never gave either of them the faintest twinge of gout. These little mutual attentions were then expected on both sides. Neither my father nor mother ever used the word "hotel" in speaking of any hostelry in the United Kingdom. Like all their contemporaries they always spoke of an "inn."

In 1860 a new contract had been signed with the Post Office by the London and North-Western Railway and the City of Dublin Steam-Packet Co., by which they jointly undertook to convey the mails between London and Dublin in eleven hours. Up to 1860, the time occupied by the journey was from fourteen to sixteen hours. Everything in this world being relative, this was rapidity itself compared to the five days my uncle, Lord John Russell, the future Prime Minister, spent on the journey in 1806. He was then a schoolboy at Westminster, his father, the sixth Duke of Bedford, being Lord-Lieutenant of Ireland. My uncle, who kept a diary from his earliest days, gives an account of this journey in it. He spent three days going by stage-coach to Holyhead, sleeping on the way at Coventry and Chester, and thirty-eight hours crossing the Channel in a sailing-packet. The wind shifting, the packet had to land her passengers at Balbriggan, twenty-one miles north of Dublin, from which my uncle took a special post-chaise to Dublin, presenting his glad parents, on his arrival, with a bill for £31 16s., a nice fare for a boy of fourteen to pay for going home for his holidays!

In order to fulfil the terms of the 1860 contract, the mail-trains had to cover the 264 miles between London and Holyhead at an average rate of 42 miles per hour; an unprecedented speed in those days. People then thought themselves most heroic in entrusting their lives to a train that travelled with such terrific velocity as the "Wild Irishman." It was to meet this acceleration that Mr. Ramsbottom, the Locomotive Superintendent of the London and North-Western Railway, devised a scheme for laying water-troughs between the rails, by which the engine could pick up water through a scoop whilst running. I have somewhere seen this claimed as an American innovation, but the North-Western engines have been picking up water daily now, ever since 1861; nearly sixty years ago.

The greatest improvement, however, was effected in the cross-Channel passage. To accomplish the sixty-five miles between Holyhead and Kingstown in the contract time of four hours, the City of Dublin Co. built four paddle-vessels, far exceeding any cross-Channel steamer then afloat in tonnage, speed and accommodation. They were over three hundred feet in length, of two thousand tons burden, and had a speed of fifteen knots. Of these the *Munster*, *Connaught*, and *Ulster* were built by Laird of Birkenhead, whilst the *Leinster* was built in London by Samuda. These boats were most elaborately and comfortably fitted up, and many people of my age, who were in the habit of travelling constantly to Ireland, retain a feeling of almost personal affection for these old paddle-wheel mail-boats which carried them so often in safety across St. George's Channel. It is possible that this feeling may be stronger in those who, like myself, are unaffected by sea-sickness. I think that we all took a pride in the finest Channel steamers then afloat, and, as a child, I was always conscious of a little added dignity and an extra ray of reflected glory when crossing in the *Leinster* or the *Connaught*, for they had four funnels each. I think that I am correct in saying that these splendid sea-boats never missed one single passage, whatever the weather, for nearly forty years, until they were superseded by the present three thousand tons, twenty-four knot twin-screw boats. The old paddle-wheelers were rejuvenated in 1883, when they were fitted with forced draught, and their paddles were submerged deeper, giving them an extra speed of two knots. Their engines being "simple," they consumed a perfectly ruinous amount of coal, sixty-four tons for the round trip; considerably more than the coal consumption of the present twenty-four knotters.

In the "sixties" a new Lord-Lieutenant crossed in a special mail-steamer, for which he had the privilege of paying.

When my father went over to be sworn-in, we arrived at Holyhead in the evening, and on going on board the special steamer *Munster*, we found a sumptuous supper awaiting us.

There is an incident connected with that supper of which, of course, I knew nothing at the time, but which was told me more than thirty years after by Mrs. Campbell, the comely septuagenarian head-stewardess of the *Munster*, who had been in the ship for forty-four years. Most habitual travellers to Ireland will cherish very kindly recollections of genial old Mrs. Campbell, with her wonderfully fresh complexion and her inexhaustible fund of stories.

It appears that the supper had been supplied by a firm of Dublin caterers, who sent four of their own waiters with it, much to the indignation of the steward's staff, who resented this as a slight on their professional abilities.

Mrs. Campbell told me the story in some such words as these :

" About ten minutes before your father, the new Lord-Lieutenant, was expected, the chief-steward put his head into the ladies' cabin and called out to me, ' Mrs. Campbell, ma'am ! For the love of God come into the saloon this minute.' ' What is it, then, Mr. Murphy ? ' says I. ' Wait till ye see,' says he. So I go into the saloon where there was the table set out for supper, so grand that ye wouldn't believe it, and them four Dublin waiters was all lying dead-drunk on the saloon floor.

" ' I put out the spirit decanters on the supper table,' says Mr. Murphy, ' and see ! Them Dublin waiters have every drop of it drunk on me,' he goes on, showing me the empty decanters. 'They have three bottles of champagne drunk on me besides. What will we do with them now? The new Lord-Lieutenant may be arriving this minute, and we have no time to move the drunk waiters for'ard. Will we put them in the little side-cabins here?' 'Ah then!' says I, 'and have them roaring and shouting, and knocking the place down maybe in half an hour or so? I'm surprised at ye, Mr. Murphy. We'll put the drunk waiters under the saloon table, and you must get another table-cloth. We'll pull it down on both sides, the way the feet of them will not show.' So I call up two stewards and the boys from the pantry, and we get the drunk waiters arranged as neat as herrings in a barrel under the saloon table. Mr. Murphy and I put on the second cloth, pulling it right down to the floor, and ye wouldn't believe the way we worked, setting out the dishes, and the flowers, and the swatemates on the table. 'Now,' says I, 'for the love of God let none of them sit down at the table, or they'll feel the waiters with their feet. Lave it to me to get His Excellency out of this, and then hurry the drunk waiters away!' And I spoke a word to the boys in the pantry. 'Boys,' says I, 'as ye value your salvation, keep up a great clatteration here by dropping the spoons and forks about, the way they'll not hear it if the drunk waiters get snoring,' and then the thrain arrives, and we run up to meet His Excellency your father.

"We went down to the saloon for a moment, and every one says that they never saw the like of that for a supper, the boys in the pantry keeping up such a clatteration by tumbling the spoons and forks about, that ye'd think the bottom of the ship would drop out with the noise of it all. Then I said, 'Supper will not be ready for ten minutes, your Excellency'—though God forgive me if every bit of it was not on the table that minute. 'Would you kindly see if the sleeping accommodation is commodious enough, for we'll alter it if it isn't,' and so I get them all out of that, and I kept talking of this, and of that, the Lord only knows what, till Mr. Murphy comes up and says, 'Supper is ready, your Excellency,' giving me a look out of the tail of his eye as much as to say, 'Glory be! We have them drunk waiters safely out of that.'"

Of course I knew nothing of the convivial waiters, but I retain vivid recollections of the splendours of the supper-table, and of the "swate-mates," for I managed to purloin a whole pocketful of preserved ginger and other good things from it, without being noticed.

We arrived at Kingstown in the early morning, and anchored in the harbour, but, by a polite fiction, the *Munster* was supposed to be absolutely invisible to ordinary eyes, for the new Lord-Lieutenant's official time of arrival from England was 11 a.m. Accordingly, every one being arrayed in their very best for the State entry into Dublin, the *Munster* got up steam and crept out of the harbour (still, of course, completely invisible), to cruise about a little, and to re-enter the harbour (obviously direct from England) amidst the booming of twenty-one guns from the guardship, a vast display of bunting, and a tornado of cheering.

Unfortunately, it had come on to blow; there was a very heavy sea outside, and the *Munster* had an unrivalled opportunity for showing off her agility, and of exhibiting her unusual capacity for pitching and rolling. My youngest brother and I have never been affected by sea-sickness; the ladies, however, had a very unpleasing half-hour, though it must be rather a novel and amusing experience to succumb to this malady when arrayed in the very latest creations of a Paris dressmaker and milliner; still I fear that neither my mother nor my sisters can have been looking quite their best when we landed amidst an incredible din of guns, whistles and cheering.

My father, as was the custom then, made his entry into Dublin on horseback. Since he had to keep his right hand free to remove his hat every minute or so, in acknowledgment of his welcome, and as his horse got alarmed by the noise, the cheering, and the waving of flags, he managed to give a very pretty exhibition of horsemanship.

By the way, Irish cheering is a thing *sui generis*. In place of the deep-throated, reverberating English cheer, it is a long, shrill, sustained note, usually very high-pitched.

The State entry into Dublin was naturally the first occasion on which I had ever driven through streets lined with soldiers and gay with bunting. If I remember right, I accepted most of it as a tribute to my own small person.

On arriving at the Viceregal Lodge in the Phœnix Park, my brother and I were much relieved at finding that we were not expected to live perpetually surrounded by men in full uniform and by ladies in smart dresses, as we had gathered that we were fated to do during the morning's ceremonies at Dublin Castle.

The Viceregal Lodge is a large, unpretentious, but most comfortable house, standing in really beautiful grounds. The 160 acres of its enclosure have been laid out with such skill as to appear to the eye double or treble the extent they actually are. The great attraction to my brother and me lay in a tract of some ten acres of woodland which had been allowed to run entirely wild. We soon peopled this very satisfactorily with two tribes of Red Indians, two bands of peculiarly bloodthirsty robbers, a sufficiency of bears, lions and tigers, and an appalling man-eating dragon. I fear that in view of the size of the little wood, these imported inhabitants must have had rather cramped quarters.

The enacting of the rôle of a Red Indian "brave" was necessarily a little fatiguing, for according to Fenimore Cooper, our guide in these matters, it was essential to keep up an uninterrupted series of guttural grunts of "Ug! Ug!" the invariable manner in which his "braves" prefaced their remarks.

There was perhaps little need for the imaginary menagerie, for the Dublin Zoological Gardens adjoined the "Lodge" grounds, and were accessible to us at any time with a private key. The Dublin Zoo had always been very successful in breeding lions, and derived a large amount of their income from the sale of the cubs. They consequently kept a number of lions, and the roaring of these lions at night was very audible at the Viceregal Lodge, only a quarter of a mile away. When I told the boys at school, with perfect truth, that in Dublin I was nightly lulled to sleep by the gentle roaring of lions round my couch, I was called a young liar.

There is a pretty lake inside the Viceregal grounds. My two elder brothers were certain that they had seen wild duck on this lake in the early morning, so getting up in the dusk of a December morning, they crept down to the lake with their guns. With the first gleam of dawn, they saw that there were plenty of wild fowl on the water, and they succeeded in shooting three or four of them. When daylight came, they retrieved them with a boat, but were dismayed at finding that these birds were neither mallards, nor pochards, nor any known form of British duck; their colouring, too, seemed strangely brilliant. Then they remembered the neighbouring Zoo, with its ornamental ponds covered with rare imported and exotic waterfowl, and they realised what they had done. It is quite

possible that they had killed some unique specimens, imported at fabulous cost from Central
Africa, or from the heart of the Australian continent, some priceless bird that was the apple of the
eye of the Curator of the Gardens, so we buried the
episode and the birds, in profound secrecy.

For my younger brother and myself, this lake
had a different attraction, for, improbable as it may
seem, it was the haunt of a gang of most abandoned
pirates. Behind a wooded island, but quite invisible
to the adult eye, the pirate craft lay, conforming in
the most orthodox fashion to the descriptions in
Ballantyne's books : "a schooner with a long, low,
black hull, and a suspicious rake to her masts. The
copper on her bottom had been burnished till it
looked like gold, and the black flag, with the skull
and cross-bones, drooped lazily from her peak."

The presence of this band of desperadoes entailed
the utmost caution and watchfulness in the neighbourhood of the lake. Unfortunately, we nearly
succeeded in drowning some young friends of ours,
whom we persuaded to accompany us in an attack
on the pirates' stronghold. We embarked on a
raft used for cutting weeds, but no sooner had we
shoved off than the raft at once, most inconsider-
ately, sank to the bottom of the lake with us.
Being Christmas time, the water was not over-
warm, and we had some difficulty in extricating
our young friends. Their parents made the most
absurd fuss about their sons having been forced to
take a cold bath in mid-December in their best

clothes. Clearly we could not be held responsible for the raft failing to prove sea-worthy, though my youngest brother, even then a nice stickler for correct English, declared that, given the circumstances, the proper epithet was "lake-worthy."

What a wonderful dream-world the child can create for himself, and having fashioned it and peopled it, he can inhabit his creation in perfect content quite regardless of his material surroundings, unless some grown-up, with his matter-of-fact bluntness, happens to break the spell.

I have endeavoured to express this peculiar faculty of the child's in rather halting blank verse. I apologise for giving it here, as I make no claim to be able to write verse. My only excuse must be that my lines attempt to convey what every man and woman must have felt, though probably the average person would express himself in far better language than I am able to command.

> " Eheu fugaces Postume !   Postume !
>   Labuntur anni.

" The memories of childhood are a web
  Of gossamer, most infinitely frail
  And tender, shot with gleaming threads of gold
  And silver, through the iridescent weft
  Of subtlest tints of azure and of rose ;
  Woven of fragile nothings, yet most dear,
  As binding us to that dim, far-off time,
  When first our lungs inhaled the fragrance sweet
  Of a new world, where all was bright and fair.
  As we approach the end of mortal things,
  The band of comrades ever smaller grows ;
  For those who have not shared our trivial round,

Nor helped with us to forge its many links,
Can only listen with dull, wearied mind.
Some few there are on whom the gods bestowed
The priceless gift of sympathy, and they,
Though knowing not themselves, yet understand.
So guard the fragile fabric, rolled away
In the sweet-scented chests of memory,
Careful lest one uncomprehending soul
Should, thoughtless, rend the filmy texture frail
Into a thousand fragments, and destroy
The precious relic of the golden dawn
Of life, when all the unknown future lay
Bathed in unending sunlight, and the heights
Of manhood, veiled in distant purple haze,
Offered ten thousand chances of success.
But why the future, when the present seemed
A flower-decked meadow in eternal spring?
When every woodland glade its secrets told
To us, and us alone.   The grown-up eye
Saw sun-flecked oaks, and tinkling, fern-fringed stream,
Nor knew that 'neath their shade most doughty Knights
Daily rode forth to deeds of chivalry;
And ruthless ruffians waged relentless war
On those who strayed (without the Talisman
Which turned their fury into impotence)
Into those leafy depths; nor dreamed there lurked,
Concealed amidst the bosky dells unseen,
Grim dragons spouting instant death; nor feared
The placid lake, along whose reed-fringed shore
Bold Buccaneers swooped down upon their prey.
Which things were hidden from maturer eyes.
To those who breathed the freshness of the morn,
Endless romance; to others, common things.
For to the Child is given to spin a web
Of golden glamour o'er the everyday.

   .   .   .   .   .   .

Happy is he who can, in spite of years,
Retain at times the spirit of the Child."

My own personal ambition at that period was
a modest one. My mother always drove out in
Dublin in a carriage-and-four, with postilions and
two outriders. We had always used black carriage-

horses, and East, the well-known job-master, had provided us for Dublin with six splendid blacks, all perfect matches. Our family colour being crimson, the crimson barouche, with the six blacks and our own black and crimson liveries, made a very smart turn-out indeed. O'Connor, the wheeler-postilion, a tiny little wizened elderly man, took charge of the carriage, and directed the outriders at turnings by a code of sharp whistles. It was my consuming ambition to ride leader-postilion to my mother's carriage, and above all to wear the big silver coat-of-arms our postilions had strapped to the left sleeves of their short jackets on a broad crimson band. I went to O'Connor in the stable-yard, and consulted him as to my chance of obtaining the coveted berth. O'Connor was distinctly encouraging. He thought nine rather young for a postilion, but when I had grown a little, and had gained more experience, he saw no insuperable objections to my obtaining the post. The leader-postilion was O'Connor's nephew, a smart-looking light-built boy of seventeen, named Byrne. Byrne was less hopeful about my chance. He assured me that such a rare combination of physical and intellectual qualities were required for a successful leader-rider, that it was but seldom that they were found, as in his case, united in the same person. That my mother had met with no accident whilst driving was solely due to his own consummate skill, and his wonderful presence of mind. Little Byrne, however, was quite affable, and allowed me to try on his livery, including the coveted big silver arm-badge and his top-boots. In my borrowed plumes I gave the stablemen to understand that I was as good as engaged already as postilion. Byrne informed me of some of the disadvantages of the position. "The heart in ye would be broke at all the claning them leathers requires." I was also told that after an extra long drive, "ye'd come home that tired that ye'd be thinking ye were losing your life, and not knowing if ye had a leg left to ye at all."

I often drove with my mother, and when we had covered more ground than usual, upon arriving home, I always ran round to the leaders to inquire anxiously if my friend little Byrne "had a leg left to him, or if he had lost his life," and was much relieved at finding him sitting on his horse in perfect health, with his normal complement of limbs encased in white leathers. I believe that I expected his legs to drop off on the road from sheer fatigue.

I knew, of course, that the Lord-Lieutenant had to confirm all death-sentences in Ireland. From much reading of Harrison Ainsworth, I insisted on calling the documents connected with this, "death-warrants." I begged and implored my father to let me see a "death-warrant." He told me that there was nothing to see, but I went on insisting, until one day he told me that I might see one of these gruesome documents. To avoid any misplaced sympathy with the condemned man, I may say that it was a peculiarly brutal murder.

A man at Cork had kicked his wife to death, and had then battered her into a shapeless mass with the poker. I went into my father's study on the tip-toe of expectation. I pictured the Private Secretary coming in slowly, probably draped for the occasion in a long black cloak, and holding a white handkerchief to his eyes. In his hand he would bear an immense sheet of paper surrounded by a three-inch black border. It would be headed DEATH in large letters, with perhaps a skull-and-crossbones below it, and from it would depend three ominous black seals attached by black ribbons. The Secretary would naturally hesitate before presenting so awful a document to my father, who, in his turn, would exhibit a little natural emotion when receiving it. At that moment my mother, specially dressed in black for the occasion, would burst into the room, and falling on her knees, with streaming eyes and outstretched arms, she would plead passionately for the condemned man's life. My father, at first obdurate, would gradually be melted by my mother's entreaties. Turning aside to brush away a furtive and not unmanly tear, he would suddenly tear the death-warrant to shreds, and taking up another huge placard headed REPRIEVE, he would quickly fill it in and sign it. He would then hand it to the Private Secretary, who would instantly start post-haste for Cork. As the condemned man was being actually conducted to the scaffold, the Private Secretary would appear, brandishing the liberating document. All then would be joy, except for the executioner, who would grind his teeth at being baulked of his prey at the last minute.

That is, at all events, the way it would have happened in a book. As it was, the Private Secretary came in just as usual, carrying an ordinary official paper, precisely similar to dozens of other official papers lying about the room.

" It is the Cork murder case, sir," he said in his everyday voice. "The sentence has to be confirmed by you."

" A bad business, Dillon," said my father. " I have seen the Chief Justice about it twice, and I have consulted the Judge who tried the case, and the Solicitor and the Attorney-General. I am afraid that there are no mitigating circumstances whatever. I shall certainly confirm it," and he wrote across the official paper, " Let the law take its course," and appended his signature, and that was all !

Could anything be more prosaic ? What a waste of an unrivalled dramatic situation !

When I returned home for the Christmas holidays in 1866, the Fenian rebellion had already broken out. The authorities had reason to believe that the Viceregal Lodge would be attacked, and various precautions had been taken. Both guards and sentries were doubled; four light field-guns stood in the garden, and a row of gas-lamps had been installed there. Stands of arms made their appearance in the passages upstairs, which were patrolled all night by constables in rubber-soled boots, but the culminating joy to my brother and me lay in the four loopholes with which the walls of the bed-room we jointly occupied were pierced. The room projected beyond the front of the main building, and was accordingly a strategic point, but to have four real loopholes, closed with wooden shutters, in the walls of our own bedroom was to the two small urchins a source of immense pride. The boys at school were hideously jealous of our loopholes when they heard of them, though they affected to despise any one who, enjoying such undreamed-of opportunities, had, on his own confession, failed to take advantage of them, and had never even fired through the loopholes, nor attempted to kill any one through them.

The Fenians were supposed to have the secret of a mysterious combustible known as " Greek Fire " which was unquenchable by water. I think that " Greek Fire " was nothing more or less than ordinary petroleum, which was practically unknown in Europe in 1866, though from personal experience I can say that it was well known in 1868, in which year my mother, three sisters, two brothers and myself narrowly escaped being burnt to death, when the Irish mail, in which we were travelling, collided with a goods train loaded with petroleum at Abergele, North Wales, an accident which resulted in thirty-four deaths.

Terrible as were the results of the Abergele accident, they might have been more disastrous still, for both lines were torn up, and the up Irish mail from Holyhead, which would be travelling at a great pace down the steep bank from Llandulas, was due at any moment. The front guard of our train had been killed by the collision, and the rear guard was seriously hurt, so there was no one to give orders. It occurred at once to my eldest brother, the late Duke, that as the train was standing on a sharp incline, the uninjured carriages would, if uncoupled, roll down the hill of their own accord. He and some other passengers accordingly managed to undo the couplings, and the uninjured coaches, detached from the burning ones, glided down the incline into safety. From the half-stunned guard my brother learned that the nearest signal-box was at Llandulas, a mile away. He ran there at the top of his speed, and arrived in time to get the up Irish mail and all other traffic stopped. On his return my brother had a prolonged fainting fit, as the strain on his heart had been very great. It took the doctors over an hour to bring him round, and we all thought that he had died.

I was eleven years old at the time, and the shock of the collision, the sight of the burning coaches, the screams of the women, the wreckage, and my brother's narrow escape from death, affected me for some little while afterwards.

It was the custom then for the Lord-Lieutenant to live for three months of the winter at the Castle, where a ceaseless round of entertainments went on. The Castle was in the heart of Dublin, and only boasted a dull little smoke-blackened garden in the place of the charming grounds of the Lodge, still there was plenty going on there. A band played daily in the Castle Yard for an hour, there was the daily guard-mounting, and the air was thick with bugle calls and rattling kettle-drums.

At " Drawing-Rooms " it was still the habit for all ladies to be kissed by the Lord-Lieutenant on being presented to him, and every lady had to be re-presented to every fresh Viceroy. This imposed an absolute orgy of compulsory osculation on the unfortunate Lord-Lieutenant, for if many of the ladies were fresh, young and pretty, the larger proportion of them were very distinctly the reverse.

There is a very fine white-and-gold throne-room in Dublin, decorated in the heavy but effective style of George IV., and it certainly compares very favourably with the one at Buckingham Palace. St. Patrick's Hall, too, with its elaborate painted ceiling, is an exceedingly handsome room, as is the Long Gallery. At my father's first Drawing-Room, when I officiated as page, the perpetual kissing tickled my fancy so, that, forgetting that to live up to my new white-satin breeches and lace ruffles I ought to wear an impassive countenance, I absolutely shook, spluttered and wriggled with laughter. The ceremony appeared to me interminable, for ten-

year-old legs soon get tired, and ten-year-old
eyelids grow very heavy as midnight approaches.
When at length it ended, and my fellow-page was
curled up fast asleep on the steps of the throne
in his official finery, in glancing at my father I
was amazed to find him prematurely aged. The
powder from eight hundred cheeks and necks had
turned his moustache and beard white ; he had to
retire to his room and spend a quarter of an hour
washing and brushing the powder out, before he
could take part in the procession through all the
state-rooms which in those days preceded supper.
My father was still a remarkably handsome man
even at fifty-six years of age, with his great height
and his full curly beard, and I thought my mother,
with all her jewels on, most beautiful, as I am
quite sure she was, though only a year younger
than my father.

The great white-and-gold throne-room brilliant
with light, the glitter of the uniforms, and the
sparkle of the jewels were attractive from their
very novelty to a ten-year-old schoolboy, perhaps
a little overwhelmed by his own gorgeous and
unfamiliar trappings. We two pages had been
ordered to stand quite motionless, one on either
side of the throne, but as the evening wore on
and we began to feel sleepy, it was difficult to
carry our instructions into effect, for there were
no facilities for playing even a game of " oughts
and crosses " in order to keep awake. The position
had its drawbacks, as we were so very conspicuous

in our new uniforms. A detail which sticks in my memory is that the guests at that Drawing-Room drank over three hundred bottles of my father's sherry, in addition to other wines.

My brother and I were not allowed in the throne-room on ordinary days, but it offered such wonderful opportunities for processions and investitures, with the sword of state and the mace lying ready to one's hand in their red velvet cradles, that we soon discovered a back way into it. Should any of the staff of Lord French, the present Viceroy, care to examine the sword of state and the mace, they will find them both heavily dented. This is due to two small boys having frequently dropped them when they proved too heavy for their strength, during strictly private processions fifty-five years ago. I often wonder what a deputation from the Corporation of Belfast must have thought when they were ushered into the throne-room, and found it already in the occupation of two small brats, one of whom, with a star cut out of silver paper pinned to his jacket to counterfeit an order, was lolling back on the throne in a lordly manner, while the other was feigning to read a long statement from a piece of paper. The small boys, after the manner of their kind, quickly vanished through a bolt-hole.

The Chapel Royal in Dublin Castle was built by my grandfather, the Duke of Bedford, who was Viceroy in 1806, and it bears the stamp of the unfortunate period of its birth on every detail of its "carpenter-Gothic" interior. It is, however, very ornate, with a profusion of gilding, stained glass and elaborate oak carving. My father and mother sat by themselves on two red velvet arm-chairs in a sort of pew-throne that projected into the Chapel. The Aide-de-Camp in waiting, an extremely youthful warrior as a rule, had to stand until the door of the pew was shut, when a folding wooden flap was lowered across the aperture, on which he seated himself, with his back resting against the pew door. At the conclusion of the service the Verger always opened the pew door with a sudden "click." Should the Aide-de-Camp be unprepared for this and happen to be leaning against the door, with any reasonable luck he was almost certain to tumble backwards into the aisle, "taking a regular toss," as hunting-men would say, and to our unspeakable delight we would see a pair of slim legs in overalls and a pair of spurred heels describing a graceful parabola as they followed their youthful owner into the aisle. This particular form of religious relaxation appealed to me enormously, and I looked forward to it every Sunday.

It was an episode that could only occur once with each person, for forewarned was forearmed ; still, as we had twelve Aides-de-Camp, and they were constantly changing, the pew door played its practical joke quite often enough to render the Services in the Chapel Royal very attractive and engrossing, and I noticed that no Aide-de-

Camp was ever warned of his possible peril. I think, too, that the Verger enjoyed his little joke.

In that same Chapel Royal I listened to the most eloquent and beautiful sermon I have ever heard in my life, preached by Dean Magee (afterwards Archbishop of York) on Christmas Day, 1866. His text was: "There were shepherds abiding in the fields." That marvellous orator must have had some peculiar gift of sympathy to captivate the attention of a child of ten so completely that he remembers portions of that sermon to this very day, fifty-four years afterwards.

To my great delight I discovered a little door near our joint bedroom which led directly into the gallery of St. Patrick's Hall. Here the big dinners of from seventy to ninety people were held, and it was my delight to creep into the gallery in my dressing-gown and slippers and watch the brilliant scene below. The stately white-and-gold hall with its fine painted ceiling, the long tables blazing with plate and lights, the display of flowers, the jewels of the ladies and the uniforms of the men, made a picture very attractive to a child. After the ladies had left, the uproar became deafening. In 1866 the old drinking habits had not yet died out, and though my father very seldom touched wine himself, he of course saw that his guests had sufficient; indeed, sufficient seems rather an elastic term, judging by what I saw and what I was told. It must have been rather like one of the scenes described by Charles Lever in his books. In 1866 political, religious, and racial animosities had not yet assumed the intensely bitter character they have since reached in Ireland, and the traditional Irish wit, at present apparently dormant, still flashed, sparkled, and scintillated. From my hiding-place in the gallery I could only hear the roars of laughter the good stories provoked, I could not hear the stories themselves, possibly to my own advantage.

Judge Keogh had a great reputation as a wit. The then Chief Justice was a remarkable-looking man on account of his great snow-white whiskers and his jet-black head of hair. My mother, commenting on this, said to Judge Keogh, "Surely Chief Justice Monaghan must dye his hair." "To my certain knowledge he does not," answered Keogh. "How, then, do you account for the difference in colour between his whiskers and his hair?" asked my mother. "To the fact that, throughout his life, he has used his jaw a great deal more than he ever has his brain," retorted Keogh.

Father Healy, most genial and delightful of men, belongs, of course, to a much later period. I was at the Castle in Lord Zetland's time, when Father Healy had just returned from a fortnight's visit to Monte Carlo, where he had been the guest (of all people in the world!) of Lord Randolph Churchill. "May I ask how you explained your absence to your flock, Father Healy?" asked Lady

Zetland. "I merely told them that I had been for a fortnight's retreat to Carlow; I thought it superfluous prefixing the Monte," answered the priest. Again at a wedding, the late Lord Morris, the possessor of the hugest brogue ever heard, observedas the young couple drove off, "I wish that I had an old shoe to throw after them for luck." "Throw your brogue after them, my dear fellow; it will do just as well," flashed out Father Healy. It was Father Healy, too, who, in posting a newly arrived lady as to Dublin notabilities, said, "You will find that there are only two people who count in Dublin, the Lady-Lieutenant and Lady Iveagh, her Ex. and her double X," for the marks on the barrels of the delicious beverage brewed by the Guinness family must be familiar to most people.

I myself heard Father Healy, in criticising a political appointment which lay between a Welsh and a Scotch M.P., say, "Well, if we get the Welshman he'll pray on his knees all Sunday, and then prey on his neighbours the other six days of the week; whilst if we get the Scotchman, he'll keep the Sabbath and any other little trifles he can lay his hand on." Healy, who was parish priest of Little Bray, used to entertain sick priests from the interior of Ireland who were ordered sea-bathing. One day he saw one of his guests, quite a young priest, rush into the sea, glass in hand, and begin drinking the sea water. "You mustn't do that, my dear fellow," cried

Father Healy, aghast. " I didn't know that there was any harm in it, Father Healy," said the young priest. " Whist! we'll not say one word about it, and maybe then they'll never miss the little drop you have taken."

Some of these stories may be old, in which case I can only apologise for giving them here.

Dublin people have always had the gift of coining extremely felicitous nicknames. I refrain from quoting those bestowed on two recent Viceroys, for they are mordant and uncomplimentary, though possibly not wholly undeserved. My father was at once christened " Old Splendid," an appellation less scarifying than some of those conferred on his successors. My father had some old friends living in the west of Ireland, a Colonel Tenison, and his wife, Lady Louisa Tenison. Colonel Tenison had one of the most gigantic noses I have ever seen, a vast, hooked eagle's beak. He was so blind that he had to feel his way about. Lady Louisa Tenison allowed herself an unusual freedom of speech, and her comments on persons and things were unconventionally outspoken. They came to stay with us at the Castle in 1867, and before they had been there twenty-four hours they were christened " Blind Hooky " and " Unlimited Loo."

In February 1867 my sister, brother and I contracted measles, and were sent out to the " Lodge " to avoid spreading infection.

We were already convalescent, when one evening

a mysterious stranger arrived from the Castle, and had an interview with the governess. As a result of that interview, the kindly old lady began clucking like a scared hen, fussed quite prodigiously, and told us to collect our things at once, as we were to start for the Castle in a quarter of an hour. After a frantically hurried packing, we were bustled into the carriage, the mysterious stranger taking his seat on the box. To our surprise we saw some thirty mounted Hussars at the door. As we moved off, to our unspeakable delight, the Hussars drew their swords and closed in on the carriage, one riding at either window. And so we drove through Dublin. We had never had an escort before, and felt immensely elated and dignified. At the Castle there seemed to be some confusion. I heard doors banging and people moving about all through the night.

Long afterwards I learnt that the great Fenian rising was fixed for that night. The authorities had heard that part of the Fenian plan was to capture the Viceregal Lodge, and to hold the Lord-Lieutenant's children as hostages, which explains the arrival at the Lodge of Chief Inspector Dunn, the frantic haste, and the escort of Hussars with drawn swords.

That night an engagement, or it might more justly be termed a skirmish, did take place between the Fenians and the troops at Tallagh, some twenty miles from Dublin. My brothers and most of my father's staff had been present, which explained the mysterious noises during the night. As a result of this fight, some three hundred prisoners were taken, and Lord Strathnairn, then Commander-in-Chief in Ireland, was very hard put to it to find sufficient men (who, of course, would have to be detached from his force) to escort the prisoners into Dublin. Lord Strathnairn suddenly got an inspiration. He had every single button, brace buttons and all, cut off the prisoners' trousers. Then the men had perforce, for decency's sake, to hold their trousers together with their hands, and I defy any one similarly situated to run more than a yard or two. The prisoners were all paraded in the Castle yard next day, and I walked out amongst them. As they had been up all night in very heavy rain, they all looked very forlorn and miserable. The Castle gates were shut that day, for the first time in the memory of the oldest inhabitant, and they remained shut for four days. I cannot remember the date when the prisoners were paraded, but I am absolutely certain as to one point: it was Shrove Tuesday, 1867, the day on which so many marriages are celebrated amongst country-folk in Ireland. Dublin was seething with unrest, so on that very afternoon my father and mother drove very slowly, quite alone, without an Aide-de-Camp or escort, in a carriage-and-four with outriders, through all the poorest quarters in Dublin. They were well received, and there was no hostile demonstration whatever. The idea of the slow drive through the slums was my mother's. She wished to show that though the Castle gates were closed, she and my father were not afraid. I saw her on her return, when she was looking very pale and drawn, but I was too young to realise what the strain must have been. My mother's courage was loudly praised, but I think that my friends O'Connor and little Byrne, the postilions, also deserve quite a good mark, for they ran the same amount of risk, and they were not entirely free agents in the matter, as my father and mother were.

Dr. Hatchell, who attended us all, had been physician to countless Viceroys and their families, and was a very well-known figure in Dublin. He was a jolly little red-faced man with a terrific brogue. There was a great epidemic of lawlessness in Dublin at that time. Many people were waylaid and stripped of their valuables in dark suburban streets. Dr. Hatchell was returning from a round of professional visits in the suburbs one evening, when his carriage was stopped by two men, who seized the horses' heads. One of the men came round to the carriage door.

" We know you, Dr. Hatchell, so you had better hand over your watch and money quietly." " You know me," answered the merry little doctor, with his tremendous brogue, " so no doubt you would like me to prescribe for you. I'll do it with all the pleasure in life. Saltpetre is a grand drug, and I often order it for my patients. Sulphur is the finest thing in the world for the blood, and charcoal is an elegant disinfectant. By a great piece of luck, I have all these drugs with me in the carriage, but "—and he suddenly covered the man with his revolver—" they are all mixed up together, and there is the least taste in life of lead in front of them, and, by God! you'll get it through you if you don't clear out of that." The men decamped immediately. I have heard Dr. Hatchell tell that story at least twenty times. Dr. Hatchell, who was invited to every single entertainment, both at the Lodge and at the Castle, was a widower. A peculiarly stupid young Aide-de-Camp once asked him why he had not brought Mrs. Hatchell with him. "Sorr," answered the doctor in his most impressive tones, "Mrs. Hatchell is an angel in heaven." A fortnight later the same foolish youth asked again why Dr. Hatchell had come alone. "Mrs. Hatchell, sorr, is still an angel in heaven," answered the indignant doctor.

It was said that no mortal eye had ever seen Dr. Hatchell in the daytime out of his professional frock-coat and high hat. I know that when he stayed with us in Scotland some years later, he went out salmon-fishing in a frock-coat and high hat (with a stethoscope clipped into the crown of it), an unusual garb for an angler.

In the spring of 1868, King Edward and Queen Alexandra (then, of course, Prince and Princess of Wales) paid us a long visit at the Castle. My father had heard a rumour that recently the Prince of

Wales had introduced the custom of smoking in
the dining-room after dinner. He was in a difficult
position; nothing would induce him to tolerate
such a practice, but how was he to avoid dis-
courtesy to his Royal guest? My mother rose
to the occasion. A little waiting-room near the
dining-room was furnished and fitted up in the
most attractive manner, and before the Prince had
been an hour in the Castle, my mother showed him
the charming little room, and told H.R.H. that it
had been specially fitted up for him to enjoy his
after-dinner cigar in. That saved the situation.
Young men of to-day will be surprised to learn
that in my time no one dreamed of smoking before
they went to a ball, as to smell of smoke was considered an affront to one's partners. I myself,
though a heavy smoker from an early age, never
touched tobacco in any form before going to a
dance, out of respect for my partners. Incredible
as it may sound, in those days all gentlemen had a
very high respect for ladies and young ladies, and
observed a certain amount of deference in their
intercourse with them. Never, to the best of my
recollection, did either we or our partners address
each other as " old thing," or " old bean." This, of
course, now is hopelessly Victorian, and as defunct
as the dodo. Present-day hostesses tell me that
all young men, and most girls, are kind enough to
flick cigarette-ash all over their drawing-rooms, and
considerately throw lighted cigarette-ends on to
fine old Persian carpets, and burn holes in pieces

of valuable old French furniture. Of course it would be too much trouble to fetch an ash-tray, or to rise to throw lighted cigarette-ends into the grate. The young generation have never been brought up to take trouble, nor to consider other people; we might perhaps put it that they never think of any one in the world but their own sweet selves. I am inclined to think that there are distinct advantages in being a confirmed, unrepentant Victorian.

During the stay of the Prince and Princess there was one unending round of festivities. The Princess was then at the height of her great beauty, and seeing H.R.H. every day, my youthful adoration of her increased tenfold. The culminating incident of the visit was to be the installation of the Prince of Wales as a Knight of St. Patrick in St. Patrick's Cathedral, with immense pomp and ceremonial. The Cathedral had undergone a complete transformation for the ceremony, and all its ordinary fittings had disappeared. The number of pages had now increased to five, and we were constantly being drilled in the Cathedral. We had all five of us to walk backwards down some steps, keeping in line and keeping step. For five small boys to do this neatly, without awkwardness, requires a great deal of practice. The procession to the Cathedral was made in full state, the streets being lined with troops, and the carriages, with their escorts of cavalry, going at a foot's pace through the principal thoroughfares of Dublin. I remember it chiefly on account of the bitter north-east wind blowing. The five pages drove together in an open carriage, and received quite an ovation from the crowd, but no one had thought of providing them with overcoats. Silk stockings, satin knee-breeches and lace ruffles are very inadequate protection against an Arctic blast, and we arrived at the Cathedral stiff and torpid with cold. From the colour of our faces, we might have been five little "Blue Noses" from Nova Scotia. The ceremony was very gorgeous and imposing, and I trust that the pages were not unduly clumsy. Every one was amazed at the beauty of the music, sung from the triforium by the combined choirs of St. Patrick's and Christ Church Cathedrals, and of the Chapel Royal, with that wonderful musician, Sir Robert Stewart, at the organ. I remember well Sir Robert Stewart's novel setting of "God save the Queen." The men sang it first in unison to the music of the massed military bands outside the Cathedral, the boys singing a "Faux Bourdon" above it. Then the organ took it up, the full choir joining in with quite original harmonies.

In honour of the Prince's visit, nearly all the Fenian prisoners who were still detained in jail were released.

Many years after, in 1885, King Edward and Queen Alexandra paid us a visit at Barons' Court. During that visit a little episode occurred which is worth recording. On the Sunday, the Princess of Wales, as she still was, inspected the Sunday School children before Morning Service. At luncheon the Rector of the parish told us that one of the Sunday scholars, a little girl, had been taken ill with congestion of the lungs a few days earlier. The child's disappointment at having missed seeing the Princess was terrible. Desperately ill as she was, she kept on harping on her lost opportunity. After luncheon the Princess drew my sister-in-law, the present Dowager Duchess of Abercorn, on one side, and inquired where the sick child lived. Upon being told that it was about four miles off, the Princess asked whether it would not be possible to get a pony-cart from the stables and drive there, as she would like to see the little girl. I myself brought a pony-cart round to the door, and the Princess and my sister-in-law having got in, we three started off alone, the Princess driving. When we reached the cottage where the child lived, H.R.H. went straight up to the little girl's room, and stayed talking to her for an hour, to the child's immense joy. Two days later the little girl died, but she had been made very happy meanwhile.

A little thing perhaps; but there are not many people in Queen Alexandra's position who would have taken an eight-mile drive in an open cart on a stormy and rainy April afternoon in order to avoid disappointing a dying child, of whose very existence she had been unaware that morning.

It is the kind heart which inspires acts like these which has drawn the British people so irresistibly to Queen Alexandra.

CHAPTER IV

I WAS sent to school as soon as I was nine, to Mr. Chittenden's, at Hoddesdon, in Hertfordshire. This remarkable man had a very rare gift: he was a born teacher, or, perhaps, more accurately, a born mind-trainer. Of the very small stock of knowledge which I have been able to accumulate during my life, I certainly owe at least one-half to Mr. Chittenden. There is a certain profusely advertised system for acquiring concentration, and for cultivating an artificial memory, the name of which will be familiar to every one. Instead of the title it actually bears, that system should be known as "Chittendism," for it is precisely the method adopted by him with his pupils fifty-four years ago. Mr. Chittenden, probably recognising that peculiar quality of mental laziness which is such a marked characteristic of the average English man or

94

woman, set himself to combat and conquer it the moment he got a pupil into his hands. Think of the extraordinary number of persons you know who never do more than half-listen, half-understand, half-attend, and who only read with their eyes, not with their brains. The other half of their brain is off wool-gathering somewhere, so naturally they forget everything they read, and the little they do remember with half their brain is usually incorrect. It seems to me that this sort of mental limitation is far more marked in the young generation, probably because foolish parents seem to think it rather an amusing trait in their offspring. Now, the boy at Chittenden's who allowed his mind to wander, and did not concentrate, promptly made the acquaintance of the "spatter," a broad leathern strap ; and the spatter hurt exceedingly, as I can testify from many personal experiences of it. On the whole, then, even the most careless boy found it to his advantage to concentrate. This clever teacher knew how quickly young brains tire, so he never devoted more than a quarter of an hour to each subject, but during that quarter of an hour he demanded, and got, the full attention of his pupils. The result was that everything absorbed remained permanently. If I enlarge at some length on Mr. Chittenden's methods, it is because the subject of education is of such vital importance, and the mere fact that the much-advertised system to which I have alluded has attained such success, would seem to indicate that many people are aware that they share that curious disability in the intellectual equipment of the average Englishman to which I have referred ; for unless they had habitually only half-listened, half-read, half-understood, there could be no need for their undergoing a course of instruction late in life Surely it is more sensible to check this peculiarly English tendency to mental laziness quite early in life, as Mr. Chittenden did with his boys. To my mind another striking characteristic of the average English man and woman is their want of observation. They don't notice : it is far too much trouble ; besides, they are probably thinking of something else. All Chittenden's boys were taught to observe ; otherwise they got into trouble. He insisted, too, on his pupils expressing themselves in correct English, with the result that Chittenden's boys were more intellectually advanced at twelve than the average Public School boy is at sixteen or seventeen. It is unusual to place such books as Paley's *Christian Evidences*, or Archbishop Whateley's *Historic Doubts as to Napoleon Bonaparte*, in the hands of little boys of twelve, with any expectation of a satisfactory result; yet we read them on Sundays, understood the point of them, and could explain the why and wherefore of them. Chittenden's one fault was his tendency to " force " a receptive boy, and to develop his intellect too quickly. As in the Pelm—— (I had very nearly written it) system, he made great use of *memoria technica*, and always taught us to link one idea with another. At the age of ten I got puzzled over Marlborough's campaigns. "'Brom,' my boy, remember 'Brom,'" said Mr. Chittenden. "That will give you Marlborough's victories in their proper sequence—Blenheim, Ramillies, Oude-narde, Malplaquet, 'Brom'"; and "Brom" I have remembered from that day to this.

Though it is now many years since Mr. Chitten-den passed away, I must pay this belated tribute to the memory of a very skilful teacher, and an exceedingly kind friend, to whom I owe an immense debt of gratitude.

My own experiences as a pedagogue are limited. During the War, I was asked to give some lessons in elementary history and rudimentary French to convalescent soldiers in a big hospital. No one ever had a more cheery and good-tempered lot of pupils than I had in my blue-clad, red-tied disciples. For remembering the order of the Kings of Eng-land, we used Mr. Chittenden's jingle, beginning:

"Billy, Billy, Harry, Ste,
Harry, Dick, Jack, Harry Three."

By repeating it all together, over and over again, the very jangle of it made it stick in my pupils' memory. Dates proved a great difficulty, yet a few dates, such as that of the Norman Conquest and of the Battle of Waterloo, were essential. "Clarke, can you remember the date of the Norman Conquest?" "Very sorry, sir; clean gone out of my 'ead." "Now, Daniels, how about the date of Waterloo?" "You've got me this time, sir." Then I had an inspiration. Feigning to take up a telephone-receiver, and to speak down it, I begged for "Willconk, One, O, double-six, please." Twenty blithesome wounded Tommies at once went through an elaborate pantomime of unhooking receivers, and asked anxiously for "Willconk—One, O, double-six, miss, please. No, miss, I didn't say, 'City, six, eight, five, four'; I said 'Willconk, One, O, double-six.' Thank you, miss; now I can let mother know I'm coming home to tea." This, accompanied by much playful badinage with the imaginary operator, proved immensely popular, but "Willconk, One, O, double-six" stuck in the brains of my blue-clothed flock. In the same way the Battle of Waterloo became "Batterloo—One, eight, one, five, please, miss," so both those dates remained in their heads.

We experienced some little trouble in mastering the French numerals, until I tried a new scheme, and called out, "From the right, number, in French!" Then my merry convalescents began shouting gleefully, "Oon," "Doo," "Troy," "Catta," "Sink," etc.; but the French numerals stuck in their heads. Never did any one, I imagine, have such a set of jolly, cheery boys in blue as pupils, and the strong remnant of the child left in many of them made them the more attractive.

When I first went to school, the selection and purchase of my outfit was, for some inscrutable reason, left to my sisters' governess, an elderly lady to whom I was quite devoted. This excellent person, though, knew very little about boys, and nothing whatever as to their requirements. Her mind harked back to the "thirties" and "forties," and she endeavoured to re-constitute the dress of little boys at that period. She ordered for me a velvet tunic for Sunday wear, of the sort seen in old prints, and a velvet cap with a peak and tassel, such as young England wore in William IV.'s days. She had large floppy limp collars specially made for me, of the pattern worn by boys in her youth; every single article of my unfortunate equipment had been obsolete for at least thirty years. In my ignorance, and luckily not knowing what was in store for me, I felt immensely proud of my new kit.

On the first Sunday after my arrival at school, I arrayed myself with great satisfaction in a big floppy collar, and my new velvet tunic, amidst the loud jeers of all the other boys in the dormitory. I was, however, hardly prepared for the yells and howls of derision with which my appearance in the schoolroom was greeted ; my unfortunate garments were held to be so unspeakably grotesque that boys laughed till the tears ran down their cheeks. As church-time approached the boys produced their high hats, which I found were worn even by little fellows of eight ; I had nothing but my terrible tasselled velvet cap, the sight of which provoked even louder jeers than the tunic had done. We marched to church two and two, in

old-fashioned style in a "crocodile," but not a boy
in the school would walk beside me in my absurd
garments, so a very forlorn little fellow trotted to
church alone behind the usher, acutely conscious
of the very grotesque figure he was presenting.
I must have been dressed very much as Henry
Fairchild was when he went to visit his little
friend Master Noble. On returning from church,
I threw my velvet cap into the water-butt, where,
for all I know, it probably is still, and nothing
would induce me to put on the velvet tunic or the
floppy collars a second time. I bombarded my
family with letters until I found myself equipped
with a high hat and Eton jackets and collars such
as the other boys wore.

We were taught French at Chittenden's by a
very pleasant old Belgian, M. Vansittart. I could
talk French then as easily as English, and after
exchanging a few sentences with M. Vansittart,
he cried, "Tiens! mais c'est un petit Français;"
but the other boys laughed so unmercifully at
what they termed my affected accent, that in self-
defence I adopted an ultra-British pronunciation,
made intentional mistakes, and, in order to conform
to type, punctiliously addressed our venerable in-
structor as "Moosoo," just as the other boys did.
M. Vansittart must have been a very old man, for
he had fought as a private in the Belgian army
at the Battle of Waterloo. He had once been
imprudent enough to admit that he and some
Belgian friends of his had . . . how shall we put

it ? . . . absented themselves from the battlefield without the permission of their superiors, and had hurriedly returned to Brussels, being doubtless fatigued by their exertions. His little tormentors never let him forget this. When we thought that we had done enough French for the day, a shrill young voice would pipe out, " Now, Moosoo, please tell us how you and all the Belgians ran away from the Battle of Waterloo." It never failed to achieve the desired end. " Ah ! tas de petits sacripants ! 'Ow dare you say dat ? " thundered the poor old gentleman, and he would go on to explain that his and his friends' retirement was only actuated by the desire to be the first bearers to Brussels of the news of Wellington's great victory, and to assuage their families' very natural anxiety as to their safety. He added, truthfully enough, " Nos jambes courraient malgrès nous." Poor M. Vansittart! He was a gentle and a kindly old man, with traces of the eighteenth-century courtliness of manner.

Mr. Chittenden was never tired of dinning into us the astonishing merits of a pupil who had been at the school eleven or twelve years before us. This model boy apparently had the most extra-ordinary mental gifts, and had never broken any of the rules. Mr. Chittenden predicted a brilliant future for him, and would not be surprised should he eventually become Prime Minister. The para-gon had had a distinguished career at Eton, and was at present at Cambridge, where he was certain to do equally well. From having this Admirable Crichton perpetually held up to us as an example, we grew rather tired of his name, much as the Athenians wearied at constantly hearing Aristides described as "the just." At length we heard that the pattern-boy would spend two days at Hoddesdon on his way back to Cambridge. We were all very anxious to see him. As Mr. Chittenden confidently predicted that he would one day become Prime Minister, I formed a mental picture of him as being like my uncle, Lord John Russell, the only Prime Minister I knew. He would be very short, and would have his neck swathed in a high black-satin stock. When the Cambridge undergraduate appeared, he was, on the contrary, very tall and thin, with a slight stoop, and so far from wearing a high stock, he had an exceedingly long neck emerging from a very low collar. His name was Arthur James Balfour.

I think Mr. Balfour and the late Mr. George Wyndham were the only pupils of Chittenden's who made names for themselves. The rest of us were content to plod along in the rut, though we had been taught to concentrate, to remember, and to observe.

Compared with the manner in which little boys are now pampered at preparatory schools, our method of life appears very Spartan. We never had fires or any heating whatever in our dormitories, and the windows were always open. We were never given warm water to wash in, and in frosty weather our jugs were frequently frozen over. Truth compels me to admit that this freak of Nature's was rather welcomed, for little boys are not as a rule over-enamoured of soap and water, and it was an excellent excuse for avoiding any ablutions whatever. We rose at six winter and summer, and were in school by half-past six. The windows of the school-room were kept open, whilst the only heating came from a microscopic stove jealously guarded by a huge iron stockade to prevent the boys from approaching it. For breakfast we were never given anything but porridge and bread and butter. We had an excellent dinner at one o'clock, but nothing for tea but bread and butter again, never cake or jam. It will horrify modern mothers to learn that all the boys, even little fellows of eight, were given two glasses of beer at dinner. And yet none of us were ever ill. I was nearly five years at Chittenden's, and I do not remember one single case of illness. We were all of us in perfect health, nor were we ever afflicted with those epidemics which seem to play such havoc with modern schools, from all of which I can only conclude that a regime of beer and cold rooms is exceedingly good for little boys.

The Grange, Mr. Chittenden's house, was one of the most perfect examples of a real Queen Anne house that I ever saw. Every room in the house was wood-panelled, and there was some fine carving on the staircase. The house, with a splendid avenue of limes leading up to it, stood

in a large old-world garden, where vast cedar trees
spread themselves duskily over shaven lawns round
a splashing fountain, and where scarlet geraniums
blazed.   Such a beautiful old place was quite
wasted as a school.

We were very well treated by both Mr. and
Mrs. Chittenden, and we were all very happy at
the Grange. During my first year there one of
my elder brothers died. A child of ten, should
death never have touched his family, looks upon
it as something infinitely remote, affecting other
people but not himself. Then when the first gap
in the home occurs, all the child's little world
tumbles to pieces, and he wonders how the birds
have the heart to go on singing as usual, and how
the sun can keep on shining. A child's grief is
very poignant and real. I can never forget Mr.
and Mrs. Chittenden's extreme kindness to a very
sorrowful little boy at that time.

There was one curious custom at Chittenden's,
and I do not know whether it obtained in other
schools in those days. Some time in the summer
term the head-boy would announce that "The
Three Sundays" had arrived, and must be duly
observed according to ancient custom. We all
obeyed him implicitly. The first Sunday was
"Cock-hat Sunday," the second "Rag Sunday,"
and the third (if I may be pardoned) "Spit-in-the-
pew Sunday." On the first Sunday we all marched
to church with our high hats at an extreme angle
over our left ears; on the second Sunday every

boy had his handkerchief trailing out of his pocket;
on the third, I am sorry to say, thirty-one little
boys expectorated surreptitiously but simultaneously in the pews, as the first words of the
Litany were repeated. I think that we were all
convinced that these were regularly appointed
festivals of the Church of England. I know that
I was, and I spent hours hunting fruitlessly
through my Prayer Book to find some allusion to
them. I found Sundays after Epiphany, Sundays
in Lent, and Sundays after Trinity, but not one
word could I discover, to my amazement, either
about "Cock-hat Sunday" or "Spit-in-the-pew
Sunday." What can have been the origin of this
singular custom I cannot say. When I, in my
turn, became head-boy, I fixed "The Three Sundays" early in May. It so happened that year
that the Thursday after "Cock-hat Sunday" was
Ascension Day, when we also went to church, but,
it being a week-day, we wore our school caps in
the place of high hats. Ascension Day thus
falling, if I may so express myself, within the
Octave of "Cock-hat Sunday," I decreed that the
customary ritual must be observed with the school
caps, and my little flock obeyed me implicitly. So
eager were some of the boys to do honour to this
religious festival, that their caps were worn at such
an impossible angle that they kept tumbling off all
the way to church. It is the only time in my life
that I have ever wielded even a semblance of
ecclesiastical authority, and I cannot help thinking

that the Archbishop of Canterbury would have
envied the unquestioning obedience with which all
my directions were received, for I gather that his
own experience has not invariably been equally
fortunate.

At thirteen I said good-bye to the pleasant
Grange, and went, as my elder brothers, my father,
and my grandfather had done before me, to
Harrow.

In the Harrow of the " seventies " there was
one unique personality, that of the Rev. John
Smith, best-loved of men. This saintly man was
certainly very eccentric. We never knew then
that his whole life had been one long fight against
the hereditary insanity which finally conquered
him. In appearance he was very tall and gaunt,
with snow-white whiskers and hair, and the kindest
eyes I have ever seen in a human face; he was
meticulously clean and neat in his dress. "John,"
as he was invariably called, on one occasion met a
poorly clad beggar shivering in the street on a cold
day, and at once stripped off his own overcoat and
insisted on the beggar taking it. John never bought
another overcoat, but wrapped himself in a plaid
in winter-time. He addressed all boys indiscrimi-
nately as "laddie," though he usually alluded to
the younger ones as "smallest of created things,"
"infinitesimal scrap of humanity," or "most diminutive of men"; but, wildly eccentric as he was,
no one ever thought of laughing at him. It was
just "old John," and that explained everything.

I was never "up" to John, for he taught a low Form, and I had come from Chittenden's, and all Chittenden's boys took high places; but he took "pupil-room" in my house, and helped my tutor generally, so I saw John daily, and, like every one else, I grew very much attached to this simple, saint-like old clergyman.

He went round every room in the house on Sunday evenings, always first scrupulously knocking at the door. An untidy room gave him positive pain, and the most slovenly boys would endeavour to get their filthy rooms into some sort of order, "just to please old John." John was passionately fond of flowers, and one would meet the most unlikely boys with bunches of roses in their hands. If one inquired what they were for, they would say half-sheepishly, "Oh, just a few roses I've bought. I thought they would please old John; you know how keen the old chap is on flowers." Now English schoolboys are not as a rule in the habit of presenting flowers to their masters. For all his apparent simplicity, John was not easy to "score off." I have known Fifth-form boys bring a particularly difficult passage of Herodotus to John in "pupil-room," knowing that he was not a great Greek scholar. John, after glancing at the passage, would say, " Laddie, you splendid fellows in the Upper Fifth know so much; I am but a humble and very ignorant old man. This passage is beyond my attainments. Go to your tutor, my child. He will doubtless make it all clear to you;

and pray accept my apologies for being unable to help you," and the Fifth-form boy would go away feeling thoroughly ashamed of himself. After his death, it was discovered from his diary that John had been in the habit of praying for twenty boys by name, every night of his life. He went right down the school list, and then he began again. Any lack of personal cleanliness drove him frantic. I myself have heard him order a boy with dirty nails and hands out of the room, crying, " Out of my sight, unclean wretch! Go and cleanse the hands God gave you, before I allow you to associate with clean gentlemen, and write out for me two hundred times, ' Cleanliness is next to godliness.' "

John took the First Fourth, and his little boys could always be detected by their neatness and extreme cleanliness. Neither of these can be called a characteristic of little boys in general, but the little fellows made an effort to overcome their natural tendencies " to please old John." When his hereditary enemy triumphed, and his reason left him, hundreds of his old pupils wished to subscribe, and to surround John for the remainder of his life with all the comforts that could be given him in his afflicted condition. It was very characteristic of John to refuse this offer, and to go of his own accord into a pauper asylum, where he combined the duties of chaplain and butler until his death. John was buried at Harrow, and by his own wish no bell was tolled, and his coffin was

covered with scarlet geraniums, as a sign of re-
joicing. I know how I should describe John, were
I preaching a sermon.

Another mildly eccentric Harrow master was the
Rev. T. Steele, invariably known as "Tommy."
His peculiarities were limited to his use of the
pronoun "we" instead of "I," as though he had
been a crowned head, and to his habit of perpetually
carrying, winter and summer, rain or sunshine,
a gigantic bright blue umbrella. He had these
umbrellas specially made for him; they were
enormous, the sort of umbrellas Mrs. Gamp must
have brought with her when her professional
services were requisitioned, and they were of the
most blatant blue I have ever beheld. Old Mr.
Steele, with his jovial rubicund face, his flowing
white beard, and his bright blue umbrella, was a
species of walking tricolour flag.

Schoolboys worship a successful athlete. There
was a very pleasant mathematical master named
Tosswill, always known as "Tosher," who at that
time held the record for a broad jump, he having
cleared, when jumping for Oxford, twenty-two and
a half feet. That record has long since been beaten.
Should one be walking with another boy when
passing "Tosher," he was almost certain to say,
"You know that Tosher holds the record for broad
jumps. Twenty-two and a half feet; he must be
an awfully decent chap!" Tosswill had the knack
of devising ingenious punishments. I was "up"
to him for mathematics, and, with my hopelessly

non-mathematical mind, I must have been a great trial to him. At that time I was playing the euphonium in the school brass band, an instrument which afforded great joy to its exponents, for in most military marches the solo in the "trio" falls to the euphonium, though I fancy that I evoked the most horrible sounds from my big brass instrument. To play a brass instrument with any degree of precision, it is first necessary to acquire a "lip" —that is to say, the centre of the lip covered by the mouthpiece must harden and thicken before "open notes" can be sounded accurately. To "get a lip" quickly, I always carried my mouthpiece in my pocket, and blew noiselessly into it perpetually, even in school. Tosher had noticed this. One day my algebra paper was even worse than usual. With the best intentions in the world to master this intricate branch of knowledge, algebra conveyed nothing whatever to my brain. To state that $A + b = xy$, seemed to me the assertion of a palpable and self-evident falsehood. After looking through my paper, Tosher called me up. "Your algebra is quite hopeless, Hamilton. You will write me out a Georgic. No; on second thoughts, as you seem to like your brass instrument, you shall bring it up to my house every morning for ten days, and as the clock strikes seven, you shall play me 'Home Sweet Home' under my window." Accordingly every morning for ten days I trudged through the High Street of Harrow with my big brass instrument under my arm, and as seven rang out from the school clock, I commenced my extremely lugubrious rendering of "Home Sweet Home" on the euphonium, to a scoffing and entirely unsympathetic audience of errand-boys and early loafers, until Tosher's soap-lathered face nodded dismissal from the window.

The school songs play a great part in Harrow life. Generation after generation of boys have sung these songs, and they form a most potent bond of union between Harrovians of all ages, for their words and music are as familiar to the old Harrovian of sixty as to the present Harrovian of sixteen.

Most of these songs are due to the genius of two men, Edward Bowen and John Farmer. Like Gilbert and Sullivan, neither of these would, I think, have risen to his full height without the aid of the other. Farmer had an inexhaustible flow of facile melody at his command, always tuneful, sometimes almost inspired. In addition to the published songs, he was continually throwing off musical settings to topical verse, written for some special occasion. These were invariably bright and catchy, and I am sorry that Farmer considered them of too ephemeral a nature to be worth preserving. "Racquets," in particular, had a de-lightfully ear-tickling refrain. Bowen's words are a little unequal at times, but at his best he is very hard to beat.

I had organ lessons from Farmer, and as I liked him extremely, I was continually at his house. I

111

enjoyed seeing him covering sheets of music paper with rapid notation, and then humming the newly born product of his musical imagination. As I had a fairly good treble voice, and could read a part easily, Farmer often selected me to try one of his new compositions at " house-singing," where the boys formed an exceedingly critical audience. Either the new song was approved of, or it was received in chilling silence. Farmer in moments of excitement perspired more than any human being I have ever seen. Going to his house one afternoon, I found him bathed in perspiration, writing away for dear life. He motioned me to remain silent, and went on writing. Presently he jumped up, and exclaimed triumphantly, " I have got it ! I have got it at last ! " He then showed me the words he was setting to music. They began :

> " Forty years on, when afar and asunder,
>   Parted are those who are singing to-day."

" I wrote another tune to it first," explained Farmer, " a bright tune, a regular bell-tinkle " (his invariable expression for a catchy tune), " but Bowen's words are too fine for that. They want something hymn-like, something grand, and now I've found it. Listen ! " and Farmer played me that majestic, stately melody which has since been heard in every country and in every corner of the globe, wherever two old Harrovians have come together. Some people may recall how, during the Boer War, " Forty years on " was sung by two mortally wounded Harrovians on the top of Spion Kop just before they died.

To my great regret my voice had broken then, else it is quite possible that Farmer might have selected me to sing " Forty years on " for the very first time. As it was, that honour fell to a boy with a remarkably sweet voice, named A. M. Wilkinson.

John Farmer's eccentricities were, I think, all assumed. He thought they helped him to manage the boys. I sang in the chapel choir, and he circulated the quaintest little notes amongst us, telling us how he wished the Psalms sung. " Psalm 136, quite gaily and cheerfully ; Psalm 137, very slowly and sorrowfully ; Psalm 138, real merry bell-tinkle, with plenty of organ.—J. F."

Long after I had left, Farmer continued to pour out a ceaseless flow of school songs. Of course they varied in merit, but in some, such as " Raleigh," and " Five Hundred Faces," he managed to touch some subtle chord of sympathy that makes them very dear to those who heard them in their youth. After Farmer left Harrow for Oxford, his successor, Eaton Faning, worthily continued the traditions. All Eaton Faning's songs are melodious, but in two of them, " Here, sir ! " and " Pray charge your glasses, gentlemen," he reaches far higher levels.

The late E. W. Howson's words to " Here, sir ! " seem to strike exactly the right note for boys. They are fine and virile, with underlying sentiment, yet free from the faintest suspicion of mawkish sentimentality. Two of the verses are worth quoting :

> " Is it nought—our long procession,
>   Father, brother, friend, and son,
> As we step in quick succession,
>   Cap and pass and hurry on?
>   One and all,
>   At the call,
>   Cap and pass and hurry on?
>   Here, sir ! Here, sir ! etc.

> " So to-day—and oh ! if ever
>   Duty's voice is ringing clear,
> Bidding men to brave endeavour,
>   Be our answer, ' We are here ! '
>   Come what will,
>   Good or ill,
>   We will answer, ' We are here ! '
>   Here, sir ! Here, sir ! " etc.

The allusion is, of course, to ": Bill," the Harrow term for the roll-call. These lines, for me, embody all that is best in the so-called " Public School spirit."

In my time the distant view from the chapel terrace was exceedingly beautiful, whilst the immediate foreground was uncompromisingly ugly. A vegetable garden then covered the space where now the steps of the " Slopes" run down through lawns and shrubberies, and rows of utilitarian cabbages and potatoes extended right up to the terrace wall. But beyond this prosaic display of kitchen-stuff, in summer-time an unbroken sea of green extended to the horizon, dotted with such splendid oaks as only a heavy clay soil can produce. London, instead of being ten miles off, might have been a hundred miles distant. Now, for fifty years London, Cobbett's "monstrous wen," has been throwing her tentative feelers into the green Harrow country. Already pioneer tentacles of red-brick houses are creeping over the fields, and before long the rural surroundings will have vanished beyond repair.

"Ducker," the Harrow bathing-place, has had scant justice done to it. It is a most attractive spot, standing demurely isolated amidst its encircling fringe of fine elms, and jealously guarded by a high wooden palisade. No unauthorised person can penetrate into "Ducker"; in summer-time it is the boys' own domain. The long, tiled pool stretches in sweeping curves for 250 feet under the great elms, a splashing fountain at one end, its far extremity gay with lawns and flower-beds. I can conceive of nothing more typical of the exuberant *joie-de-vivre* of youth than the sight of Ducker on a warm summer evening, when the place is ringing with the shouts and laughter of some four hundred boys, all naked as when they were born, swimming, diving, ducking each other, splashing and rollicking in the water, whilst others stretched out on the grass, *puris naturalibus*, are basking in the sun, or regaling themselves on buns and cocoa. The whole place is vibrant with the intense zest the young feel in life, and with the whole-hearted powers of enjoyment of boyhood. A school-song set to a captivating

waltz-lilt record the charms of Ducker. One verse
of it,

" Oh ! the effervescing tingle,
    How it rushes in the veins !
Till the water seems to mingle
    With the pulses and the brains,"

exactly expresses the reason why, as a boy, I loved
Ducker so.

Unfortunately, I never played cricket for Harrow
at " Lords," as my two brothers George and Ernest
did. My youngest brother would, I think, have
made a great name for himself as a cricketer, had
not the fairies endowed him at his birth with a
fatal facility for doing everything easily. As the
result of this versatility, his ambitions were continually changing. He accordingly abandoned
cricket for steeplechase riding, at which he distinguished himself until politics ousted steeplechase
riding. After some years, politics gave place to
golf and music, which were in their turn supplanted
by photography. He then tried writing a few
novels, and very successful some of them were,
until it finally dawned on him that his real voca-
tion in life was that of a historian. My brother
was naturally frequently rallied by his family on
his inconstancy of purpose, but he pleaded in
extenuation that versatility had very marked
charms of its own. He produced one day a copy
of verses, written in the Gilbertian metre, to illus-
trate his mental attitude, and they strike me as so
neatly worded, that I will reproduce them in full.

116

THE DAYS BEFORE YESTERDAY

"THE CURSE OF VERSATILITY"

" It is possible the student of Political Economy
    Might otherwise have cultivated Fame,
And the Scientist whose energies are given to Astronomy
    May sacrifice a literary name.
In the Royal Academician may be buried a facility
    For prosecuting Chemical Research,
But he knows that if he truckles to the Curse of Versatility,
    Competitors will leave him in the lurch.

" If an eminent physician should develop a proclivity
    For singing on the operatic stage,
He will find that though his patients may apparently
    forgive it, he
Will temporal'ly cease to be the rage.
And the lawyer who depreciates his logical ability
    And covets a poetical renown,
Will discover on his Circuit that the Curse of Versatility
    Has limited the office of his gown.

" The costermonger yonder, if he had the opportunity,
    Might rival the political career
Of the orator who poses as the pride of the community,
    The Radical Hereditary Peer.
And the genius who fattens on a chronic inability
    To widen the horizon of his brain,
May be stupider than others, whom the Curse of Versatility
    Has fettered with a mediocre chain.

" Should a Civil Servant woo the panegyrics of Society,
    And hanker after posthumous applause,
It *may* happen that possession of a prodigal variety
    Of talents will invalidate his cause.
He must learn to put a tether on his cerebral agility,
    And focus all his energies of aim
On *one* isolated idol, or the Curse of Versatility
    Will drag him from the pinnacle of Fame.

" Though the Curse may be upon us, and condemn us for
    Eternity
    To jostle with the ordinary horde;
Though we grovel at the shrine of the professional fraternity
    Who harp upon one solitary chord;

117

Still . . . we face the situation with an imperturbability
   Of spirit, from the knowledge that we owe
To the witchery that lingers in the Curse of Versatility
   The balance of our happiness below."

Of course, to some temperaments variety will appeal; whilst others revel in monotony. The latter are like a District Railway train, going perpetually round and round the same Inner Circle. As far as my experience goes, the former are the more interesting people to meet.

To persons of my time of life, the last verse of "Forty years on" has a tendency to linger in the memory. It runs—

" Forty years on, growing older and older,
   Shorter in wind, as in memory long,
Feeble of foot, and rheumatic of shoulder,
   What will it help you that once you were strong ? "

Although it is now fifty, instead of "forty years on," I indignantly disclaim the "feeble of foot," whilst reluctantly pleading guilty to "rheumatic of shoulder." It is common to most people, as they advance in life, to note with a sorrowful satisfaction the gradual decay of the physical powers of their contemporaries, though they always seem to imagine that they themselves have retained all their pristine vigour, and have successfully resisted every assault of Time's battering-ram. The particular sentiment described in German as "Schadenfreude," " pleasure over another's troubles " (how characteristic it is that there should be no equivalent in any other language for this peculiarly Teutonic emo-

tion!), makes but little appeal to the average Briton
except where questions of age and of failing powers
come into play, and obviously this only applies to
men: no lady ever grows old for those who are
really fond of her; one always sees her as one likes
best to think of her.

I have already divulged one family secret, so I
will reveal another. Some few years ago my three
eldest brothers were dining together. Each of
them professed deep concern at the palpable signs
of physical decay which he detected in his brethren,
whilst congratulating himself on remaining untouched by advancing years. The dispute became
acrimonious to a degree; the grossest personalities
were freely bandied about. At length it was
decided to put the matter to a practical test, and
it was agreed (I tell this in the strictest confidence)
that the three brothers should run a hundred yards
race in the street then and there. Accordingly,
a nephew of mine paced one hundred yards in
Montagu Street, Portman Square, and stood im-
movable as winning-post. The Chairman of the
British South African Chartered Company, the
Chairman of the Great Eastern Railway Company,
and the Secretary of State for India took up their
positions in the street and started. The Chairman
of the Great Eastern romped home. We are all
of us creatures of our environment, and we may
become unconsciously coloured by that environment; as the Great Eastern Railway has always
adopted a go-ahead policy, it is possible that some

particle of the momentum which would naturally result from this may have been subconsciously absorbed by the Chairman, thus giving him an unfair advantage over his brothers. It is unusual for a Duke, a Chairman of an important Railway Company, and a Secretary of State to run races in a London street at ten o'clock at night, especially when two of them, at least, were long past their sixtieth year, but I feel certain that my confidence about this little episode will be respected.

I fear that this habit of running races late in life may be a family failing. During my father's second tenure of office as Lord-Lieutenant of Ireland, he was still an enthusiastic cricketer, and played regularly in the Viceregal team in spite of his sixty-four years. The Rev. Dr. Mahaffy, Professor of Ancient History at Trinity College, Dublin, also played for the Viceregal Lodge in his capacity of Chaplain to the Viceroy. Dr. Mahaffy, though a fine bowler, was the worst runner I have ever seen. He waddled and paddled slowly over the ground like a duck, with his feet turned outwards, exactly as that uninteresting fowl moves. My father frequently rallied Dr. Mahaffy on his defective locomotive powers, and finally challenged him to a two hundred yards race. My father being sixty-four years old, and Dr. Mahaffy only thirty-six, it was agreed that the Professor should be handicapped by wearing cricket-pads, and by carrying a cricket bat. I was present at the race, which came off in the gardens of the Viceregal Lodge, before

120

quite a number of people. My father won with the utmost ease, to the delirious joy of the two policemen on duty, who had never before seen a Lord-Lieutenant of Ireland racing a Professor of Trinity College.

I myself must plead guilty to having entered for a " Veterans' Race " two years ago, at the age of sixty-one, at some Sunday School sports in Ireland. I ran against a butler, a gardener, two foremen-mechanics, and four farmers, but only achieved second place, and that at the price of a sprained tendon, so possibly the "feeble of foot" of the song really is applicable to me after all. The butler, who won, started off with the lead and kept it, though one would naturally have expected a butler to run a "waiting" race.

I was at Harrow with the Duke of Aosta, brother to the beautiful Queen Margherita of Italy. H.R.H. sported a full curly yellow beard at the age of sixteen, a somewhat unusual adornment for an English schoolboy. When I accompanied my father's special Mission to Rome in 1878, at a luncheon at the Quirinal Palace, Queen Margherita alluded to her brother having been at Harrow, and added, " I am told that Harrow is the best school in England." The Harrovians present, including my father, my brother Claud, myself, the late Lord Bradford, and my brother-in-law the late Lord Mount Edgcumbe, welcomed this indisputable proposition warmly—nay, enthusiastically. The Etonians who were there, Sir Augustus

Paget, then British Ambassador in Rome, the late Lord Northampton, and others, contravened her Majesty's obviously true statement with great heat, quite oblivious of the fact that it is opposed to all etiquette to contradict a Crowned Head. The dispute engendered considerable heat on either side ; the walls of that hall in the Quirinal rang with our angered protests, until the Italians present became quite alarmed. Our discussion having taken place in English, they had been unable to follow it, and they felt the gravest apprehensions as to the plot the foreigners were evidently hatching. When told that we were merely discussing the rival merits of two schools in England, they were more than ever confirmed in their opinion that all English people were hopelessly mad.

To one like myself, to whom it has fallen to visit almost every country on the face of the globe, there is always a tinge of melancholy in revisiting the familiar High Street of Harrow. It is like returning to the starting-point at the conclusion of a long race. The externals remain unchanged. Outwardly, the New Schools, the Chapel, the Vaughan Library, and the Head-Master's House all wear exactly the same aspect that they bore half a century ago. They have not changed, and the ever-renewed stream of young life flows through the place as joyously as it did fifty years ago. But . . . .

> " Oh, the great days, in the distance enchanted,
>   Days of fresh air, in the rain and the sun."

THE DAYS BEFORE YESTERDAY

At times the imagination is apt to play tricks and to set back the hands of the clock, until one pictures oneself again in a short jacket and Eton collar, going up to school, with a pile of books hugged under the left arm, and the intervening half-century wiped out. But, as they would put it in Ireland, these lucky, fresh-faced youngsters of to-day have their futures in front of them, not behind them. Then it is that Bowen's words, wedded to John Farmer's haunting refrain, come back to the mind—

> " Yet the time may come as the years go by,
>   When your heart will thrill
>   At the thought of ' The Hill,'
> And the day that you came, so strange and shy."

CHAPTER V

As it had already been settled that I was to
enter the Diplomatic Service, my father very wisely
determined that I should leave Harrow as soon as
I was seventeen to go to France, in order to learn
French thoroughly. As he pointed out, it would
take three years at least to become proficient in
French and German, and it would be as well to
begin at once.

The French tutor selected for me enjoyed a
great reputation at that time. Oddly enough,
she was a woman, but it will be gathered that she
was quite an exceptional woman, when I say
that she had for years ruled four unruly British
cubs, varying in age from seventeen to twenty,
with an absolute rod of iron. Mme. Ducros was

the wife of a French judge, she spoke English perfectly, and must have been in her youth a wonderfully good-looking woman. She was very tall, and still adhered to the dress and head-dress of the "sixties," wearing little bunches of curls over each ears—a becoming fashion, even if rather reminiscent of a spaniel.

The Ducros lived at Nyons in the south of France. Nyons lay twenty-five miles east of the main line from Paris to Marseilles, and could only be reached by *diligence*. I think that I can safely say that no foreigner (with the exception of the Ducros' pupils) had ever set foot in Nyons, for the place was quite unknown, and there was nothing to draw strangers there. It was an extraordinarily attractive spot, lying in a little circular cup of a valley of the Dauphiné Alps, through which a brawling river had bored its way. Nyons was celebrated for its wine, its olive oil, its silk, and its truffles, all of them superlatively good. The ancient little walled town, basking in this sun-trap of a valley, stood out ochre-coloured against the silver-grey background of olive trees, whilst the jagged profiles of the encircling hills were always mistily blue, with that intense blue of which the Provence hills seem alone to have the secret. So few English people knew anything about the conditions of life in a little out-of-the-way French provincial town, where no foreigners have ever set foot, that it may be worth while saying something about them. In the first place it must have been

deadly dull for the inhabitants, for nothing whatever happened there. Even the familiar "tea and
tennis," the stereotyped mild dissipation of little
English towns, was quite unknown. There was no
entertaining of any sort, beyond the formal visits
the ladies were perpetually paying each other. The
Ducros alone, occasionally, asked their legal friends
to dinner, invitations accepted with the utmost
enthusiasm, for the culinary genius who presided
over the Ducros' kitchen (M. Ducros' own sister)
deservedly enjoyed an enormous local reputation.

Most people must be familiar with Alphonse
Daudet's immortal work, *Tartarin de Tarascon*, in
which the typical "Méridional" of Southern France
is portrayed with such unerring exactitude that
Daudet himself, after writing the book, was never
able to set foot in Tarascon again.

We had a *cercle* in Nyons, in the Place
Napoléon (re-christened Place de la République
after September 4, 1870), housed in three rather
stately, sparsely furnished, eighteenth-century
rooms. Here, with the exception of Tartarin himself, the counterparts of all Daudet's characters
were to be found. "Le Capitaine Bravida" was represented by Colonel Olivier, a fiercely moustached
and imperialled Crimean veteran, who perpetually
breathed fire and swords on any potential enemy
of France. "Costecalde" found his prototype in
M. Sichap, who, although he had in all probability
never fired off a gun in his life, could never see a
tame pigeon, or even a sparrow flying over him,

without instantly putting his walking-stick to his shoulder and loudly ejaculating, "Pan, pan," which was intended to counterfeit the firing of both barrels of a gun. I once asked M. Sichap why so excellent a shot as he (with a walking-stick) invariably missed his bird with his first barrel, and only brought him down with his second. This was quite a new light to M. Sichap, who had hitherto considered the double "Pan, pan," an indispensable adjunct to the pantomime of firing a gun; much as my young brother and I had once imagined "Ug, ug," an obligatory commencement to any remark made by a Red Indian "brave."

In so remote a place as Nyons, over four hundred miles from the capital, the glamour of Paris exercised a magical attraction. The few inhabitants of Nyons who had ever visited Paris, or even merely passed through it, were never quite as other people, some little remnant of an aureole encircled them. The dowdy little wife of M. Pélissier, who had first seen the light in some grubby suburb of Paris, either Levallois-Perret or Clichy, held an immense position in Nyons on the strength of being "une vraie Parisienne," and most questions of taste were referred to her. M. Sisteron, the collector of taxes, himself a native of Nyons, had twenty years before gone to Paris on business, and spent four days there. There were the darkest rumours current in Nyons, to the effect that M. Sisteron had spent these four days in a whirl of the most frantic and abandoned dissipation. It

was popularly supposed that these four days in
Paris, twenty years ago, had so completely un-
settled M. Sisteron that life in Nyons had lost all
zest for him. He was perpetually hungering
for the delirious joys of the metropolis; even the
collection of taxes no longer afforded him the
faintest gratification. Every inhabitant of Nyons
was secretly proud of being able to claim so dare-
devil a roysterer as a fellow-townsman. The
memory of those rumoured four hectic days in
Paris clung round him like a halo; it became
almost a pleasure to pay taxes to so celebrated a
character. M. Sisteron was short, paunchy, bald,
and bearded. He was a model husband and a
pattern as a father. I am persuaded that he had
spent those four days in Paris in the most blameless
and innocuous fashion, living in the cheapest hotel
he could find, and, after the manner of the people
of Nyons, never spending one unnecessary franc.
Still, the legend of his lurid four days, and of the
amount of champagne he had consumed during
them, persisted. In moments of expansion, his
intimate friends would dig him in the ribs, remembering those four feverish days, with a facetious
"Ah! vieux polisson de Sisteron, va! Nous autres,
nous n'avons pas fait des farces à Paris dans notre
jeunesse!" to M. Sisteron's unbounded delight. It
was in the genuine spirit of Tartarin de Tarascon,
with all the mutual make-believe on both sides.
His wife, Mme. Sisteron, was fond of assuring her
friends that she owed her excellent health to the

fact that she invariably took a bath twice a year, whether she required it or not.

The other members of the *cercle* were also mostly short, tubby, black-bearded, and olive-complexioned. When not engaged in playing "manille" for infinitesimal points, they would all shout and gesticulate violently, as only Southern Frenchmen can, relapsing as the discussion grew more heated into their native Provençal, for though Nyons is geographically in Dauphiné, climatically and racially it is in Provence. In Southern France the "Langue d'Oïl," the literary language of Paris and Northern France, has never succeeded in ousting the "Langue d'Oc," the language of the Troubadours. From hearing so much Provençal talked round me, I could not help picking up some of it. It was years before I could rid myself of the habit of inquiring *quézaco?* instead of "qu'est ce que c'est?" and of substituting for "Comment cela va-t-il?" the Provençal *Commoun as?* I found, too, that it was unusual elsewhere to address people in our Nyons fashion as "Té, mon bon!"

Those swarthy, amply waistcoated, voluble little men were really very good fellows in spite of their excitability and torrents of talk.

The Southern Frenchmen divide Europe into the "Nord" and the "Midi." The "Nord" is hardly worth talking about, the sun never really shines there, and no garlic or oil is used in cookery in those benighted regions. The town of Lyons is considered to be in the "Nord," although we should consider it well in the south of France. To the curious in such matters, it may be pointed out that the line of demarcation between "Nord" and "Midi" is perfectly well defined. In travelling from Paris to Marseilles, between Valence and Montélimar, the observer will note that quite abruptly the type of house changes. In place of the high-pitched roof of Northern Europe the farm-houses suddenly assume flat roofs of fluted tiles, with projecting eaves, after the Italian fashion; at the same time the grey-green olive trees put in a first appearance. Then you are in the "Midi," and any black-bearded, olive-complexioned, stumpy little men in the carriage will give a sigh of relief, for now, at last, the sun will begin to shine.

Nyons had been for two hundred years a Huguenot stronghold, so for a French town an unusual proportion of its inhabitants were Protestants, and there was, oddly enough, a colony of French Wesleyans there.

M. Ducros' father had been the Protestant *pasteur* of Nyons for forty-four years. He was eighty-six years old, and on week-days the old gentleman dozed in the sun all day, and was quite senile and *gaga*. On Sundays, no sooner had he ascended the pulpit than his faculties seemed to return to him, and he would preach interminable but perfectly coherent sermons with a vigour astonishing in so old a man, only to relapse into childishness again on returning home, and to remain senile till the following Sunday.

The Ducros lived in a large farm-house on the outskirts of the town. It was a farm without any live-stock, for there is no grass whatever in that part of France, and consequently no pasture for cattle or sheep. Every one in Nyons kept goats for milk, and, quaintly enough, they fed them on the dried mulberry leaves the silkworms had left over. For every one reared silkworms too, a most lucrative industry. The French speak of " making " silkworms (*faire des vers-à-soie*). Lucrative as it is, it would never succeed in England even if the white mulberry could be induced to grow, for successful silkworm rearing demands such continual watchfulness and meticulous attention as only French people can give ; English people " couldn't be bothered " to expend such minute care on anything they were doing.

Every foot of the Ducros' property was carefully cultivated, with vineyards above on the terraced hill-side, olive-yards below, and mulberry trees on the lower levels. Our black mulberry, with its cloying, luscious fruit, is not the sort used for silkworms, it is the white mulberry, which does not fruit, that these clever little alchemists transmute into glossy, profitable cocoons of silk. The Ducros made their own olive-oil, and their own admirable wine.

In that sun-drenched cup amongst the hills, roses bloomed all the year round. I always see Nyons with my inner eyes from the terrace in front of the house, the air fragrant with roses, and the soothing gurgle of the fountain below in my ears as it splashed melodiously into its stone reservoir, the little town standing out a vivid yellow against the silver background of olive trees, and the fantastic outlines of the surrounding hills steeped in that wonderful deep Provençal blue. In spite of its dullness, I and the three other pupils liked the place. We all grew very fond of the charming Ducros family, we appreciated the wonderful beauty of the little spot, we climbed all the hills, and, above all, we had each hired a velocipede. Not a bicycle (except that it certainly had two wheels); not a so-called "ordinary," as those machines with one immensely high, shining, nickel-plated wheel and a little dwarf brother following it, were for some inexplicable reason termed; but an original antediluvian velocipede, a genuine "bone-shaker": a clumsy contrivance with two high wooden wheels of equal height, and direct action. Even on the level they required an immense amount of muscle to drive them along, and up the smallest hill every ounce of available strength had to be brought into play. They did not steer well, were very difficult to get on and off, and gave us some awful falls; still we got an immense amount of fun out of them, and we scoured all the surrounding country on them, until all four of us developed gigantic calves which would have done credit to any coal-heaver.

M. Ducros' sister was a brilliant culinary genius such as is only found in France. We were given truffled omelets, wonderful salads of eggs, anchovies, and tunny-fish, ducks with oranges and olives, and other delicacies of the Provençal cuisine prepared by a consummate artist, and those four English cubs termed them all "muck," and clamoured for plain roast mutton and boiled potatoes. It really was a case of casting pearls before swine! Those ignorant hobbledehoys actually turned up their noses at the admirable "Côtes du Rhône" wine, and begged for beer. In justice I must add that we were none of us used to truffles or olives, nor to the oil which replaces butter in Provençal cookery. Mlle. Louise, the sister, was pained, but not surprised. She had never left Nyons, and, from her experience of a long string of English pupils, was convinced that all Englishmen were savages. They inhabited an island enveloped in dense fog from year's end to year's end. They had never seen the sun, and habitually lived on half-raw "rosbif." It was only natural that such young barbarians should fail to appreciate the cookery of so celebrated a *cordon-bleu*, which term, I may add, is only applicable to a woman-cook, and can never be used of a man. This truly admirable woman made us *terrines* of truffled *foie-gras* such as even Strasburg could not surpass, and gave them to us for breakfast. I blush to own that those four benighted boys asked for eggs and bacon instead.

Although M. Ducros had heard English talked around him for so many years, he had all the average Frenchman's difficulty in assimilating any foreign language. His knowledge of our tongue was confined to one word only, and that a most curiously chosen word. "Slop-basin" was the beginning and end of his knowledge of the English language. M. Ducros used his one word of English only in moments of great elation. Should, for instance, his sister Mlle. Louise have surpassed herself in the kitchen, M. Ducros, after tasting her *chef d'œuvre*, would joyously ejaculate, "Slop-basin!" several times over. It was understood in his family that "slop-basin" always indicated that the master of the house was in an extremely contented frame of mind.

The judicial system of France is not as concentrated as ours. Every Sous-préfecture in France has its local Civil Court with a Presiding Judge, an Assistant Judge, and a "Substitut." The latter, in small towns, is the substitute for the Procureur de la République, or Public Prosecutor. The legal profession in France is far more "clannish" than with us, for lawyers have always played a great part in the history of France. The so-called "Parlements" (not to be confounded with our Parliament) had had, up to the time of the French Revolution, very large powers indeed. They were orginally Supreme Courts of Justice, but by the fifteenth century they could not only make, on their own account, regulations having the force of laws, but had acquired independent administrative powers. Originally the "Parlement de Paris" stood alone, but as time went on, in addition to this, thirteen or fourteen local "Parlements" administered France. After the Revolution, the term was only applied to Supreme Courts, without administrative powers. M. Ducros was Assistant Judge of the Nyons Tribunal, and the Ducros were rather fond of insisting that they belonged to the old *noblesse de robe.*

As a child I could speak French as easily as English, and even after eight years of French lessons at school, my French was still tucked away in some corner of my head; but I had, of course, only a child's vocabulary, sufficient for a child's simple wants. Under Madame Ducros' skilful tuition I soon began to acquire an adult vocabulary, and it became no effort to me whatever to talk.

The French judicial system seems to demand perpetual judicial inquiries (*enquêtes*) in little country places. M. Ducros invited me to accompany him, the Président, and the "Substitut" on one of these *enquêtes*, and these three, with their tremendous spirits, their perpetual jokes, and above all with their delightful *gaieté française*, amused me so enormously, that I jumped at a second invitation. So it came about in time, that I invariably accompanied them, and when we started in the shabby old one-horse cabriolet soon after 7 a.m., "notre ami le petit *Angliche*" was always perched on the box. My suspicions may be unfounded, but I somehow think that these *enquêtes* were conducted not so much on account of legal exigencies as for the gastronomic possibilities at the end of the journey, for all our inquiries were made in little towns celebrated for some local *chef*. These three merry *bons-vivants* revelled in the pleasures of the table, and on our arrival at our destinations, before the day's work was entered upon, there were anxious and even heated discussions with "Papa Charron," "Père Vinay," or whatever the name of the local artist might be, as to the comparative merits of truffles or olives as an accompaniment to a *filet*, or the rival claims of mushrooms or tunny-fish as a worthy lining of an omelet. The legal business being all disposed of by two o'clock, we four would approach the great ceremony of the day, the mid-day dinner, with tense expectancy. The Président could never keep out of the kitchen, from which he returned with most assuring reports: "Cette fois ça y est, mes amis," he would jubilantly exclaim, rubbing his hands, and even "Papa Charron" himself bearing in the first dish, his face scorched scarlet from his cooking-stove, would confidently aver that "MM. les juges seront contents aujourd'hui."

The crowning seal of approbation was always put on by M. Ducros, who, after tasting the masterpiece, would cry exultantly, "Bravo! Slop-basin! Slop-basin!" should it fulfil his expecta-

tions. I have previously explained that M. Ducros'
solitary word of English expressed supreme satisfaction, whilst his friends looked on, with uncon-
cealed admiration at their colleague's linguistic
powers. It sounds like a record of three gorman-
dising middle-aged men; but it was not quite
that, though, like most French people, they
appreciated artistic cookery. It is impossible for
me to convey in words the charm of that delightful *gaieté française*, especially amongst southern
Frenchmen. It bubbles up as spontaneously as
the sparkle of champagne; they were all as merry
as children, full of little quips and jokes, and plays
upon words. Our English "pun" is a clumsy
thing compared to the finesse of a neatly-turned
French *calembour*. They all three, too, had
an inexhaustible supply of those peculiarly French
pleasantries known as *petites gauloiseries*. I know
that I have never laughed so much in my
life. It is only southern Frenchmen who can
preserve this unquenchable torrent of animal
spirits into middle life. I was only seventeen;
they were from twenty to thirty years my seniors,
yet I do not think that we mutually bored each
other the least. They did not need the stimulus
of alcohol to aid this flow of spirits, for, like most
Frenchmen of that class, they were very abstemious,
although the "Patron" always produced for us
"un bon vieux vin de derrière les fagots," or
"un petit vin qui fait rire." It was sheer "*joie
de-vivre*" stimulated by the good food and that

spontaneous *gaieté française* which appeals so irresistibly to me. The "Substitut" always preserved a rather deferential attitude before the Président and M. Ducros, for they belonged to the *magistrature assise*, whilst he merely formed part of the *magistrature debout*. The French word *magistrat* is not the equivalent of our magistrate, the French term for which is "Juge de Paix." A *magistrat* means a Judge or a Public Prosecutor.

From being so much with the judges, I grew quite learned in French legal terms, talked of the *parquet* (which means the Bar), and invariably termed the grubby little Nyons law-court the *Palais*. I rather fancy that I considered myself a sort of honorary member of the French Bar. Strictly speaking, *Palais* only applies to a Court of Law; old-fashioned Frenchmen always speak of the *Château* de Versailles, or the *Château* de Fontainebleau, never of the *Palais*.

There was always plenty to see in these little southern towns whilst the judges were at work In one village there was a perfume factory, where essential oils of sweet-scented geranium, verbena, lavender, and thyme were distilled for the wholesale Paris perfumers ; a fragrant place, where every operation was carried on with that minute attention to detail which the French carry into most things that they do, for, unlike the inhabitants of an adjacent island, they consider that if a thing is worth doing at all, it is worth taking trouble over.

In another village there was a wholesale dealer in silkworms' eggs, imported direct from China. Besides the eggs, he had a host of Chinese curios to dispose of, besides quaint little objects in everyday use in China.

Above all there was Grignan, with its huge and woefully dilapidated château, the home of Mme. de Sévigné's daughter, the Comtesse de Grignan. It was to Grignan that this queen of letter-writers addressed much of her correspondence to her adored daughter, between 1670 and 1695, and Mme. de Sévigné herself was frequently a visitor there.

Occasionally the judges, the Substitut, and I made excursions further afield by *diligence* to Orange, Vaucluse, and Avignon, quite outside our judicial orbit. Orange, a drowsy little spot, has still a splendid Roman triumphal arch and a Roman theatre in the most perfect state of preservation. Orange was once a little independent principality, and gives its name to the Royal Family of Holland, the sister of the last of the Princes of Orange having married the Count of Nassau, whence the House of Orange-Nassau. Indirectly, sleepy little Orange has also given its name to a widely-spread political and religious organisation of some influence.

Vaucluse, most charming of places, in its narrow leafy valley, surrounded by towering cliffs, is celebrated as having been the home of Petrarch for sixteen years during the thirteen hundreds. We may hope that his worshipped Laura sometimes brightened his home there with her presence. The famous Fountain of Vaucluse rushes out from its cave a full-grown river. It wastes no time in infant frivolities, but settles down to work at once, turning a mill within two hundred yards of its birthplace.

Avignon is another somnolent spot. The gigantic and gloomy Palace of the Popes dominates the place, though it is far more like a fortress than a palace. Here the Popes lived from 1309 to 1377 during their enforced abandonment of Rome, and Avignon remained part of the Papal dominions until the French Revolution. The Président took less interest in the Palace of the Popes than he did in a famous cook at one of the Avignon hotels. He could hardly recall some of the *plats* of this noted artist without displaying signs of deep emotion. These ancient towns on the banks of the swift-rushing green Rhone seemed to me to be perpetually dozing in the warm sun, like old men, dreaming of their historic and varied past since the days of the Romans.

My French legal friends were much exercised by a recent decision of the High Court. M. Thiers had been President of the Republic from 1870 to 1873. A distant cousin of his living in Marseilles, being in pecuniary difficulties, had applied ineffectually to M. Thiers for assistance. Whereupon the resourceful lady had opened a restaurant in Marseilles, and had had painted over the house-front in gigantic letters, " Restaurant tenu par la cousine de Monsieur Thiers." She was proceeded against for bringing the Head of the State into contempt, was fined heavily, and made to remove the offending inscription. My French friends hotly contested the legality of this decision. They declared that it was straining the sense of the particular Article of the Code to make it applicable in such a case, and that it was illogical to apply the law of Lèse-majesté to the Head of a Republican State. The Président pertinently added that no evidence as to the quality of food supplied in the restaurant had been taken. If bad, it might unquestionably reflect injuriously on the Head of the State; if good, on the other hand, in view of the admitted relationship of the proprietress of the restaurant to him, it could only redound to M. Thiers' credit. This opens up interesting possibilities. If relationship to a prominent politician may be utilised for business purposes, we may yet see in English watering-places the façades of houses blazoned with huge inscriptions: "This Private Hotel is kept by a fourth cousin of Lord Rose——," whilst facing it, gold lettering proudly proclaims that "The Proprietress of this Establishment is a distant relative of Mr. Ar—— Bal——"; or, to impart variety, at the next turning the public might perhaps be informed in gleaming capitals that "The Cashier in this Hotel is connected by marriage with Mr. As——." The idea really offers an unlimited field for private enterprise.

The political situation in France was very strained at the beginning of 1874. Marshal MacMahon had succeeded M. Thiers as President of the Republic, and it was well known that the Marshal, as well as the Royalist majority in the French Chamber, favoured the restoration of the Bourbon Monarchy, represented by the Comte de Chambord, as head of the elder branch. People of the type of M. Ducros, and of the Président of the Nyons Tribunal, viewed the possible return of a Legitimist Bourbon Monarchy with the gravest apprehension. Given the character of the Comte de Chambord, they felt it would be a purely reactionary regime. Traditionally, the elder branch of the Bourbons were incapable of learning anything, and equally incapable of forgetting anything. These two shrewd lawyers had both been vigorous opponents of the Bonapartist regime, but they pinned their faith on the Orleans branch, inexplicably enough to me, considering the treacherous record of that family. They never could mention the name of a member of the Orleans family without adding, " Ah ! les braves gens ! " the very last epithet in the world I should have dreamed of applying to them. All the negotiations with the Comte de Chambord fell through, owing to his obstinacy (to which I have referred earlier) in refusing to accept the Tricolor as the national flag. Possibly pig-headed obstinacy ; but in these days of undisguised opportunism, it is rare to find a man who deliberately refuses a throne on account of his convictions. I do not think that the Comte de Chambord would have been a success in present-day British politics. A crisis was averted by extending Marshal MacMahon's tenure of the Presidency to seven years, the "Septennat," as it was called. Before two years the Orleanists, who had always a keen appreciation of the side on which their bread was buttered, "rallied" to the Republic. I rather fancy that some question connected with the return of the confiscated Orleans fortunes came into play here. The adherents of the Comte de Chambord always spoke of him as Henri V. For some reason (perhaps euphony) they were invariably known as "Henri Quinquists." In the same way, French people speak of the Emperor Charles V. as "Charles Quint," never as "Charles Cinq."

My friends the Nyons lawyers were fond of alluding to themselves as forming part of the *bonne bourgeoisie*.

It is this *bonne bourgeoisie* who form the backbone of France. Frugal, immensely industrious, cultured, and with a very high standard of honour, they are far removed from the frivolous, irresponsible types of French people to be seen at smart watering-places, and they are less dominated by that inordinate love of money which is an unpleasant element in the national character, and obscures the good qualities of the hard-working French peasants, making them grasping and avaricious.

It must be admitted that this class of the French bourgeoisie surveys the world from rather a Chinese standpoint. The Celestial, as is well known, considers all real civilisation confined to China.

Every one outside the bounds of the Middle Kingdom is a barbarian. This is rather the view of the
French bourgeois. He is convinced that all true
civilisation is centred in France, and that other
countries are only civilised in proportion as French
influence has filtered through to them. He will
hardly admit that other countries can have an art
and literature of their own, especially should neither
of them conform to French standards. This is
easily understood, for the average Frenchman
knows no language but his own, has never travelled,
and has no curiosity whatever about countries
outside France. When, in addition, it is remembered how paramount French literary and artistic
influence was during the greater portion of the
seventeenth and eighteenth centuries, and how
universal the use of the French language was in
Northern Continental Europe amongst educated
people, the point of view becomes quite intelligible.

In spite of this, I enjoyed my excursions with
these delightful French lawyers quite enormously.
The other pupils never accompanied us, for they
found it difficult to keep up a conversation in
French.

The average intellectual level is unquestionably
far higher in France than in England, nor is it
necessary to give, to a people accustomed for
generations to understand *à demi-mot*, the elaborate explanations usually necessary in England
when the conversation has got beyond the mental
standards of a child six years old. The French,

too, are not addicted to perpetual wool-gathering. Nor can I conceive of a Frenchwoman endeavouring to make herself attractive by representing herself as so hopelessly " vague " that she can never be trusted to remember anything, or to avoid losing all her personal possessions. Idiocy, whether genuine or feigned, does not appeal to the French temperament. The would-be fascinating lady would most certainly be referred to as "une dinde de première classe."

The French are the only thoroughly logical people in the world, and their excessive development of the logical faculty leads them at times into pitfalls. " Ils ont les défauts de leurs qualités." In this country we have found out that systems, absolutely indefensible in theory, at times work admirably well in practice, and give excellent results. No Frenchman would ever admit that anything unjustifiable in theory could possibly succeed in practice—" Ce n'est pas logique," he would object, and there would be the end of it.

The Substitut informed me one day that he was making a " retreat " for three days at the Monastery of La Trappe d'Aiguebelle, and asked me if I would care to accompany him. To pass three days in a Trappist Monastery certainly promised a novel experience, but I pointed out that I was a Protestant, and that I could hardly expect the monks to welcome me with open arms. He answered that he would explain matters, and that the difference of religion would be overlooked. So

L

off we started, and after an interminable drive reached a huge, gaunt pile of buildings in very arid surroundings. The " Hospice " where visitors were lodged stood apart from the Monastery proper, the Chapel lying in between. It was explained to me that I must observe the rule of absolute silence within the building, and that I would be expected to be in bed by 8.15 p.m. and to rise at 5 a.m. like the rest of the guests. It was further conveyed to me that they hoped that I would see my way to attend Chapel at 5.30 a.m., afterwards I should be free for the remainder of the day. Talking and smoking were both permitted in the garden. I was given a microscopic whitewashed cell, most beautifully clean, containing a very small bed, one chair, a gas-jet, a *prie-Dieu*, a real human skull, and nothing else whatever. We went to dinner in a great arched refectory, where a monk, perched up in a high pulpit, read us Thomas à Kempis in a droning monotone. Complete silence was observed. At La Trappe no meat or butter is ever used, but we were given a most excellent dinner of vegetable soup, fish, omelets, and artichokes dressed with oil, accompanied by the monks' admirable home-grown wine. There were quite a number of visitors making "retreats," and I had hard work keeping the muscles of my face steady, as they made pantomimic signs to the lay-brothers who waited on us, for more omelet or more wine. After dinner the " Frère Hospitalier," a jolly, rotund little lay-brother, who wore a black

stole over his brown habit as a sign that he was
allowed to talk, drew me on one side in the garden.
As I was a heretic (he put it more politely) and
had the day to myself, would I do him a favour?
He was hard put to it to find enough fish for all
these guests; would I catch him some trout in the
streams in the forest? I asked for nothing better,
but I had no trout-rod with me. He produced a
rod, *such* a trout-rod! A long bamboo with a piece
of string tied to it! To fish for trout with a worm
was contrary to every tradition in which I had been
reared, but adaptability is a great thing, so with
two turns of a spade I got enough worms for the
afternoon, and started off. The Forêt d'Aiguebelle
is not a forest in our acceptation of the term, but
an endless series of little bare rocky hills, dotted
with pines, and fragrant with tufts of wild lavender,
thyme and rosemary. It was intersected with two
rushing, beautifully clear streams. I cannot conceive where all the water comes from in that arid
land. In sun-baked Nyons, water could be got
anywhere by driving a tunnel into the parched
hill-sides, when sooner or later an abundant spring
would be tapped. These French trout were either
ridiculously unsophisticated, or else very weary of
life: they simply asked to be caught. I got quite
a heavy basket, to the great joy of the "Frère
Hospitalier," and I got far more next day. Though
we had to rise at five, we got no breakfast till
eight, and a very curious breakfast it was. Every
guest had a yard of bread, and two saucers placed

in front of him ; one containing honey, the other shelled walnuts. We dipped the walnuts in the honey, and ate them with the bread, and excellent they were. In the place of coffee, which was forbidden, we had hot milk boiled with borage to flavour it, quite a pleasant beverage. The washing arrangements being primitive, I waited until every one was safely occupied in Chapel for an hour and a half, and then had a swim in the reservoir which supplied the monastery with water, and can only trust that I did not dirty it much. I was greatly disappointed with the singing in the severe, unadorned Chapel ; it was plainsong, without any organ or instrument. The effect of so great a body of voices might have been imposing had not the intonation (as kindly critics say at times of a debutante) been a little uncertain. As Trappists never speak, one could understand their losing their voices, but it seems curious that they should have lost their ears as well, though possibly it was only the visitors who sang so terribly out of tune.

I was taken all over the Monastery next day by the " Père Hospitalier," who, like his brown-frocked lay-brother, wore a black stole over his white habit, as a badge of office. With the exception of the fine cloisters, there were no architectural features whatever about the squat, massive pile of buildings. The modern chapel, studiously severe in its details, bore the unmistakable imprint of Viollet-le-Duc's soulless, mathematically correct Gothic. Personally, I think that Viollet-le-Duc spoiled every

ancient building in France which he "restored."
I was taken into the refectory to see the monks'
dinners already laid out for them.   They consisted
of nothing but bread and salad, but with such vast
quantities of each!   Each monk had a yard-long
loaf of bread, a bottle of wine and an absolute
stable-bucket of salad, liberally dressed with oil
and vinegar.   The oil supplied the fat necessary
for nutrition, still it was a meagre enough dinner
for men who had been up since 3 a.m. and had
done two hours' hard work in the vegetable gardens.
The " Père Hospitalier " told me that not one scrap
of bread or lettuce would be left at the conclusion
of the repast.   The immense austerity of the place
impressed me very much.   The monks all slept on
plank-beds, but they were not allowed to remain
on these hard resting-places after 3 a.m.   Their
" Rule " was certainly a very severe one.   I was
told that the monks prepared Tincture of Arnica
for medicinal purposes in an adjoining factory,
arnica growing wild everywhere in the Forest, and
that the sums realised by the sale of this drug
added materially to their revenues.

Next day both the Substitut and I were to be
received by the Abbot.   It struck me as desirable
that we should have our interviews separately, for
as the Substitut was making a "retreat," he might
wish to say many private things to the Abbot
which he would not like me, a heretic, to overhear.
As soon as he had finished, I was ushered in alone
to the Abbot's parlour.   I found the Abbot very

dignified and very friendly, but what possible subject of conversation could a Protestant youth of seventeen find which would interest the Father Superior of a French Monastery, presumably indifferent to everything that passed outside its walls? Suddenly I had an inspiration: the Arian Heresy! We had had four lessons on this interesting topic at Chittenden's five years earlier (surely rather an advanced subject for little boys of twelve!), and some of the details still stuck in my head. A brilliant idea! Soon we were at it hammer and tongs; discussing Arius, Alexander, and Athanasius; the Council of Nicæa, Hosius of Cordova, *homo-ousion* and *homoi-ousion*; Eusebius of Nicomedia, and his namesake of Cæsarea.

Without intending any disrespect to these two eminent Fathers of the Church, the two Eusebius' always reminded me irresistibly of the two Ajaxes of Offenbach's *opéra-bouffe*, *La Belle Hélène*, or, later on, of the "Two Macs" of the music-hall stage of the "nineties." I blessed Mr. Chittenden for having so thoughtfully provided me with conversational small-change suitable for Abbots. The Abbot was, I think, a little surprised at my theological lore. He asked me where I had acquired it, and when I told him that it was at school, he presumed that I had been at a seminary for youths destined for the priesthood, an idea which would have greatly shocked the ultra-Evangelical Mr. Chittenden.

I was very glad that I had passed those three

days at La Trappe, for it gave one a glimpse into a wholly unsuspected world. The impression of the tremendous severity with which the lives of the monks were regulated, remained with me. The excellent monks made the most absurdly small charges for our board and lodging. Years afterwards I spent a night in an Orthodox Monastery in Russia, when I regretfully recalled the scrupulous cleanliness of La Trappe. Never have I shared a couch with so many uninvited guests, and never have I been so ruthlessly devoured as in that Russian Monastery.

With June at Nyons, silkworm time arrived. Three old women, celebrated for their skill in rearing silkworms, came down from the mountains, and the *magnanerie*, as lofts devoted to silkworm culture are called, was filled with huge trays fashioned with reeds. The old women had a very strenuous fortnight or so, for silkworms demand immense care and attention. The trays have to be perpetually cleaned out, and all stale mulberry leaves removed, for the quality and quantity of the silk depend on the most scrupulous cleanliness. To preserve an even temperature, charcoal fires were lighted at night in the *magnanerie*, until the little black caterpillars, having transformed themselves into repulsive flabby white worms, these worms became obsessed with the desire to increase the world's supply of silk, and to gratify them, twigs were placed in the trays for them to spin their cocoons on. The cocoons spun, they were all picked off, and baked in the public ovens of the town, in order to kill the chrysalis inside. Nothing prettier can be imagined than the streets of Nyons, with white sheets laid in front of every house, each sheet heaped high with glittering, shimmering, gleaming piles of silk-cocoons, varying in shade from palest straw-colour to deep orange. If pleasant to the eye, they were less grateful to the nose, for freshly baked cocoons have the most offensive odour. The silk-buyers from Lyons then made their appearance, and these shining heaps of gold thread were transformed into a more portable form of gold, which found its way into the pockets of the inhabitants.

The peculiarly French capacity for taking infinite pains, of which a good example is this silkworm culture, has its drawbacks when carried into administrative work. My friend M. David, the post-master of Nyons, showed me his official instructions. They formed a volume as big as a family Bible. It would have taken years to learn all these regulations. The simplest operations were made enormously complicated. Let any one compare the time required for registering a letter or a parcel in England, with the time a similar operation in France will demand. M. David showed me the lithographed sheet giving the special forms of numerals, 1, 2, 3, and so on, which French postal officials are required to make. These differ widely from the forms in general use.

I have my own suspicions that similar sheets are

issued to the cashiers in French restaurants. Personally, I can never read one single item in the bill, much less the cost, and I can only gaze in hopeless bewilderment at the long-tailed hieroglyphics, recalling a backward child's first attempts at "pot-hooks."

The infinite capacity of the French for taking trouble, and their minute attention to detail, tend towards unnecessary complications of simple matters. Thus, on English railways we find two main types of signals sufficient for our wants, whereas on French lines there are five different main types of signal. On English lines we have two secondary signals, against eight in France, all differing widely in shape and appearance. Again, on a French locomotive the driver has far more combinations at his command for efficient working, under varying conditions, than is the case in England. The trend of the national mind is towards complicating details rather than simplifying them.

Delightful as was the winter climate of Nyons, that sun-scorched little cup amongst the hills became a place of positive torment as the summer advanced. The heat was absolutely unendurable. Day and night, thousands of cicadas (the *cigales* of the French) kept up their incessant "dzig, dzig, dzig," a sound very familiar to those who have sojourned in the tropics. Has Nature given this singular insect the power of dispensing with sleep? What possible object can it hope to attain by keeping up this incessant din? If a love-song, surely the most optimistic cicada must realise that his amorous strains can never reach the ears of his lady-love, since hundreds of his brethren are all keeping up the same perpetual purposeless chirping, which must obviously drown any individual effort. Have the cicadas a double dose of *gaieté française* in their composition, and is this their manner of expressing it? Are they, like some young men we know, always yearning to turn night into day? All these are, and will remain, unsolved problems.

As I found the summer heat of Nyons unbearable, I went back to England for a holiday, and, on the morning of my departure, climbed some olive trees and captured fourteen live cicadas, whom I imprisoned in a perforated cardboard box, and took back to London with me. Twelve of them survived the journey, and as soon as I had arrived, I carefully placed the cicadas on the boughs of the trees in our garden in Green Street, Grosvenor Square. Conceive the surprise of these travelled insects at finding themselves on the soot-laden branches of a grimy London tree! The dauntless little creatures at once recommenced their "dzig, dzig, dzig," in their novel environment, and kept it up uninterruptedly for twenty-four hours, in spite of the lack of appreciation of my family, who complained that their night's rest had been seriously interfered with by the unaccustomed noise. Next evening the cicadas were silent. Possibly they

had been choked with soot, or had fallen a prey
to London cats; but my own theory is that they
succumbed to the after-effects of a rough Channel
passage, to which, of course, they would not have
been accustomed. Anyhow, for the first time in
the history of the world, the purlieus of Grosvenor
Square rang with the shrill chirping of cicadas for
twenty-four hours on end.

Six months later I regretfully bid farewell to
Nyons, and went direct from there to Germany.
After studying the Teutonic tongue for two and a
half years at Harrow I was master of just two
words in it, *ja* and *nein*, so unquestionably there
were gaps to fill up.

I was exceedingly sorry to leave the delightful
Ducros family who had treated me so kindly, and
I owe a deep debt of gratitude to comely Mme.
Ducros for the careful way in which she taught
me history. In teaching history she used what I
may call the synoptic method, taking periods of
fifty years, and explaining contemporaneous events
in France, Italy, Germany, and England during
that period.

With the exception of one friendly visit to the
Ducros, I have never seen pleasant Nyons again.
Of late years I have often meditated a pilgrimage
to that sunny little cup in the Dauphiné hills, but
have hesitated owing to one of the sad penalties
advancing years bring with them; every single
one of my friends, man or woman, must have
passed away long since. I can see Nyons, with

its encircling fringe of blue hills, just as vividly, perhaps, with my inner eyes as I could if it lay actually before me, and now I can still people it with the noisy, gesticulating inhabitants whom I knew and liked so much.

CHAPTER VI

BRUNSWICK had been selected for me as a
suitable spot in which to learn German, and to
Brunswick I accordingly went. As I was then
eighteen years old, I did not care to go to a
regular tutor's, but wished to live in a German
family, where I was convinced I could pick up the
language in far shorter time. I was exceedingly
fortunate in this respect. A well-to-do Managing
Director of some jute-spinning mills had recently
built himself a large house. Mr. Spiegelberg found
not only that his new house was unnecessarily big
for his family, but he also discovered that it had
cost him a great deal more than he had anticipated.

He was quite willing, therefore, to enter into an arrangement for our mutual benefit.

Brunswick is one of the most beautiful old towns in Europe. Its narrow, winding streets are (or, perhaps, were) lined with fifteenth and sixteenth century timbered houses, each storey projecting some two feet further over the street than the one immediately below it, and these wooden house-fronts were one mass of the most beautiful and elaborate carving. Imagine Staples Inn in Holborn double its present height, and with every structural detail chiselled with patient care into intricate patterns of fruit and foliage, and you will get some idea of a Brunswick street. The town contained four or five splendid old churches, and their mediæval builders had taken advantage of the dead-flat, featureless plain in which Brunswick stands, to erect such lofty towers as only the architects in the Low Countries ever devised; towers which served as landmarks for miles around, their soaring height silhouetted against the pale northern sky. The irregular streets and open places contained one or two gems of Renaissance architecture, such as the stone-built Town Hall and "Guild House," both very similar in character to buildings of the same date in sleepy old Flemish towns. The many gushing fountains of mediæval bronze and iron-work in the streets added to the extraordinary picturesqueness of the place. It was like a scene from an opera in real life. It always puzzled me to think how the water for these fountains can have been provided on that dead-flat plain in pre-steam days. There must have been pumps of some sort. Before 1914, tens of thousands of tourists visited Nuremberg annually, but the guide-books are almost silent about Brunswick, which is fully as picturesque.

The standard of material comfort appeared far higher in Brunswick than in a French provincial town. The manner in which the Spiegelbergs' house was fitted up seemed very elaborate after the simple appointments of the Ducros' farm-house, though nothing in the world would have induced me to own one single object that this Teutonic residence contained. The Spiegelbergs treated me extremely kindly, and I was fortunate in being quartered on such agreeable people.

At Nyons there was not one single bookseller, but Brunswick bristled with book-shops, and, in addition, there were two of those most excellent lending libraries to be found in every German town. Here almost every book ever published in German or English was to be found, as well as a few very cautiously selected French ones, for German parents were careful then as to what their daughters read.

The great resource of Brunswick was the theatre, such a theatre as does not exist in any French provincial town, and such a theatre as has never even been dreamed of in any British town. It was fully as large as Drury Lane, and was subsidised by the State. I really believe that every opera ever written was given here, and given quite admirably. In this town of 60,000 inhabitants, in addition to the opera company, there was a fine dramatic company, as well as a light opera company, and a corps de ballet. Sunday, Tuesday and Saturday were devoted to grand opera, Monday to classical drama (Schiller or Shakespeare), Wednesday to modern comedy, Friday to light opera or farce. The bill was constantly changing, and every new piece produced in Berlin or Vienna was duly presented to the Brunswick public. There are certainly some things we can learn from Germany! The mounting of the operas was most excellent, and I have never seen better lighting effects than on the Brunswick stage, and this, too, was all done by gas, incandescent electric light not then being dreamed of even. I had imagined in my simplicity that effects were far easier to produce on the modern stage since the introduction of electric light. Sir Johnston Forbes-Robertson, than whom there can be no greater authority, tells me that this is not so. To my surprise, he declares that electric light is too crude and white, and that it destroys all illusion. He informs me that it is impossible to obtain a convincing moonlight effect with electricity, or to give a sense of atmosphere. Gas-light was yellow, and colour-effects were obtained by dropping thin screens of coloured silk over the gas-battens in the flies. This diffused the light, which a crude blue or red electric bulb does not do. Sir Johnston

Forbes-Robertson astonished me by telling me that Henry Irving always refused to have electric light on the stage at the Lyceum, though he had it in the auditorium. All those marvellous and complicated effects, which old playgoers must well recollect in Irving's Lyceum productions, were obtained with gas. I remember the lovely sunset, with its after-glow fading slowly into night, in the garden scene of the Lyceum version of *Faust*, and this was all done with gas. The factor of safety is another matter. With rows of flaming gas-battens in the flies, however carefully screened off, and another row of " gas lengths " in the wings, and flaring "ground-rows" in close proximity to highly inflammable painted canvas, the inevitable destiny of a gas-lit theatre is only a question of time. The London theatres of the "sixties" all had a smell of mingled gas and orange-peel, which I thought delicious.

Mr. Spiegelberg most sensibly suggested that as I was absolutely ignorant of German, the easiest manner in which I could accustom my ears to the sound of the language would be to take an *abonnement* at the theatre, and to go there nightly. So for the modest sum of thirty shillings per month, I found myself entitled to a stall in the second row, with the right of seeing thirty performances a month. I went every night to the theatre, and there was no monotony about it, for the same performance was never repeated twice in one month. I have seen, I think, every opera

M

ever written, and every single one of Shakespeare's tragedies. A curious trait in the German character is petty vindictiveness. A certain Herr Behrens had signed a contract as principal bass with the Brunswick management. Getting a far more lucrative offer from Vienna, the prudent Behrens had paid a fine, and thrown over the Brunswick theatre. For eighteen months the unfortunate man was pilloried every night on the theatre programmes. Every play-bill had printed on it in large letters, "Kontrakt brüchig Herr Behrens," never allowing the audience to forget that poor Behrens was a convicted "contract-breaker."

Half Brunswick went to the theatre every night of its life. The ladies made no pretence of elaborate toilets, but contented themselves with putting two tacks into the necks of their day gowns so as to make a V-shaped opening. (With present fashions this would not be necessary.) Over this they placed one of those appalling little arrangements of imitation lace and blue or pink bows, to be seen in the shop windows of every German town, and known, I think, as *Theater-Garnitures*. They then drew on a pair of dark plum-coloured gloves, and their toilet was complete. The contrast between the handsome white-and-gold theatre and the rows of portly, dowdy matrons, each one with her ample bosom swathed in a piece of antimacassar, was very comical. Every *abonné* had his own peg for hanging his coat and hat on, and this, and the fact that one's neighbours in the stalls were invariably the same, gave quite a family atmosphere to the Brunswick theatre.

The conductor was Franz Abt the composer, and the musical standard of the operatic performances was very high indeed. The mounting was always excellent, but going to the theatre night after night, some of the scenery became very familiar. There was a certain Gothic hall which seemed to share the mobile facilities of Aladdin's palace. This hall was ubiquitous, whether the action of the piece lay in Germany, Italy, France, or England. Mary Queen of Scots sobbed in this hall; Wallenstein in Schiller's tragedy ranted in it; Rigoletto reproved his flighty daughter in it. It seemed curious that personages so widely different should all have selected the same firm of upholsterers to fit up their sanctums.

The Spiegelbergs had many friends in the theatrical world, and I was immensely thrilled one evening at learning that after the performance of *Lohengrin*, Elsa and the Knight of the Swan were coming home to supper with us. When Elsa appeared on the balcony in the second act, and the moon most obligingly immediately appeared to light up her ethereal white draperies, I was much excited at reflecting that in two hours' time I might be handing this lovely maiden the mustard, and it seemed hardly credible that the resplendent Lohengrin would so soon abandon his swan in favour of the homely goose that was awaiting him at the Spiegelbergs', although the latter would enjoy the advantage of being roasted.

I was on the tip-toe of expectation until the singers arrived. Fraülein Scheuerlein, the soprano, was fat, fair, and forty, all of them perhaps on the liberal side. As she burst into the room, the first words I heard from the romantic Elsa, whom I had last seen sobbing over her matrimonial difficulties, were: " Dearest Frau Spiegelberg, my . . ." (Elsa here used a blunt dissyllable to indicate her receptacle for food) " is hanging positively crooked with hunger. Quick! For the love of Heaven, some bread and butter and sausage, or I shall faint;" so the first words the heroine of the evening addressed to me were somewhat blurred owing to her mouth being full of sausage, which destroyed most of the glamour of the situation. Hedwig Scheuerlein was a big, jolly, cheery South-German, and she was a consummate artist in spite of her large appetite, as was the tenor Schrötter too. Schrötter was a fair-bearded giant, who was certainly well equipped physically for playing " heroic" parts. He had one of those penetrating virile German tenor voices that appeal to me. These good-natured artists would sing us anything we wanted, but it was from them that I first got an inkling of those petty jealousies that are such a disagreeable feature of the theatrical world in every country. Buxom Scheuerlein was a very good sort, and I used to feel immensely elated at receiving in my stall a friendly nod over the footlights from

Isolde, Aïda, Marguerite, or Lucia, as the case might be.

I wonder why none of Meyerbeer's operas are ever given in London. The "books," being by Scribe, are all very dramatic, and lend themselves to great spectacular display; Meyerbeer's music is always melodious, and has a certain obvious character about it that would appeal to an average London audience. This is particularly true with regard to the *Prophète*. The Coronation scene can be made as gorgeous as a Drury Lane pantomime, and the *finale* of the opera is thrilling, though the three Anabaptists are frankly terrible bores. As given at Brunswick, in the last scene the Prophet, John of Leyden, is discovered at supper with some boon companions in rather doubtful female society. In the middle of his drinking-song the palace is blown up. There is a loud crash; the stage grows dark; hall, supper-table, and revellers all disappear; and the curtain comes down slowly on moonlight shining over some ruins, and the open country beyond. A splendid climax! Again, the third act of *Robert le Diable* is magnificently dramatic. Bertram, the Evil One in person, leads Robert to a deserted convent whose nuns, having broken the most important of their vows, have all been put to death. The curtain goes up on the dim cloisters of the convent, the cloister-garth, visible through the Gothic arches of the arcade, bathed in bright moonlight beyond. Bertram begins his incantations, recalling the erring nuns from the dead. Very

165

slowly the tombs in the cloister open, and dim grey figures, barely visible in the darkness, creep silently out from the graves. Bertram waves his arms over the cloister-garth, and there, too, the tombs gape apart, and more shadowy spectres emerge. Soon the stage is full of these faint grey spectral forms. Bertram lifts his arms. The wicked nuns throw off their grey wrappers, and appear glittering in scarlet and gold; the stage blazes with light, and the ballet, the famous "Pas de Fascination," begins. When really well done, this scene is tremendously impressive.

I once heard in Paris, Levasseur, the French counterpart of our own Corney Grain, giving a skit on *Robert le Diable*, illustrating various stage conventions. Levasseur, seated at his piano, and keeping up an incessant ripple of melody, talked something like this:—

"The stage represents Isabelle's bedroom. As is usual with stage bed-rooms, Isabelle's bower is about the size of an average cathedral. It is very sparsely furnished, but near the footlights is a large gilt couch, on which Isabelle is lying fast asleep. Robert enters on tip-toe very very gently, so as not to disturb his beloved, and sings in a voice that you could hear two miles off, 'Isa-belle!' dropping a full octave on the last note. Isabelle half awakes, and murmurs, 'I do believe I heard something. I feel so nervous!' Robert advances a yard, and sings again, if anything rather louder, 'Isa-belle!' Isabelle says: 'Really, my nerves do play me such tricks! I can't help fancying that there is some one in the room, and I am so terribly afraid of burglars! Perhaps it is only a mouse.' Robert advances right up to Isabelle's bed, and shouts for the third time in a voice that makes the chandelier ring again, 'Isa-belle!' Isabelle says, 'I don't think that I can have imagined that. There really is some one in the room. I'm terribly frightened, and don't quite know what to do,' so she gets out of bed, and anxiously scans the stalls and boxes over the footlights for signs of an intruder. Finding no one there but the audience, she then searches the gallery fruitlessly, and getting a sudden inspiration, she looks behind her, and, to her immense astonishment, finds her lover standing within a foot of her." This, as told with Levasseur's inimitable drollery, was really excruciatingly funny.

Robert is an expensive opera to put on, for, owing to hideous jealousies at the Paris Opéra, Meyerbeer was compelled to write two *prima-donna* parts which afforded the rival ladies exactly equal opportunities. In the same way Halévy, the composer of *La Juive*, had to re-arrange and transpose his score, for Adolphe Nourrit, the great Paris tenor, in 1835, when the opera was first produced, was jealous of the splendid part the bass had been given, the tenor's rôle being quite insignificant. So it came about that *La Juive* is the only opera in which the grey-bearded old father is played by the principal tenor, whilst the lover is the light tenor. Méhul's Biblical *Joseph and his Brethren* is the one opera in which there are no female characters, though "Benjamin" is played by the leading soprano. In both the *Prophète* and *Favorita* the contralto plays the principal part, the soprano having a very subsidiary rôle. Meyerbeer wrote the part of the Prophet himself specially for Roger, the great tenor, and that of "Fides" for Mme. Viardot. By the way, the famous skating scene in the *Prophète* was part of the original production in Paris of 1849, and yet we think roller-skating an invention of yesterday.

I had German lessons from a Professor Hentze. This old man was the first example of a militant German that I had come across. He was always talking of Germany's inevitable and splendid destiny. Although a Hanoverian by birth, he was a passionate admirer of Bismarck and Bismarck's policy, and was a furious Pan-German in sentiment. "Where the German tongue is heard, there will be the German Fatherland," he was fond of quoting in the original. As he declared that both Dutch and Flemish were but variants of Low German, he included Holland and Belgium in the Greater Germany of the future, as well as the German-speaking Cantons of Switzerland, and Upper and Lower Austria. Mentally, he possibly included a certain island lying between the North Sea and the Atlantic as well, though, out of regard for my feelings, he never mentioned it. Hentze taught English and French in half a dozen boys' and girls' schools in Brunswick, and his brother taught history in the " Gymnasium." These two mild-mannered be-spectacled old bachelors, who in their leisure moments took snuff and played with their poodle, were tremendous fire-eaters. They were both enormously proud of the exploits of a cousin of theirs who, under the guise of a harmless commercial traveller in wines, had been engaged in spying and map-making for five years in Eastern France prior to 1870. It was, they averred (no doubt truthfully enough), owing to the labours of their cousin and of countless others like him, that the Franco-Prussian War of 1870-71 had been such an overwhelming success for Germany. Where German interests were concerned, these two old brothers could see nothing under a white light. And remember that they were teachers and trainers of youth ; it was they who had the mould-ing of the minds of the young generation. I think that any one who knows Germany well will agree with me that it is the influence of the teaching class, whether in school or university, that has transformed the German mentality so greatly during the last forty years. These two mild-mannered old Hentzes must have infected scores and hundreds of lads with their own aggressively militant views. By perpetually holding up to them their own dream of a Germany covering half Europe, they must have transmitted some of their own enthusiasm to their pupils, and underlying that enthusiasm was a tacit assumption that the end justified any means ; that provided the goal were attained, the manner in which it had been arrived at was a matter of quite secondary importance. I maintain that the damnable spirit of modern Germany is mainly due to the teaching profession, and to the doctrines it consistently instilled into German youth.

The Hentzes took in eight resident German pupils who attended the various schools in the town, mostly sons of wealthy Hamburg business-people. Hentze was always urging me to associate more with these lads, three of whom were of my own age, but I could discover no common ground whatever on which to meet them. The things that interested me did not appeal to them, and *vice versa.* They seemed to me dull youths, heavy alike in mind and body. From lack of sufficient fresh air and exercise they had all dull eyes, and flabby, white faces that quivered like blancmanges when they walked. In addition, they obstinately refused to talk German with me, looking on me as affording an excellent opportunity for obtaining a gratuitous lesson in English. One of Hentze's pupils was a great contrast, physically, to the rest, for he was very spare and thin, and seldom opened his mouth. I was to see a great deal of this silent, slim lad later on.

Mr. Spiegelberg was a prominent member of the so-called English and French Club in Brunswick. This was not in the least what its name would seem to indicate; the members of the Club were not bursting with overwhelming love for our language and institutions, nor were they consumed with enthusiastic admiration for French art and literature. They were merely some fifteen very practical Brunswick commercial men, who, realising that a good working knowledge of English and French would prove extremely useful to them in their business relations, met at each other's houses in rotation on one night a week during the winter months, when the host of the evening provided copious supplies of wine, beer and cigars. For one hour and a half the members of the Club had to talk English or French as the case might be, under a penalty of a fine of one thaler (three shillings) for every lapse into their native German. Mr. Spiegelberg informed me that I had been elected an honorary member of the English and French Club, which flattered my vanity enormously at the time. In the light of more mature experience I quite understand that the presence of a youth to whom knotty points in both languages could be submitted would be a considerable asset to the Club, but I then attributed my election solely to my engaging personality. These Club evenings amused me enormously, though incidentally they resulted in my acquiring a precocious love of strong, rank, Hamburg cigars. Let us imagine fifteen portly, be-spectacled, middle-aged or elderly men seated round a table groaning under a collection of bottles of all shapes and sizes, addressing each other in laboured inverted English. The German love of titles is a matter of common knowledge. All these business men had honorific appellations which they translated into English, and introduced scrupulously into every sentence. The conversation was something like this :—

"But, Mr. Over-Inspector of Railways, I do not think that you understand rightly what Mr. Factory Director Spiegelberg says. Mr. Factory Director also spins jute. To make concurrenz with Dundee in Schottland, he must produce cheaply. To produce cheaply he must become . . . no, obtain new machinery from Leeds in England. If that machinery is duty-payable, Mr. Factory Director cannot produce so cheaply. That seems to me clear. Once our German industries established are, then we will see. That is another matter."

"I take the liberty to differ, Mr. Councillor of Commerce. How then shall our German industries flourish, if they not protected be? What for a doctrine is that? Mr. Factory Director Spiegelberg thinks only of jute. Outside jute, the German world of commerce is greater, and with in-the-near-future-to-be-given railways facilities, vast and imposing shortly shall be."

"What Mr. Councillor of Commerce just has said, is true. You, Mr. Over-Inspector of Railways, and also you, Mr. Ducal Supervisor of Forests, are not merchants like us, but much-skilled specialists; so is the point of view different. Mr. Town Councillor Balhorn, you have given us most brilliant beer to-night. This is no beer of here, it must be real Munich. It tastes famous. Prosit!"

"I thank you, Mr. Court Councillor. In the place, gentlemen, of with-anger-discussing Free Trade, let us all drink some Munich beer. Discussion is good, but beer with content is better."

Now I put it to you—could any one picture fifteen English business men in Manchester, Liverpool, or Leeds doing anything so sensible as to meet once a week amongst themselves, to acquire proficiency and fluency in French, Spanish, or German, all of which languages they must presumably require at times for the purposes of their business. Every one knows that it is unthinkable. No Englishman could be bothered to take the trouble. Why is it that English people have this extraordinary reluctance to learn any foreign language? It is certainly not from want of natural ability to do so, though this natural aptitude may be discounted by the difficulty most English people experience in keeping their minds concentrated. I venture to assert unhesitatingly that, with the exception of Dutch and Russian people, English folk learn foreign languages with greater ease than any other nationality. This is notably true with regard to Russian and Spanish. The English throat is more flexible than that of the Frenchman or German, and, with the one exception of French, there are no unwonted sounds in any European language that an Englishman cannot reproduce fairly accurately. We have something like the hard Russian "l" in the last syllable of "impossible," and to the Scottish or Irish throat the Dutch hard initial guttural, and the Spanish soft guttural, offer but little difficulty. "Jorje," which looks like "George" spelt phonetically, but is pronounced so very differently, can easily be mastered, and that real teaser "gracht," the Dutch for "canal," with a strong guttural at either end of it, comes easily out of a Scottish throat. The power to acquire these tongues is there, but the inclination is woefully lacking.

Some ten years ago I went out to Panama to have a look at the canal works. On board the mail-steamer there were twelve commercial travellers representing British firms, bound for the West Coast of South America. Ten of these twelve were Germans, all speaking English and Spanish fluently in addition to their native German. The other two were English, not knowing one word of any language but their own. I had a long talk with these two Englishmen, and asked them whether they were familiar with the varying monetary standards of the countries they were going to visit; for the nominal dollar represents a widely different value in each South American State. No, they knew nothing whatever about this, and were quite ignorant of Spanish-American weights and measures. Now what possible object did the firms sending out these ill-equipped representatives hope to attain? Could they in their wildest

174

moments have supposed that they would get one single order through their agency? And how came it about that these young men were so ignorant of the language and customs of the countries they were proposing to travel? During the voyage I noticed the German travellers constantly conversing with South Americans from the Pacific Coast, in an endeavour to improve their working knowledge of Spanish; meanwhile the young Englishmen played deck-quoits and talked English. That in itself is quite sufficiently characteristic. In Manchester there is a firm who do a large business in manufacturing brightly coloured horse-trappings for the South American market. I speak with some confidence about this, for I have myself watched those trappings being made. Most of the "ponchos" used in the Argentine are woven in Glasgow. Why is it that in these two great industrial centres no one seems to have thought of establishing a special class in any of the numerous schools and colleges for training youths as commercial travellers in foreign countries? They would have, in addition to learning two or three languages, to get used to making quick calculations in dollars and cents, and in dollars of very varying values; they would also have to learn to *think* quickly in weights and measures different to those to which they had been accustomed. Why should British firms be compelled to use German travellers, owing to the ineptitude of their own countrymen? The power to learn is there;

it is only the will that is lacking, and in justice I must add, perhaps the necessary facilities. People who do not mind taking trouble will always in the end get a pull over people who hate all trouble. I think that our present King once cried, "Buck up, England!" and his Majesty spoke true; very few things can be done in this world without taking a little trouble.

To return, after this long digression, to the portly German middle-aged business men who met weekly in Brunswick to improve their working knowledge of French and English, I must candidly say that I never detected the faintest shadow of animosity to Great Britain in them. They were not Prussians—they were Hanoverians and Brunswickers. They felt proud, I think, that the throne of Britain was then occupied by a branch of their own ancient House of Guelph; they remembered the hundred years' connection between Britain and Hanover; as business men they acknowledged Britain's then unquestioned industrial supremacy, and they recognised that men of their class enjoyed in England a position and a power which was not accorded to them in Germany. Certainly they never lost an opportunity of pointing out that Britain was neither a military nor a fighting nation, and would never venture again to conduct a campaign on the Continent. Recent events will show how correct they were in their forecasts.

I liked the society of these shrewd, practical men

for from being so much with the French judges,
I had become accustomed to associating with men
double or treble my own age. There was nothing
corresponding to the *gaieté française* about them,
though at times a ponderous playfulness marked
their lighter moments, and flashes of elephantine
jocularity enlivened the proceedings of the Club.
I picked up some useful items of knowledge from
them, for I regret to admit that up to that time I
had no idea what a bill of lading was, or a ship's
manifest; after a while, even such cryptic expressions, too, as *f.o.b.* and *c.i.f.* ceased to have any
mysteries for me. Let the inexperienced beware
of " Swedish Punch," a sickly, highly-scented preparation of arrack. I do not speak from personal
experience, for I detest the sweet, cloying stuff;
but it occasionally fell to my lot to guide downstairs the uncertain footsteps of some ventripotent
Kommerzien-Rath, or even of Mr. Over-Inspector
of Railways himself, both temporarily incapaci-
tated by injudicious indulgence in Swedish Punch.
"So, Herr Ober-Inspector, endlich sind wir glück-
lich herunter gekommen-Jetz konnen Sie nach
Hause immer auf gleichem Fusse gehen-Natür-
lich! Jedermann weisst wie abscheulich kräftig
Schwedischer Punsch ist. Die Strasse ist ganz
leer. Glückliche Heimkehr, Herr Ober-Inspector!"
It was difficult to attend the Club without becoming a connoisseur in various kinds of German
beer. Brunswick boasts a special local sweet black
beer, brewed from malted wheat instead of barley,

known as "Mumme"—heavy, unpalatable stuff.
If any one will take the trouble to consult
Whitaker's Almanac, and turn to "Customs Tariff
of the United Kingdom," they will find the very
first article on the list is "mum." "Berlin white
beer" follows this. One of the few occasions when
I have ever known Mr. Gladstone nonplussed for
an answer, was in a debate on the Budget (I
think in 1886) on a proposed increase of excise
duties. Mr. Gladstone was asked what "mum"
was, and confessed that he had not the smallest
idea. The opportunity for instructing the om-
niscient Mr. Gladstone seemed such a unique one,
that I nearly jumped up in my place to tell him
that it was a sweet black beer brewed from wheat,
and peculiar to Brunswick; but being a very young
Member of the House then, I refrained, as it looked
presumptuous and too much like self-advertisement. "White beer" is only made in Berlin; it
is not unlike our ginger-beer, and is pleasant
enough. The orthodox way of ordering it in
Berlin is to ask the waiter for "eine kühle
Blonde." I do not suppose that one drop of
either of these beverages has been imported into
the United Kingdom for a hundred years; equally
I imagine that the first two Georges loved them
as recalling their beloved Hanover, and indulged
freely in them; whence their place in our Customs
tariff.

One of the members of the English and French
Club was a Mr. Vieweg, at that time, I believe,

the largest manufacturer of sulphate of quinine in
Europe. Mr. Vieweg was that *rara avis* amongst
middle-class German business-men, a born sportsman. He had already made two sporting trips to
Central Africa after big game, and rented a large
shooting estate near Brunswick. In common with
the other members of the Club, he treated me very
kindly and hospitably, and I often had quaint
repasts at his house, beginning with sweet chocolate soup, and continuing with eels stewed in beer,
carp with horseradish, "sour-goose," and other
Teutonic delicacies. Mr. Vieweg's son was one
of Hentze's pupils, and was the thin, silent boy I
have already noticed. I remember well how young
Vieweg introduced himself to me in laboured
English. "Are you a friend to fishing with the
fly?" he asked. "I also fish most gladly, and if
you wish, we will together to the Harz Mountains
go, and there many trout catch." As the Harz
Mountains are within an hour of Brunswick by
train, off we went, and young Vieweg was certainly
a most expert fisherman. My respect for him was
increased enormously when I found that he did not
mind in the least how wet he got whilst fishing.
Most German boys of his age would have thought
standing in cold water up to their knees a certain
forerunner of immediate death.

Vieweg told me, with perfect justice, that he
knew every path and every track in the Northern
Harz, and that he had climbed every single hill.
He complained that none of his German friends

cared for climbing or walking, and asked whether
I would accompany him on one of his expeditions.
So a week later we went again to the Harz, and
Vieweg led me an interminable and very rough
walk up-hill and down-dale. He afterwards confessed that he was trying to tire me out, in which
he failed signally, for I have always been, and am still,
able to walk very long distances without fatigue.
He had taken four of his fellow-pupils from Hentze's
over the same road, and they had all collapsed, and
had to be driven back to the railway in a hay-cart,
in the last stages of exhaustion. Finding that he
could not walk me down, Vieweg developed an
odd sort of liking for me, just as I had admired
him for standing up to his knees in very cold water
for a couple of hours on end whilst fishing. So a
queer sort of friendship sprang up between me and
this taciturn youth. The only subject which moved
Vieweg to eloquence was quinine, out of which his
father had made his fortune. I confess that at that
time I knew no more about that admirable pro-
phylactic than the Queen of Sheba knew about
dry-fly fishing, and had not the faintest idea of
how quinine was made. Vieweg, warming to his
subject, explained to me that the cinchona bark
was treated with lime and alcohol, and informed
me that his father now obtained the bark from
Java instead of from South America as formerly.
He did his utmost to endeavour to kindle a little
enthusiasm in me on the subject of this valuable
febrifuge. When not talking of quinine, he kept

silence. This singular youth was obsessed with a passionate devotion to the lucrative drug.

The Harz Mountains are pretty without being grand. The far-famed Brocken is not 4000 ft. high, but rising as these hills do out of the dead-flat North German plain, the Harz have been glorified and magnified by a people accustomed to monotonous levels, and are the setting for innumerable German legends. The Brocken is, of course, the traditional scene of the "Witches' Sabbath" on *Walpurgis-Nacht*, and many of the rock-strewn valleys seem to have pleasant traditions of bloodthirsty ogres and gnomes associated with them. There is no real climbing in the Harz, easy tracks lead to all the local lions. As is customary in methodical Germany, signposts direct the pedestrian to every view and every waterfall, and I need hardly add that if one post indicates the *Aussichtspunkt*, a corresponding one will show the way to the restaurant without which no view in Germany would be complete. Through rocky defiles and pine-woods, over swelling hills and past waterfalls, Vieweg and I trudged once a week in sociable silence, broken only by a few scraps of information from my companion as to the prospects of that year's crop of cinchona bark, and the varying wholesale price of that interesting commodity. At times, before a fine view, Vieweg would make quite a long speech for him: "Du Fritz! Schön was?" using, of course, the German diminutive to my christian name, after which he would gaze on the prospect and relapse into silence and dreamy meditations on sulphate of quinine and its possibilities.

I think Vieweg enjoyed these excursions, for on returning to Brunswick after about four hours' unbroken silence, he would always say on parting, " Du Fritz ! War nicht so übel ; " or, " Fritz, it wasn't so bad," very high praise from so sparing a talker.

Mr. Vieweg senior invited me to shoot with him on several occasions during the winter months. The " Kettle-drive " (*Kessel-Treib*) is the local manner of shooting hares. Guns and beaters form themselves into an immense circle, a mile in diameter, over the treeless, hedgeless flats, and all advance slowly towards the centre of the circle. At first, it is perfectly safe to fire into the circle, but as it diminishes in size, a horn is sounded, the guns face round, back to back, and as the beaters advance alone, hares are only killed as they run out of the ring. Hares are very plentiful in North Germany, and " Kettle-drives " usually resulted in a bag of from thirty to forty of them. To my surprise, in the patches of oak-scrub on the moorlands, there were usually some woodcock, a bird which I had hitherto associated only with Ireland. Young Vieweg was an excellent shot ; in common with all his father's other guests, he was arrayed in high boots, and in one of those grey-green suits faced with dark green, dear to the heart of the German sportsman. The guns all looked like the chorus in the *Freischütz*, and I expected them to break at any moment into the "Huntsmen's Chorus." Young Vieweg was greatly pained at my unorthodox costume, for I wore ordinary homespun knickerbockers, and sported neither a green Tyrolese hat with a blackcock's tail in it, nor high boots; my gun had no green sling attached to it, nor did I carry a game-bag covered with green tassels, all of which, it appeared, were absolutely essential concomitants to a *Jagd-Partie*.

In these country districts round Brunswick nothing but Low German ("Platt-Deutsch") was talked. Low German is curiously like English at times. The sentence, "the water is deep," is identical in both tongues. "Mudder," "brudder," and "sister" have all a familiar ring about them, too. The word "watershed," as applied to the ridge separating two river systems, had always puzzled me. In High German it is "Wasserscheide," *i. e.* water-parting; in Low German it is "Water-shed," with the same meaning, thus making our own term perfectly clear. "Low" German, of course, only means the dialect spoken in the low-lying North German plains: "High" German, the language spoken in the hilly country south of the Harz Mountains. High German only became the literary language of the country owing to Luther having deliberately chosen that dialect for the translation of the Bible. The Nibelungen-Lied and the poems of the twelfth and thirteenth centuries were all in Middle-High German (Mittel-Hoch Deutsch).

THE DAYS BEFORE YESTERDAY

I remember being told as a boy, when standing on the terrace of Windsor Castle, that in a straight line due east of us there was no such corresponding an elevation until the Ural Mountains were reached, on the boundary between Europe and Asia. This will give some idea of the extreme flatness of Northern Europe, for the terrace at Windsor can hardly be called a commanding eminence.

I am sorry to say that for over forty years I have quite lost sight of Vieweg. My connection with quinine, too, has been usually quite involuntary. I have had two very serious bouts of malarial fever, one in South America, the other in the West Indies, and on both occasions I owed my life to quinine. Whilst taking this bitter, if beneficent drug, I sometimes wondered whether it had been prepared under the auspices of the friend of my youth. So ignorant am I of the quinine world, that I do not know whether the firm of Buchler & Vieweg still exists. One thing I do know. Vieweg must be now sixty-three years old, should he be still alive, and I am convinced that he remains an upright and honourable gentleman. I would also venture a surmise that business competitors find it very hard to overreach him, and that he has escaped the garrulous tendencies of old age.

One of the curses of German towns is the prevalence of malicious and venomous gossip. This is almost entirely due to that pestilent institution the " Coffee Circle," or *Kaffee Klatsch*, that standing feature of German provincial life.

Amongst the bourgeoisie, the ladies form associations, and meet once a week in turn at each others' houses. They bring their work with them, and sit for two hours, eating sweet cakes, drinking coffee, and tearing every reputation in the town to tatters. All males are jealously excluded from these gatherings. Mrs. Spiegelberg was a pretty, fluffy little English woman, without one ounce of malice in her composition. She had lived long enough in Germany, though, to know that she would not be welcomed at her "Coffee Circle" unless she brought her budget of pungent gossip with her, so she collected it in the usual way. The instant the cook returned from market, Mrs. Spiegelberg would rush into the kitchen with a breathless, "Na, Minna, was gibt's neues?" or "Now, Minna, what is the news?" Minna, the cook, knowing what was expected of her, proceeded to unfold her items of carefully gathered gossip: Lieutenant von Trinksekt had lost three hundred marks at cards, and had been unable to pay; it was rumoured that Fraülein Unsittlich's six weeks' retirement from the world was not due to an attack of scarlet fever, as was alleged, but to a more interesting cause, and so on, and so on. The same thing was happening, simultaneously, in every kitchen in Brunswick, and at the next "Coffee Circle" all these rumours would be put into circulation and magnified, and the worst possible interpretation would be given them. All German women love spying, as is testified by those little external mirrors fixed outside almost every German window, by which the mistress of the house can herself remain unseen, whilst noting every one who passes down the street, or goes into the houses on either side. I speak with some bitterness of the poisonous tongues of these women, for I cannot forget how a harmless episode, when I happened to meet a charming friend of mine, and volunteered to carry her parcels home, was distorted and perverted.

One of Hentze's pupils, a heavy, bovine youth, invited me to Hamburg to his parents' silver wedding festivities. I was anxious to see Hamburg, so I accepted. Möser's parents inhabited an opulent and unimaginably hideous villa on the outskirts of Hamburg. They treated me most hospitably and kindly, but never had I pictured such vast eatings and drinkings as took place in their house. Möser's other relations were equally hospitable, until I became stupid and comatose from excessive nourishment. I could not discover the faintest trace of hostility to England amongst these wealthy Hamburg merchants. They had nearly all traditional business connections with England, and most of them had commenced their commercial careers in London. They resented, on the other hand, the manner in which they were looked down on by the Prussian Junkers, who, on the ground of their having no " von " before their names, tried to exclude them from every branch of the public service. The whole of Germany had not yet become Prussianised.

These Hamburg men were intensely proud of their city. They boasted, and I believe with perfect reason, that the dock and harbour facilities of Hamburg far exceeded anything to be found in the United Kingdom. I was taken all over the docks, and treated indeed with such lavish hospitality that every seam of my garments strained under the unwonted pressure of these enormous repasts. Hamburg being a Free Port, travellers leaving for any other part of Germany had to undergo a regular Customs examination at the railway station, as though it were a frontier post. Hamburg impressed me as a vastly prosperous, handsome, well-kept town. The attractive feature of the place is the " Alster Bassin," the clear, fresh-water lake running into the very heart of the town. All the best houses and hotels were built on the stone quays of the Alster facing the lake. Geneva, Stockholm, and Copenhagen are the only other European towns I know of with clear lakes running into the middle of the city. The Möser family's silver wedding festivities did not err on the side of niggardliness. The guests all assembled in full evening dress at three in the afternoon, when there was a conjuring and magic-lantern performance for the children. This was followed by an excellent concert, which in its turn was succeeded by a vast and Gargantuan dinner. Then came an elaborate display of fireworks, after which dancing continued till 4 a.m., only interrupted by a second colossal meal, thus affording, as young Möser

187

proudly pointed out, thirteen hours' uninterrupted amusement.

As I felt certain that I should promptly succumb to apoplexy, had I to devour any more food, I left next day for Heligoland, then, of course, still a British Colony, an island I had always had the greatest curiosity to see. A longer stay in Hamburg might have broadened my mind, but it would also unqestionably have broadened my waist-belt as well.

The steamer accomplished the journey from Hamburg in seven hours, the last three over the angry waters of the open North Sea. To my surprise the steamer, though island-owned, did not fly the British red ensign, but the Heligoland flag of horizontal bars of white, green, and red. There is a local quatrain explaining these colours, which may be roughly Englished as—

> " White is the strand,
> But green the land,
> Red the rocks stand
> Round Heligoland."

Heligoland is the quaintest little spot imaginable, shaped like an isosceles triangle with the apex pointing northwards. The area of the whole island is only three-fourths of a square mile; it is barely a mile long, and at its widest only 500 yards broad. It is divided into Underland and Overland; the former a patch of shore on the sheltered side of the island, covered with the neatest little toy streets and houses. In its neatness and smallness it is rather like a Japanese town, and has its little theatre and its little Kurhaus complete. There are actually a few trees in the Underland. Above it, the red ramparts of rock rise like a wall to the Overland, only to be reached by an endless flight of steps. On the green tableland of the Overland, the houses nestle and huddle together for shelter on the leeward side of the island, the prevailing winds being westerly. The whole population let lodgings, simply appointed, but beautifully neat and clean, as one would expect amongst a seafaring population. There are a few patches of cabbages and potatoes trying to grow in spite of the gales, and all the rest is green turf. There is not one tree on the wind-swept Overland. I heard nothing but German and Frisian talked around me, and the only signs of British occupation were the Union Jack flying in front of Government House (surely the most modest edifice ever dignified with that title), and a notice-board in front of the powder-magazine on the northern point of the island. This notice-board was inscribed, " V.R. Trespassers will be prosecuted," which at once gave a homelike feeling, and made one realise that it was British soil on which one was standing.

The island had only been ceded to us in 1814, and we handed it over to Germany in 1890, so our tenure was too brief for us to have struck root deeply into the soil. Heligoland was a splendid recruiting ground for the Royal Navy, for the islanders were a hardy race of seafarers, and made ideal material for bluejackets. There was not a horse or cow on the island, ewes supplying all the milk. As sheep's milk has an unappetising green tinge about it, it took a day or two to get used to this unfamiliar-looking fluid. There being no fresh water on Heligoland, the rain water from the roofs was all caught and stored in tanks. On that rain-swept rock I cannot conceive it likely that the water supply would ever fail. Somehow the idea was prevalent in England that Heligoland was undermined by rabbits. There was not one single rabbit on the island, for even rabbits find it hard to burrow into solid rock.

Professor Gätke's books on the migrations of birds are well known. Heligoland lies in the track of migrating birds, and Dr. Gätke had established himself there for some years to observe them, and there was a really wonderful ornithological museum close to the lighthouse. The Heligoland light-house is a very powerful one, and every single one of these stuffed birds had committed suicide against the thick glass of the lantern. The lighthouse keepers told me that during the migratory periods, they sometimes found as many as a hundred dead birds on the external gallery of the light in the morning, all of whom had killed themselves against the light.

From 1830 to 1871 there were public gaming-tables in Heligoland, and the Concessionaire paid such a high price for his permit that the colonial finances were in the most flourishing condition.

In 1871, Downing Street stopped this, with disastrous effect on the island budget. Fortunately, Germans took to coming over in vast numbers for the excellent sea-bathing, and so money began to flow in again. The place attracted them with its glorious sea air; it had all the advantages of a ship, without the ship's motion.

I paid a second visit to Heligoland three years later, when I was Attaché at our Berlin Embassy. Sir Fitzhardinge Maxse,. the uncle of Mr. Leo Maxse of the *National Review*, was Governor then. Sir Fitzhardinge had done his utmost to anglicise the island, and the " Königstrasse " and " Oststrasse " had now become " King Street " and " East Street." He had induced, too, some of the shop-keepers to write the signs over their shops in English, at times with somewhat eccentric spelling; for one individual proclaimed himself a " Familie Grozer." How astonished the Governor and I would have been to know that in twenty years' time his much-loved island would be transformed into one solid concreted German fortress! Sir Fitzhardinge had a great love for the theatre. He was, I believe, the only person who had ever tried to write plays in two languages. His German plays had been very successful, and two one-act plays he wrote in English had been produced on the London stage. He always managed to engage a good German company to play in the little Heligoland theatre during the summer months, and having married the leading tragic actress of the Austrian stage, both he and Lady Maxse occasionally appeared on the boards themselves, playing, of course, in German. It looked curious seeing a bill of the "Theatre Royal on Heligoland," announcing Shakespeare's tragedy of *Macbeth*, with "His Excellency the Governor as Macbeth, and Lady Maxse as Lady Macbeth."

There is a fine old Lutheran Church on Heligoland. It is the only Protestant church in which I have ever seen *ex votos*. When the island fishermen had weathered an unusually severe gale, it was their custom to make a model of their craft, and to present it as a thank-offering to the church. There were dozens of these models, all beautifully finished, suspended from the roof of the church by wires, and the fronts of the galleries were all hung with fishing-nets. The singing in that church was remarkably good.

It was a pleasant, unsophisticated little island; a place of fresh breezes, and red cliffs with great sweeping surges breaking against them; a place of sunshine, and huge expanses of pale dappled sky.

Lady Maxse told me that it was impossible for any one to picture the unutterable dreariness of Heligoland in winter; when little Government House rocked ceaselessly under the fierce gales, and the whole island was drenched in clouds of spindrift; the rain pounding on the window-panes like small-shot, and the howling of the wind drowning all other sounds. She said that they were frequently cut off from the mainland for

three weeks on end, without either letters, newspapers, or fresh meat, as the steamers were unable
to make the passage. There was nothing to do,
nowhere to go, and no one to speak to. It must
have been a considerable change for any one
accustomed to the life of careless, easy-going,
glittering Vienna in the old days. Even Sir Fitzhardinge confessed that during the winter gales he
had frequently to make his way on all fours from
the stairs from the Underland to Government
House, to avoid being blown over the cliffs. Lady
Maxse hung an extra pair of pink muslin curtains
over every window in Government House, to shut
out the sight of the wintry sea, but the angry,
grey and white rollers of the restless North Sea
asserted themselves even through the pink muslin.

I am glad that I saw this wind-swept little rock
whilst it was still a scrap of British territory.

When my time came for leaving Brunswick, I
was genuinely sorry to go. I confess that I liked
Germany and the Germans; I had been extremely
well treated, and had got used to German ways.

The teaching profession were only then sowing
broadcast the seed which was to come to maturity
thirty years later. They were moulding the minds
of the rising generation to the ideals which find
their most candid exponent in Nietzsche. The
seed was sown, but had not yet germinated; the
greater portion of Germany in 1875 was still un-
Prussianised, but effect followed cause, and we all
know the rest.

CHAPTER VII

THE London of 1876 boasted an extraordinary
constellation of lovely women. First and fore-
most came the two peerless Moncreiffe sisters,
Georgiana Lady Dudley, and Helen Lady Forbes.
Lady Dudley was then a radiant apparition, and
her sister, the most perfect example of classical
beauty I have ever seen, had features as clean-cut
as those of a cameo. Lady Forbes always wore
her hair simply parted in the middle, a thing that
not one woman in a thousand can afford to do,
and glorious auburn hair it was, with a natural
ripple in it. I have seldom seen a head so perfectly
placed on the shoulders as that of Lady Forbes.
The Dowager Lady Ormonde and the late Lady
Ripon were then still unmarried; the first, Lady
Leila Grosvenor, with the face of a Raphael

Madonna, the other, Lady Gladys Herbert, a splendid, slender, Juno-like young goddess. The rather cruelly named "professional beauties" had just come into prominence, the three great rivals being Mrs. Langtry, then fresh from Jersey, Mrs. Cornwallis West, and Mrs. Wheeler. Unlike most people, I should myself have given the prize to the second of these ladies. I do not think that any one now could occupy the commanding position in London which Constance Duchess of Westminster and the Duchess of Manchester (afterwards Duchess of Devonshire) then held. In fact, with skirts to the knee, and an unending expanse of stocking below them, it would be difficult to assume the dignity with which these great ladies, in their flowing Victorian draperies, swept into a room. The stately Duchess of Westminster, in spite of her massive outline, had still a fine classical head, and the Duchess of Manchester was one of the hand-somest women in Europe. London society was so much smaller then, that it was a sort of enlarged family party, and I, having six married sisters, found myself with unnumbered hosts of relations and connections. I retain delightful recollections of the mid-Victorian girl. These maidens, in their airy clouds of white, pink, or green tulle, and their untouched faces, had a deliciously fresh, flower-like look which is wholly lacking in their sisters of to-day. A young girl's charm is her freshness, and if she persists in coating her face with powder and rouge that freshness vanishes, and one sees merely rows of vapid little doll-like faces, all absolutely alike, and all equally artificial and devoid of expression. The present skimpy draperies cause one to reflect that Nature has not lavished broadcast the gift of good feet and neat ankles; possibly some girls might lengthen their skirts if they realised this truth.

In the "seventies" there was a wonderful galaxy of talent at the old Gaiety Theatre, Nellie Farren, Kate Vaughan, Edward Terry, and Royce forming a matchless quartette. Young men, of course, will always be foolish, up to the end of time. Nellie Farren, Kate Vaughan and Emily Duncan all had their "colours." Nellie Farren's were dark blue, light blue, and white; Kate Vaughan's were pink and grey; Emily Duncan's black and white; the leading hosiers "stocked" silk scarves of these colours, and we foolish young men bought the colours of the lady we especially admired, and sat in the stalls of the Gaiety flaunting the scarves of our favourite round our necks. As I then thought, and still think, that Nellie Farren was one of the daintiest and most graceful little creatures ever seen on the stage, with a *gaminerie* all her own, I, in common with many other youths, sat in the stalls of the Gaiety wrapped in a blue-and-white scarf. Each lady showered smiles over the footlights at her avowed admirers, whilst contemptuously ignoring those who sported her rival's colours. One silly youth, to testify to his admiration for Emily Duncan, actually had white kid gloves with black fingers, specially manufactured for him. He was, we hope, repaid for his outlay by extra smiles from his enchantress.

Traces of the witty early nineteenth century still lingered into the "seventies," "eighties," and "nineties." Lady Constance Leslie, who is still living, and the late Lady Cork were almost the last descendants of the brilliant wits of Sydney Smith and Theodore Hook's days. The hurry of modern life, and the tendency of the age to scratch the surface of things only, are not favourable to the development of this type of keen intellect, which was based on a thorough knowledge of the English classics, and on such a high level of culture as modern trouble-hating women could but seldom hope to attain. Time and time again I have asked Lady Cork for the origin of some quotation. She invariably gave it me at once, usually quoting some lines of the context at the same time. When I complimented her on her wonderful knowledge of English literature of the seventeenth and eighteenth centuries, she answered, " In my young days we studied the ' Belles Lettres '; modern women only study ' Belle's Letters,' " an allusion to a weekly summary of social events then appearing in the *World* under that title, a chronicle voraciously devoured by thousands of women. When the early prejudice against railways was alluded to by some one who recalled the storms of protest that the conveyance of the Duke of Sussex's body by train to Windsor for burial provoked, as being derogatory to the dignity of a Royal Duke, it was Lady Cork who rapped out, "I presume in those days, a novel apposition of the quick and the dead." A certain peer was remarkable alike for his extreme parsimony and his unusual plainness of face. His wife shared these characteristics, both facial and temperamental, to the full, and yet this childless, unprepossessing and eminently economical couple were absolutely wrapped up in one another; after his death she only lingered on for three months. Some one commenting on this, said, "They were certainly the stingiest and probably the ugliest couple in England, yet their devotion to each other was very beautiful. They could neither of them bear to part with anything, not even with each other. After his death she was like a watch that had lost its mainspring." "Surely," flashed Lady Constance Leslie, "more like a vessel which had lost her auxiliary screw." The main characteristic of both Lady Cork and Lady Constance Leslie's humour was its lightning speed. It is superfluous to add, with these quick-witted ladies it was never necessary to *explain* anything, as it is to the majority of English people; they understood before you had finished saying it.

Many years after, in the late "eighties," Lady Constance Leslie's two elder daughters, now Mrs. Crawshay and Lady Hope, developed a singular gift. They could improvise blank verse indefinitely, and with their father, Sir John Leslie, they acted little mock-Shakespearean dramas, in their ordinary clothes, and without any scenery or accessories. Every word was impromptu, and yet the even flow of blank verse never ceased. I always thought it a singularly clever performance, for Mrs. Crawshay can only have been nineteen then, and her sister eighteen. Mrs. Crawshay invariably played the heroine, Lady Hope the confidante, and Sir John Leslie any male part requisite. No matter what the subject given them might be, they would start in blank verse at once. Let us suppose so unpromising a subject as the collection of railway tickets outside a London terminus had been selected. Lady Hope, with pleading eyes, and all the conventional gestures of sympathy of a stage confidante, would at once start apostrophising her sister in some such fashion as this:—

" Fair Semolina, dry those radiant orbs;
   Thy swain doth beg thee but a token small
   Of that great love which thou dost bear to him.
   Prithee, sweet mistress, take now heart of grace,
   At times we all credentials have to show,
   Eftsoons at Willesden halts the panting train,
   Each traveller knows inexorable fate
   Hath trapped him in her toils; loud rings the tread
   Of brass-bound despot as he wends his way
   From door to door, claiming with gesture rude
   His pound of flesh, or eke the pasteboard slip,
   Punched with much care, all travel-worn and stained,
   For which perchance ten ducats have been paid,
   Granting full access from some distant spot.
   Then trembles he, who reckless loves to sip
   The joys of travel free of all expense;
   Knowing the fate that will pursue him, when
   To stern collector he hath naught to show."

To which her sister, Mrs. Crawshay, would reply,

without one instant's hesitation, somewhat after this style:—

> " Sweet Tapioca, firm and faithful friend,
> Thy words have kindled in my guilty breast
> Pangs of remorse; to thee I will confess.
> Craving a journey to the salt sea waves
> Before this moon had waxed her full, I stood
> Crouching, and feigning infant's stature small
> Before the wicket, whence the precious slips
> Are issued, and declared my years but ten.
> Thus did I falsely pretext tender age,
> And claimed but half the wonted price, and now
> Bitter remorse my stricken conscience sears,
> And hot tears flow at my duplicity."

The lines would probably have been more neatly worded than this, but the flow of improvised blank verse from both sisters was inexhaustible. The somewhat unusual names of Semolina and Tapioca had been adopted for the heroine and confidante on account of their rhythmical advantages, and a certain pleasant Shakespearean ring about them.

I know another family who from long practice have acquired the habit of addressing each other in flowing periods of Johnsonian English. They never hesitate for an epithet, and manage to round off all their sentences in Dr. Johnson's best manner. I was following the hounds on foot one day, with the eldest daughter of this family, when, as we struggled through a particularly sticky and heavy ploughed field, she panted out, " Pray let us hasten to the summit of yonder commanding eminence, whence we can with greater comfort to ourselves witness the further progress of the chase," and all this without the tiniest hesitation; a most enviable gift! A son of this family was once riding in the same steeplechase as a nephew of mine. The youth had lost his cap, and turning round in his saddle, he shouted to my nephew in the middle of the race, between two fences, "You will perceive that I have already sacrificed my cap, and laid it as a votive offering on the altar of Diana." One would hardly have anticipated that a youthful cavalry subaltern, in the middle of a steeplechase, would have been able to lay his hands on such choice flowers of speech. Unfortunately, owing to the time lost by these well-turned periods, both the speaker and my nephew merely figured as "also ran."

In the "seventies" some of the curious tricks of pronunciation of the eighteenth century still survived. My aunts, who had been born with, or before the nineteenth century, invariably pronounced "yellow" as "yaller." "Lilac" and "cucumber" became "laylock" and "cowcumber," and a gold bracelet was referred to as a "goold brasslet." They always spoke of "Proosia" and "Roosia," drank tea out of a "chaney" cup, and the eldest of them was still "much obleeged" for any little service rendered to her, played at "cyards," and took a stroll in the "gyarden." My grandfather, who was born in 1766, insisted to the end of his life on terming the capital of these islands "Lunnon," in eighteenth-century fashion.

Possibly people were more cultured in those

days, or, at all events, more in the habit of using
their brains. Imbecility, whether real or simu-
lated, had not come into fashion. My mother told
me that in her young days a very favourite amusement in country houses was to write imitations or
parodies of some well-known poet, and every one
took part in this. Nowadays no one would have
read the originals, much less be able to imitate
them. My mother had a commonplace book into
which she had copied the cleverest of these skits, and
Landseer illustrated it charmingly in pen-and-ink
for her.

Any one reading the novels of the commencement of the nineteenth century must have noticed
how wonderfully popular practical jokes, often of
the crudest nature, then were. A brutal practical
joke always seems to me to indicate a very rudimentary and undeveloped sense of humour in its
perpetrator. Some people with paleolithic intel-
lects seem to think it exquisitely humorous to see
a man fall down and hurt himself. A practical
joke which hurts no one is another matter. All
those privileged to enjoy the friendship of the late
Admiral Lord Charles Beresford will always
treasure the memory of that genial and delightful
personality. About thirty years ago an elderly
gentleman named Bankes-Stanhope seemed to
imagine that he had some proprietary rights in the
Carlton Club. Mr. Bankes-Stanhope had his own
chair, lamp, and table there, and was exceedingly
zealous in reminding members of the various rules

of the club. Smoking was strictly forbidden in the hall of the Carlton at that time. I was standing in the hall one night when Lord Charles came out of the writing-room, a big bundle of newly written letters in his hand, and a large cigar in his mouth. He had just received a shilling's-worth of stamps from the waiter, when old Mr. Bankes-Stanhope, who habitually puffed and blew like Mr. Jogglebury-Crowdey of *Sponge's Sporting Tour*, noticed the forbidden cigar through a glass, door, and came puffing and blowing into the hall in hot indignation. He reproved Lord Charles Beresford for his breach of the club rules in, as I thought, quite unnecessarily severe tones. The genial Admiral kept his temper, but detached one penny stamp from his roll, licked it, and placed it on his forefinger. "My dear Mr. Stanhope," he began, "it was a little oversight of mine. I was writing in there, do you see?" (a friendly little tap on Mr. Bankes-Stanhope's shirt-front, and on went a penny stamp), "and I moved in here, you see" (another friendly tap, and on went a second stamp), "and forgot about my cigar, you see" (a third tap, and a third stamp left adhering). The breezy Admiral kept up this conversation, punctuated with little taps, each one of which left its crimson trace on the old gentleman's white shirt-front, until the whole shilling's-worth was placed in position. Mr. Bankes-Stanhope was too irate to notice these little manœuvres; he maintained his hectoring tone, and never glanced down at his shirt-front. Finally

Lord Charles left, and the old gentleman, still puffing and blowing with wrath, struggled into his overcoat, and went off to an official party at Sir Michael Hicks-Beach's, where his appearance with twelve red penny stamps adhering to his shirt-front must have created some little astonishment.

In the '86 Parliament there was a certain Member, sitting on the Conservative side, who had the objectionable habit of removing his boots (spring-sided ones, too!) in the House, and of sitting in a pair of very dubious-coloured grey woollen socks, apparently much in want of the laundress's attentions. Many Members strongly objected to this practice, but the delinquent persisted in it, in spite of protests. One night a brother of mine, knowing that there would shortly be a Division, succeeded in purloining the offending boots by covering them with his " Order paper," and got them safely out of the House. He hid them behind some books in the Division Lobby, and soon after the Division was called. The House emptied, but the discalced legislator retained his seat. " A Division having been called, the honourable Member will now withdraw," ordered Mr. Speaker Peel, most awe-inspiring of men. " Mr. Speaker, I have lost my boots," protested the shoeless one. " The honourable Member will at once withdraw," ordered the Speaker for the second time, in his sternest tones ; so down the floor of the House came the unfortunate man—hop, hop, hop, like the " little hare " in *Shockheaded Peter*. The iron ventilating gratings were apparently uncomfortable to shoeless feet, so he went hopping and limping through the Division Lobby, affording ample glimpses of his deplorably discoloured woollen foot-wear.   Later in the evening an attendant handed him a paper parcel containing his boots, the attendant having, of course, no idea where the parcel had come from. This incident effectually cured the offender of his unpleasing habit.   The accusation of neglecting his laundress may have been an unfounded one. In my early youth I was given a book to read about a tiresome little girl named Ellen Montgomery, who apparently divided her time between reading her pocket-Bible and indulging in paroxysms of tears. The only incident in the book I remember is that this lachrymose child had an aunt, a Miss Fortune, who objected on principle to clean stockings. She accordingly dyed all Ellen's stockings dirt-colour, to save the washing.   It would be charitable to assume that this particular Member of Parliament had an aunt with the same economical instincts.

I must plead guilty to two episodes where my sole desire was to avoid disappointment to others, and to prevent the reality falling short of the expectation. One was in India. Barrackpore, the Viceroy of India's official country house, is justly celebrated for its beautiful gardens. In these gardens every description of tropical tree, shrub and flower grows luxuriantly. In a far-off corner there is a splendid group of fan-bananas,

otherwise known as the " Traveller's Palm." Owing
to the habit of growth of this tree, every drop of
rain or dew that falls on its broad, fan-shaped
crown of leaves is caught, and runs down the
grooved stalks of the plant into receptacles that
cunning Nature has fashioned just where the stalk
meets the trunk. Even in the driest weather,
these little natural tanks will, if gashed with a
knife, yield nearly a tumblerful of pure sweet
water, whence the popular name for the tree. A
certain dull M.P., on his travels, had come down
to Barrackpore for Sunday, and inquired eagerly
whether there were any Travellers' Trees either in
the park or the gardens there, as he had heard
of them, but had never yet seen one. We assured
him that in the cool of the evening we would show
him quite a thicket of Travellers' Trees. It
occurred to the Viceroy's son and myself that it
would be a pity should the globe-trotting M.P.'s
expectations not be realised, after the long spell of
drought we had had. So the two of us went off
and carefully filled up the natural reservoirs of
some six fan-bananas with fresh spring-water till
they were brimful. Suddenly we had a simul-
taneous inspiration, and returning to the house we
fetched two bottles of light claret, which we poured
carefully into the natural cisterns of two more trees,
which we marked. Late in the afternoon we conducted the M.P. to the grove of Travellers' Trees,
handed him a glass, and made him gash the stem
of one of them with his pen knife. Thanks to our

preparation, it gushed water like one of the Trafalgar Square fountains, and the touring legislator
was able to satisfy himself that it was good drinking-
water. He had previously been making some inquiries about so-called " Palm-wine," which is
merely the fermented juice of the toddy-palm.
We told him that some Travellers' Palms produced
this wine, and with a slight exercise of ingenuity
we induced him to tap one of the trees we had
doctored with claret. Naturally, a crimson liquid
spouted into his glass in response to the thrust of
his pen-knife, and after tasting it two or three times,
he reluctantly admitted that its flavour was not
unlike that of red wine. It ought to have been,
considering that we had poured an entire bottle of
good sound claret into that tree. The ex-M.P.
possibly reflects now on the difficulties with which
any attempts to introduce " Pussyfoot " legislation
into India would be confronted in a land where
some trees produce red wine spontaneously.

On another occasion I was going by sea from
Calcutta to Ceylon. On board the steamer there
were a number of Americans, principally ladies,
connected, I think, with some missionary undertaking. When we got within about a hundred
miles of Ceylon, these American ladies all began
repeating to each other the verse of the well-known
hymn :

" What though the spicy breezes
    Blow soft o'er Ceylon's isle,"

over and over again, until I loathed Bishop Heber

for having written the lines. They even asked the captain how far out to sea the spicy breezes would be perceptible. I suddenly got an idea, and, going below, I obtained from the steward half a dozen nutmegs and a handful of cinnamon. I grated the nutmegs and pounded the cinnamon up, and then, with one hand full of each, I went on deck, and walked slowly up and down in front of the American tourists. Soon I heard an ecstatic cry, "My dear, I distinctly smelt spice then!" Another turn, and another jubilant exclamation: "It's quite true about the spicy breezes. I got a delicious whiff just then. Who would have thought that they would have carried so far out to sea?" A sceptical elderly gentleman was summoned from below, and he, after a while, was reluctantly forced to avow that he, too, had noticed the spicy fragrance. No wonder! when I had about a quarter of a pound of grated nutmeg in one hand, and as much pounded cinnamon in the other. Now these people will go on declaring to the end of their lives that they smelt the spicy odours of Ceylon a full hundred miles out at sea, just as the travelling M.P. will assert that a tree in India produces a very good imitation of red wine. It is a nice point determining how far one is morally responsible one-self for the unconscious falsehoods into which these people have been betrayed. I should like to have had the advice of Mrs. Fairchild, of the *Fairchild Family*, upon this delicate question. I feel convinced that that estimable lady, with her inexhaustible repertory of supplications, would instantly have recited by heart "a prayer against the temptation to lead others into uttering untruths unconsciously," which would have met the situation adequately, for not once in the book, when appealed to, did she fail to produce a lengthy and elaborately worded petition, adapted to the most unexpected emergencies, and I feel confident that her moral armoury would have included a prayer against tendencies to "leg-pulling."

To return to the London of the "seventies" and "eighties" after this brief journey to the East, nothing is more noticeable than the way public interest in Parliamentary proceedings has vanished. When I was a boy, all five of the great London dailies, *The Times*, *Morning Post*, *Standard*, *Daily Telegraph*, and *Daily News*, published the fullest reports of Parliamentary news, and the big provincial dailies followed their example. Every one then seemed to follow the proceedings of Parliament with the utmost interest; even at Harrow the elder boys read the Parliamentary news and discussed it, and I have heard keen-witted Lancashire artisans eagerly debating the previous night's Parliamentary encounters. Now the most popular newspapers give the scantiest and baldest summaries of proceedings in the House of Commons. It is an editor's business to know the tastes of his readers; if Parliamentary reports are reduced to a minimum, it must be because they no longer interest the public. This, again, is quite intelligible.

THE DAYS BEFORE YESTERDAY

When I first entered Parliament in 1885 (to which Parliament, by the way, all four Hamilton brothers had been elected), there were commanding personalities and great orators in the House: Mr. Gladstone, John Bright, Joseph Chamberlain, Lord Hartington, Henry James and Randolph Churchill. When any of these rose to speak, the House filled at once, they were listened to with eager attention, and every word they uttered would be read by hundreds of thousands of people next day. Nowadays proceedings in Parliament seem to be limited to a very occasional solo from the one star-performer, the rest of the time being occupied by uninteresting interludes by his understudies, all of which may serve to explain the decline in public interest. At the time of the Peace of Paris of 1856, on the termination of the Crimean War, there were in the House of Commons such outstanding figures as Gladstone, Disraeli, Lord John Russell, John Bright, and Palmerston; the statesman had not yet dwindled into the lawyer-politician.

I only heard Mr. Gladstone speak in his old age, when his voice had acquired a slight roughness which detracted, I thought, from his wonderful gift of oratory. Mr. Gladstone, too, had certain peculiarities of pronunciation; he always spoke of "constitootional" and of "noos." John Bright was a most impressive speaker; he obtained his effects by the simplest means, for he seldom used long words; indeed, he was supposed to limit himself to words of Saxon origin, with all their condensed vigour. Is not Newman's hymn, "Lead, Kindly Light," considered to be a model of English, as it is composed almost entirely of monosyllables, and, with six exceptions, of words of Saxon origin? John Bright's speaking had the same quality as Cardinal Newman's hymn. In spite of his eloquence, John Bright's prophecies were invariably falsified by subsequent events. I have never heard any one speak with such facility as Joseph Chamberlain. His utterance was so singularly clear that, though he habitually spoke in a very low voice, every syllable penetrated to all parts of the House. When Chamberlain was really in a dangerous mood, his voice became ominously bland, and his manner quieter than ever. Then was the time for his enemies to tremble. I heard him once roll out and demolish a poor facile-tongued professional spouter so completely and remorselessly that the unfortunate man never dared to open his mouth in the House of Commons again. I think that any old Member of Parliament will agree with me when I place David Plunkett, afterwards Lord Rathmore, who represented for many years Trinity College, Dublin, in the very front rank as an orator. Plunkett was an indolent man, and spoke very rarely indeed. When really roused, and on a subject which he had genuinely at heart, he could rise to heights of splendid eloquence. Plunkett had a slight impediment in his speech; when wound up, this impediment, so far from detracting from, added to the effect he produced. I heard Mr. Gladstone's last speech in Parliament, on March 1, 1894. It was frankly a great disappointment. I sat then on the Opposition side, but we Unionists had all assembled to cheer the old man who was to make his farewell speech to the Assembly in which he had sat for sixty years, and of which he had been so dominating and so unique a personality, although we were bitterly opposed to him politically. The tone of his speech made this difficult for us. Instead of being a dignified farewell to the House, as we had anticipated, it was querulous and personal, with a peevish and minatory note in it that made anything but perfunctory applause from the Opposition side very hard to produce. Two days afterwards, on March 3, 1894, Mr. Gladstone resigned. In the light of recent revelations, we know now that his failing eyesight was but a pretext. Lord Spencer, then First Lord of the Admiralty, had framed his Naval Estimates, and declared that the shipbuilding programme outlined in those Estimates was absolutely necessary for the national safety. Mr. Gladstone, supported by some of his colleagues, refused to sanction these Estimates. Some long-headed Members of the Cabinet saw clearly that if Lord Spencer insisted on his Estimates, in the then temper of the country, the Liberal party would go to certain defeat. Accordingly, Mr. Gladstone was induced to resign, as the easiest way out of the difficulty. I do not gather, though, that those of his colleagues who, with him, disapproved of the Naval Estimates, thought it their duty to follow their chief into retirement.

I am amused on seeing on contents bills of newspapers, as a rare item of news, "All-night sitting of Commons."

In the 1886 Parliament practically every night was an all-night sitting. Under the old rules of Procedure, as the Session advanced, we were kept up night after night till 5 a.m. Some Members, notably the late Henry Labouchere, took a sort of impish delight in keeping the House sitting late. Many Front-Bench men had their lives shortened by the strain these late hours imposed on them, notably Edward Stanhope and Mr. W. H. Smith. Mr. W. H. Smith occupied a very extraordinary position. This plain-faced man, who could hardly string two words together, was regarded by all his friends with deep respect, almost with affection. My brother George has told me that, were there any disputes in the Cabinet of which he was a member, the invariable advice of the older men was to "go and take Smith's advice about it." Men carried their private, domestic, and even financial troubles to this wise counsellor, confident that the advice given would be sound. Mr. Smith had none of the more ornamental qualities, but his fund of common sense was inexhaustible, he never spared himself in his friends' service, and his high sense of honour and strength of character earned him the genuine regard of all those who really knew him. He was a very fine specimen of the unassuming, honourable, high-minded English gentleman.

In the 1886 Parliament, Mr. Akers-Douglas, now Lord Chilston, was Chief Conservative Whip, and he was singularly fortunate in his Assistant Whips. Sir William Walrond, now Lord Waleran, Sir Herbert Maxwell, and the late Sidney Herbert, afterwards fourteenth Earl of Pembroke, formed a wonderful trio, for Nature had bestowed on each of them a singularly engaging personality. The strain put on Members of the Opposition was very severe; our constant attendance was demanded, and we spent practically our whole lives in the precincts of the House. However much we longed for a little relaxation and a little change, it was really impossible to resist the blandishments of the Assistant Whips. They made it a sort of personal appeal, and a test of personal friendship to themselves, so grudgingly the contemplated visit to the theatre was abandoned, and we resigned ourselves to six more hours inside the over-familiar building.

Sir William Hart-Dyke had been Chief Conservative Whip in the 1868–1873 Parliament. He married in May 1870, in the middle of the session at a very critical political period. He most unselfishly consented to forego his honeymoon, or to postpone it, and there were rumours that on the very evening of his wedding-day, his sense of duty had been so strong that he had appeared in the House of Commons to "tell" in an important Division.

When Disraeli was asked if this were true, he shook his head, and said, " I hardly think so. Hart-Dyke was married that day. Hart-Dyke is a gentleman; he would never kiss *and* 'tell.' " As a *pendant* to this, there was another Sir William, a baronet whose name I will suppress. With execrable taste, he was fond of boasting by name of his amatory successes. He was always known as " William Tell."

In 1886 the long hours in the House of Commons hung very heavily on our hands, once the always voluminous daily correspondence of an M.P. had been disposed of. My youngest brother and I, both then well under thirty, used to hire tricycles from the dining-room attendants, and have races up and down the long river terrace, much to the interest of passers-by on Westminster Bridge. We projected, to pass the time, a " Soulful Song-Cycle," which was frankly to be an attempt at pulling the public's leg. Our Song-Cycle never matured, though I did write the first one of the series, an imaginative effort entitled " In Listless Frenzy." It was, and was intended to be, utter nonsense, devoid alike of grammar and of meaning. I quoted my " Listless Frenzy" one night to an " intense " and gushing lady, as an example of the pitiable rubbish decadent minor poets were then turning out. It began—

" Crimson wreaths of passionless flowers
Down in the golden glen;
Silvery sheen of autumnal showers;
When, my beloved one, when? "

She assured me that the fault lay in myself, not
in the lines; that I was of too material a temperament to appreciate the subtle beauty of so-and-so's
work.   I forget to whom I had attributed the
verses, but I felt quite depressed at reflecting that
I was too material to understand the lines I had
myself written.

My brother was a great admirer of the *Ingoldsby
Legends*, and could himself handle Richard Barham's fascinating metre very effectively.   He
was meditating "A Pseudo-Ingoldsbean Lay,"
dealing with leading personalities in the then
House of Commons.   The idea came to nothing,
as an "Ingoldsby Legend" must, from its very
essence, be cast in a narrative form, and the
subject did not lend itself to narrative.   Although
it has nothing to do with the subject in hand,
I must quote some lines from "The Raid of
Carlisle," another "Pseudo-Ingoldsbean Lay" of
my brother's, to show how easily he could use
Barham's metre, with its ear-tickling doublerhyme,
and how thoroughly he had assimilated the spirit
of the *Ingoldsby Legends*.   The extracts are
from an account of an incident which occurred in
1596, when Lord Scroop was Warden of the
Western or English Marches on behalf of Elizabeth,
while Buccleuch, on the Scottish side, was Warden
of the Middle Marches on behalf of James VI.

. . . . . .

"Now I'd better explain, while I'm still in the vein,
   That towards the close of Elizabeth's reign,

THE DAYS BEFORE YESTERDAY

Though the ' thistle and rose ' were no longer at blows,
They'd a way of disturbing each other's repose.
A mode of proceeding most clearly exceeding
The rules of decorum, and palpably needing
Some clear understanding between the two nations,
By which to adjust their unhappy relations.
With this object in view, it occurred to Buccleuch
That a great deal of mutual good would accrue
If they settled that he and Lord Scroop's nominee
Should meet once a year, and between them agree
To arbitrate all controversial cases
And grant an award on an equable basis.
A brilliant idea, that promised to be a
Corrective, if not a complete panacea—
For it really appears that for several years,
These fines of ' poll'd Angus ' and Galloway steers
Did greatly conduce, during seasons of truce,
To abating traditional forms of abuse,
And to giving the *roués* of Border society
Some little sense of domestic propriety.

.   .   .   .   .   .

So finding himself, so to speak, up a tree,
And unable to think of a neat repartee,
He wisely concluded (as Brian Boru did,
On seeing his ' illigant counthry ' denuded
Of cattle and grain that were swept from the plain
By the barbarous hand of the pillaging Dane)
To bandy no words with a dominant foe,
But to wait for a chance of returning the blow,
And then let him have it *in more suo*."

.   .   .   .   .   .

These extracts make me regret that the leading
personalities in the Parliament of 1886 were not
commemorated in the same pleasant, jingling metre.

CHAPTER VIII

HAVING successfully defeated the Civil Service
Examiners, I entered the Foreign Office in 1876,
for the six or eight months' training which all
Attachés had to undergo before being sent abroad.
The typewriter had not then been invented,
so everything was copied by hand—a wearisome
and deadening occupation where very lengthy
documents were concerned.

The older men in the Foreign Office were great
sticklers for observing all the traditional forms.
Lord Granville, in obedience to political pressure,
had appointed the son of a leading politician as one
of his unpaid private secretaries. The youth had
been previously in his father's office in Leeds. On
the day on which he started work in the Foreign

Office he was given a bundle of letters to acknowledge. "You know, of course, the ordinary form of acknowledgment," said his chief. "Just acknowledge all these, and say that the matter will be attended to." When the young man from Leeds brought the letters he had written, for signature that evening, it was currently reported that they were all worded in the same way :—"Dear Sirs,— your esteemed favour of yesterday's date duly to hand, and contents noted. Our Lord Granville has your matter in hand." The horror-stricken official gasped at such a departure from established routine.

As was the custom then, after one month in the Foreign Office, my immediate chief gave me a little lecture on the traditional high standard of honour of the Foreign Office, which he was sure I would observe, and then handed me a Cabinet key which he made me attach to my watch-chain in his presence. This Cabinet key unlocked all the boxes in which the most confidential papers of the Cabinet were circulated. As things were then arranged, this key was essential to our work, but a boy just turned twenty naturally felt immensely proud of such a proof of the confidence reposed in him. I think, too, that the Foreign Office can feel justifiably proud of the fact that the trust reposed in its most junior members was never once betrayed, and that the most weighty secrets were absolutely safe in their keeping.

I have narrated elsewhere my early experiences

at Berlin and Petrograd. In every capital the Diplomatists must always be, in a sense, sojourners in a strange land, and many of them who find a difficulty in amalgamating with the people of the country must always be thrown to a great extent on their own resources. It is probably for this reason that theatricals were so popular amongst the Diplomats in Petrograd, the plays being naturally always acted in French.

Here I felt more or less at home. My grandmother, the Duchess of Bedford, was passionately fond of acting, and in my grandfather's time, one room at Woburn Abbey was permanently fitted up as a theatre. Here, every winter during my mother's girlhood, there was a succession of performances in which she, her mother and brothers and sisters all took part, the Russell family having a natural gift for acting. Probably the very name of Charles Matthews is unfamiliar to the present generation, so it is sufficient to say that he was *the* light comedian of the early nineteenth century. The Garrick Club possesses a fine collection of portraits of Charles Matthews in some of his most popular parts. Charles Matthews acted regularly with the Russell family at Woburn, my mother playing the lead. I have a large collection of Woburn Abbey play-bills, from 1831–1839, all printed on white satin, and some of the pieces they put on were quite ambitious ones. My mother had a very sweet singing voice, which she retained till late in life; indeed a tiny thread of voice remained

until her ninety-third year, with a faint remnant of
its old sweetness still clinging to it. After her
marriage, her love of theatricals still persisted, so
we were often having performances at home, as my
brothers and sisters shared her tastes. I made my
first appearance on the stage at the age of seven,
and I can still remember most of my lines.

At Petrograd, in the French theatricals, I was
always cast for old men, and I must have played
countless fathers, uncles, generals, and family
lawyers. As unmarried girls took part in these
performances, the French pieces had to be considerably "bowdlerised," but they still remained
as excruciatingly funny as only French pieces
can be.

If I may be permitted a rather lengthy digression,
"bowdlerised" derives its name from Thomas
Bowdler, who in 1818 published an expurgated
edition of Shakespeare. It would be rather interesting to make a list of words which have passed
into common parlance but which were originally
derived from some peculiarity of the person whose
surname they perpetuate. A few occur to me.
In addition to "bowdlerise," there is "sandwich."
As is well known, this compact form of nourishment derives its name from John, fourth Earl of
Sandwich, who lived between 1718–1792. Lord
Sandwich was a confirmed gambler, and such was
his anxiety to lose still more money, and to
impoverish further himself, his family, and his
descendants, that he grudged the time necessary

for meals, and had slices of bread and slices of meat placed by his side. The inventive faculty being apparently but little developed during the eighteenth century, he was the first person who thought of placing meat between two slices of bread. Owing to the economy of time thus effected, he was able to ruin himself very satisfactorily, and his name is now familiar all over the world, thanks to the condensed form of food he introduced.

Again, Admiral Edward Vernon was Naval Commander-in-Chief in the West Indies in 1740. The Admiral was known as "Old Grog," from his habit of always having his breeches and the linings of his boat-cloaks made of grogram, a species of coarse white poplin (from the French *gros-grain*). It occurred to "Old Grog" that, in view of the ravages of yellow fever amongst the men of the Fleet, it would be advisable, in the burning climate of the West Indies, to dilute the bluejackets' rations of rum with water before serving them out. This was accordingly done, to the immense dissatisfaction of the men, who probably regarded it as a forerunner of "Pussyfoot" legislation. They at once christened the mixture "grog," after the Admiral's nickname, and "grog" as a term for spirits and water has spread all over the world, and is used just as much in French as in English.

The origin of the expression "to burke an inquiry," in the sense of suppressing or stifling it, is due to Burke and Hare, two enterprising male-factors who supplied the medical schools of Edinburgh with "subjects" for anatomical research, early in the nineteenth century. Their procedure was simple. Creeping behind unsuspecting citizens in lonely streets, they stifled them to death by placing pitch-plasters over their mouths and noses. Burke was hanged for this in Edinburgh in 1829.

In our own time, an almost unknown man has enriched the language with a new verb. A Captain Boycott of Lough Mask House, Co. Mayo, was a small Irish land-agent in 1880. The means that were adopted to try and drive him out of the country are well known. Since that time the expression to "boycott" a person, in the sense of combining with others to refuse to have any dealings with him, has become a recognised English term, and is just as widely used in France as with us.

A less familiar term is a "Collins," for the usual letter of thanks which a grateful visitor addresses to his recent host. This, of course, is derived from the Rev. Mr. Collins of Jane Austen's *Pride and Prejudice*, who prided himself on the dexterity with which he worded these acknowledgments of favours received. As another example, most bridge-players are but too familiar with the name of a certain defunct Earl of Yarborough, who, whatever his other good qualities may have been, scarcely seems to have been a consistently good card-holder.

There must be quite a long list of similar words, and they would make an interesting study.

To return to the Diplomatic Theatricals at Petrograd, Labiche's piece, *La Cagnotte*, is extraordinarily funny, though written over sixty years ago. We gave a very successful performance of this, in which I played the restaurant waiter—a capital part. *La Lettre Chargée* and *Le Sous-Préfet* are both most amusing pieces, which can be played, with very slight "cuts," before any audience, and they both bubble over with that *gaieté française* which appeals so to me. We were coached at Petrograd by Andrieux, the *jeune premier* of the Théâtre Michel, and we all became very professional indeed, never talking of *Au Seconde Acte*, but saying *Au Deux*, in proper French stage style. We also endeavoured to cultivate the long-drawn-out " a's " of the Comédie Française, and pronounced " adorahtion " and " imaginahtion " in the traditional manner of the " Maison de Molière."

The British business community in Petrograd were also extremely fond of getting up theatricals, in this case, of course, in English. If in the French plays I was invariably cast for old men, in the English ones I was always allotted the extremely juvenile parts, being still very slim and able to " make up " young. I must confess to having appeared on the stage in an Eton jacket and collar at the age of twenty-four, as the schoolboy in *Peril*.

Russians are extremely clever at parody. Two brothers Narishkin wrote an intensely amusing mock-serious opera, entitled *Gargouillada, ou la Belle de Venise*. It was written half in French and mock-Italian, and half in Russian, and was an excellent skit on an old-fashioned Italian opera. All the ladies fought shy of the part of " Countess Gorganzola," the heroine's grandmother. This was partly due to the boldness of some of " Gorganzola's " lines, and also to the fact that whoever played the rôle would have to make-up frankly as an old woman. I was asked to take " Countess Gorganzola " instead of the villain of the piece, which I had rehearsed, and I did so, turning it into a sort of *Charley's Aunt* part. *Gargouillada* went with a roar from the opening chorus to the final tableau, and so persistently enthusiastic were the audience that we agreed to give the opera again four nights in succession.

I was at work in the Chancery of the Embassy next morning when three people were ushered in to me. They were a family from either St. Helens, Runcorn, or Widnes, I forget which, all speaking the broadest Lancashire. The navigation of the Neva being again opened, they had come on a little trip to Russia on a tramp-steamer belonging to a friend of theirs. There was the father, a short, thickset man in shiny black broadcloth, with a shaven upper lip, and a voluminous red " Newgate-frill " framing his face—exactly the type of face one associates with the Deacon of a

Calvinistic-Methodist Chapel; there was the mother, a very grim-looking female; and the son, a nondescript hobbledehoy with goggle-eyes. It appeared that after their passports had been inspected on landing, the goggle-eyed boy had laid his down somewhere and had lost it. No hotel would take him in without a passport, but these people were so obviously genuine, that I had no hesitation in issuing a fresh passport to the lad, after swearing the father to an affidavit that the protuberant-eyed youth was his lawful son. After a few kind words as to the grave effects of any carelessness with passports in a country like Russia, I let the trio from Runcorn (or St. Helens) depart.

That evening I had just finished dressing and making-up as Countess Gorganzola, when I was told that three English people who had come on from the Embassy wished to see me. The curtain would be going up in ten minutes, so I got an obliging Russian friend who spoke English to go down and interview them. The strong Lancashire accent defeated him. All he could tell me was that it was something about a passport, and that it was important. I was in a difficulty. It would have taken at least half an hour to change and make-up again, and the curtain was going up almost at once, so after some little hesitation I decided to go down as I was. I was wearing a white wig with a large black lace cap, and a gown of black moiré-antique trimmed with flounces and hanging sleeves of an abominable material known as black Chantilly lace. Any one who has ever had to wear this hateful fabric knows how it catches in every possible thing it can do. Down I went, and the trio from Widnes (or Runcorn) seemed surprised at seeing an old lady enter the room. But when I spoke, and they recognised in the old lady the frock-coated (and I trust sympathetic) official they had interviewed earlier in the day, their astonishment knew no bounds. The father gazed at me horror-stricken, as though I were a madman ; the mother kept on swallowing, as ladies of her type do when they wish to convey strong dis- approbation ; and the prominent-orbed boy's eyes nearly fell out of his head. I explained that some theatricals were in progress, but that did not mend matters ; evidently in the serious circles in which they moved in St. Helens (or Widnes), theatricals were regarded as one of the snares of the Evil One. To make matters worse, one of my Chantilly lace sleeves caught in the handle of a drawer, and perhaps excusably, but quite audibly, I condemned all Chantilly lace to eternal punishment, but in a much shorter form. After that they looked on me as clearly beyond the pale. The difficulty about the passport was easily adjusted. The police had threatened to arrest the young man, as his new passport was clearly not the one with which he had entered Russia. The Russian Minister of the Interior happened to be in the green-room, and on my personal guarantee as to the identity of the

Widnes youth, he wrote an order to the police on his visiting-card, bidding them to leave the goggle-eyed boy in peace. I really tremble to think of the reports this family must have circulated upon their return to Widnes (or Runcorn) as to the frivolity of junior members of the British Diplomatic Service, who dressed up as old women, and used bad language about Chantilly lace.

There is a wearisome formality known as "legalising" which took up much time at the Berlin Embassy. Commercial agreements, if they are to be binding in two countries, say Germany and England, have to be "legalised," and this must be done at the Embassy, not at the Consulate. The individual bringing the document has to make a sworn affidavit that the contents of his papers are true; he then signs it, the dry-seal of the Embassy is embossed on it, and a rubber stamp impressed, declaring that the affidavit has been duly sworn to before a member of the Embassy staff. This is then signed and dated, and the process is complete. There were strings of people daily in Berlin with documents to be legalised, and on a little shelf in the Chancery reposed an Authorized Version of the Bible, a German Bible, a Vulgate version of the Gospels in Latin, and a Pentateuch in Hebrew, for the purpose of administering the oath, according to the religion professed by the individual. I was duly instructed how to administer the oath in German, and was told that my first question must be as to the religion the applicant professed, and that I was then to choose my Book accordingly. My great friend at Berlin was my fellow-attaché Maude, a most delightful little fellow, who was universally popular. Poor Maude, who was a near relation of Mr. Cyril Maude the actor's, died four years afterwards in China. Most of the applicants for legalisation were of one particular faith. I admired the way in which little Maude, without putting the usual question as to religion, would scan the features of the applicant closely and then hand him the Hebrew Pentateuch, and request him to put on his hat. (Jews are always sworn covered.) About a month after my arrival in Berlin, I was alone in the Chancery when a man arrived with a document for legalisation. I was only twenty at the time, and felt rather "bucked" at administering my first oath. I thought that I would copy little Maude's methods, and after a good look at my visitor's prominent features, I handed him the Pentateuch and requested him to put on his hat. He was perfectly furious, and declared that both he and his father had been pillars of the Lutheran Church all their lives. I apologised profusely, but all the same I am convinced that the original family seat had been situated in the valley of the Jordan. I avoided, however, guesses as to religions for the future.

Both at Berlin and at Petrograd I kept what are known as the "Extraordinary Accounts" of the Embassies. I am therefore in a position to give the exact amount spent on Secret Service, but I have not the faintest intention of doing anything of the sort. Suffice it to say that it is less than one-twentieth of the sum the average person would imagine. Bought information is nearly always unreliable information. A moment's consideration will show that, should a man be base enough to sell his country's secrets to his country's possible enemy, he would also unhesitatingly cheat, if he could, the man who purchases that information, which, from the very nature of the case, it is almost impossible to verify. In all probability the so-called information would have been carefully prepared at the General Staff for the express purpose of fooling the briber. There is a different class of information which, it seems to me, is more legitimate to acquire. The Russian Ministries of Commerce and Finance always imagined that they could overrule economic laws by decrees and stratagems. For instance, they were perpetually endeavouring to divert the flow of trade from its accustomed channels to some port they wished to stimulate artificially into prosperity, by granting rebates, and by exceptionally favourable railway rates. Large quantities of jute sacking were imported from Dundee to be made into bags for the shipment of Russian wheat. One Minister of Commerce elaborated an intricate scheme for supplanting the jute sacking by coarse linen sacking of Russian manufacture, by granting a bonus to the makers of the latter, and by doubling the import duties on the Scottish-woven material. I could multiply these economic schemes indefinitely. Now let us suppose that we had some source of information in the Ministry of Commerce, it was obviously of advantage to the British Government and to British traders to be warned of the pending economic changes some two years in advance, for nothing is ever done quickly in Russia. People in England then knew what to expect, and could make their arrangements accordingly. I can see nothing repugnant to the most rigid code of honour in obtaining information of this kind.

On May 6, 1882, Lord Frederick Cavendish, the newly appointed Irish Secretary, and Mr. Burke, the Permanent Under-Secretary for Ireland, were assassinated in the Phœnix Park, Dublin. I knew Tom Burke very well indeed. The British Government offered a reward of ten thousand pounds for the apprehension of the murderers, and every policeman in Europe had rosy dreams of securing this great prize, and was constantly on the alert for the criminals and the reward.

In July 1882, the Ambassador and half the Embassy staff were on leave in England. As matters were very slack just then, the Chargé d'Affaires and the Second Secretary had gone to Finland for four days' fishing, leaving me in charge of the Embassy, with an Attaché to help me. My servant came to me early one morning as I was in bed, and told me that an official of the Higher Police was outside my front door, and begged for permission to come into my flat. I have explained elsewhere that Ambassadors, their families, their staffs, and even all the Embassy servants, enjoy what is called exterritoriality; that is, that by a polite fiction the Embassy and the houses or apartments of the Secretaries are supposed to be on the actual soil of the country they represent. Consequently, the police of the country cannot enter them except by special permission, and both the Secretaries and their servants are immune from arrest, and are not subject to the laws of the country, though they can, of course, be expelled from it. I gave the policeman leave to enter, and he came into my bedroom. " I have caught one of the Phœnix Park murderers," he told me triumphantly in Russian, visions of the possible ten thousand pounds wreathing his face in smiles. I jumped up incredulously. He went on to inform me that a man had landed from the Stockholm steamer early that morning. Though he declared that he had no arms with him, a revolver and a dagger had been found in his trunk. His passport had only been issued at the British Legation in Stockholm, and his description tallied exactly with the *signalement* issued by Scotland Yard in eight languages. The *policier* showed me the description: "height about five feet nine; complexion sallow, with dark eyes. Thickset build; probably with some recent cuts on face and hands." The policeman declared that the cuts were there, and that it was unquestionably the man wanted.

Then he put the question point-blank, would the Embassy sanction this man's arrest? I was only twenty-five at the time. I had to act on "my own," and I had to decide quickly. "Yes, arrest him," I said, "but you are not to take him to prison. Confine him to his room at his hotel, with two or three of your men to watch him. I will dress and come there as quickly as I can."

Half an hour later I was in a grubby room of a grubby hotel, where a short, sallow, thickset man, with three recent cuts on his face, was walking up and down, smoking cigarettes feverishly, and throwing frightened glances at three sinister-looking plain-clothes men, who pretended to be quite at their ease. I looked again at the description and at the man. There could be no doubt about it. I asked him for his own account of himself. He told me that he was the Manager of the Gothenburg Tramway Company in Sweden, an English concern, and that he had come to Russia for a little holiday. He accounted for the cuts on his face and hands by saying that he had slipped and fallen on his face whilst alighting from a moving tram-car. He declared that he was well known in Stockholm, and that his wife, when packing his things, must have put in the revolver and dagger without his knowledge. It all sounded grotesquely improbable, but I promised to telegraph both to Stockholm and Gothenburg, and to return to him as soon as I had received the answers. In the meanwhile I feared that he must

consider himself as under close arrest. He himself was under the impression that all the trouble
was due to the concealed arms; the Phœnix Park
murders had never once been mentioned. I sent
off a long telegram in cypher to the Stockholm
Legation, making certain inquiries, and a longer
one *en clair* to the British Consul at Gothenburg.
By nagging at the Attaché, and by keeping that
dapper young gentleman's nose pretty close to the
grindstone, I got the first telegram cyphered and
dispatched by 10 a.m.; the answers arrived about
4 p.m. The man's story was true in every particular. He *had* fallen off a moving tram and cut
his face; his wife, terrified at the idea of unknown
dangers in Russia, *had* borrowed a revolver and
dagger from a friend, and had packed them in
her husband's trunk without his knowledge. Mr.
D—— (I remember his name perfectly) was well
known in Stockholm, and was a man of the highest
respectability. I drove as fast as I could to the
grubby hotel, where I found the poor fellow still
restlessly pacing the room, and still smoking cigarette after cigarette. There was a perfect Mont
Blanc of cigarette stumps on a plate, and the
shifty-looking plain-clothes men were still watching
their man like hawks. I told the police that they
had got hold of the wrong man, that the Embassy
was quite satisfied about him, and that they must
release the gentleman at once. They accordingly
did so, and the alluring vision of the ten thousand
pounds vanished into thin air! The poor man

was quite touchingly grateful to me; he had formed the most terrible ideas about a Russian State prison, and seemed to think that he owed his escape entirely to me. I had not the moral courage to tell him that I had myself ordered his arrest that morning, still less of the awful crime of which he had been suspected. Looking back, I do not see how I could have acted otherwise; the primâ facie case against him was so strong; never was circumstantial evidence apparently clearer. Mr. D—— went back to Sweden next day, as he had had enough of Russia. Should Mr. D—— still be alive, and should he by any chance read these lines, may I beg of him to accept my humblest apologies for the way I behaved to him thirty-eight years ago.

I happened to see the four assassins of Alexander II. driven through the streets of Petrograd on their way to execution. They were seated in chairs on large tumbrils, with their backs to the horses. Each one had a placard on his, or her breast, inscribed " Regicide " ("Tsaryubeeyetz" in Russian). Two military brass bands, playing loudly, followed the tumbrils. This was to make it impossible for the condemned persons to address the crowd, but the music might have been selected more carefully. One band played the well-known march from *Fatinitza*. There was a ghastly incongruity between the merry strains of this captivating march and the terrible fate that awaited the people escorted by the band at the end of their last drive on earth. When the first band rested, the second replaced it instantly to avoid any possibilities of a speech. The second band seemed to me to have made an equally unhappy selection of music. "Kaiser Alexander," written as a complimentary tribute to the murdered Emperor by a German composer, is a spirited and tuneful march, but as "Kaiser Alexander" was dead, and had been killed by the very people who were now going to expiate their crime, the familiar tune jarred horribly. A jaunty, lively march tune, and death at the end of it, and in a sense at the beginning of it too. At times even now I can conjure up a vision of the broad, sombre Petrograd streets, with the dull cotton-wool sky pressing down almost on to the house-tops; the vast silent crowds thronging the thoroughfares, and the tumbrils rolling slowly forward through the crowded streets to the place of execution, accompanied by the gay strains of the march from *Fatinitza*. The hideous incongruity between the tune and the occasion made one positively shudder.

There is in the Russian temperament a peculiar unbalanced hysterical element. This, joined to a distinct bent towards the mystic, and to a large amount of credulity, has made Russia for two hundred years the happy hunting-ground of charlatans and impostors of various sorts claiming supernatural powers: clairvoyants, mediums, yogis, and all the rest of the tribe who batten on human weaknesses, and the perpetual desire to tear away the veil from the Unseen. It so happened that my chief at Lisbon had in his youth dabbled in the Black Art. Sir Charles Wyke was a dear old man, who had spent most of his Diplomatic career in Mexico and the South American Republics. He spoke Spanish better than any other Englishman I ever knew, with the one exception of Sir William Barrington. He was unmarried, and was a most distinguished-looking old gentleman with his snow-white imperial and moustache. He was unquestionably a little eccentric in his habits. He had rendered some signal service to the Mexican Government whilst British Minister there, by settling a dispute between them and the French authorities. The Mexican Government had out of gratitude presented him with a splendid Mexican saddle, with pommel, stirrups and bit of solid silver, and with the leather of the saddle most elaborately embroidered in silver. Sir Charles kept this trophy on a saddle-tree in his study at Lisbon, and it was his custom to sit on it daily for an hour or so. He said that as he was too old to ride, the feel of a saddle under him reminded him of his youth. When every morning I brought the old gentleman the day's dispatches, I always found him seated on his saddle, a cigar in his mouth, a skull-cap on his head, and his feet in the silver shoe-stirrups. Sir Charles had been a great friend of the first Lord Lytton, the novelist, and they had together dabbled in Black Magic. Sir Charles declared that the last chapters in Bulwer-

Lytton's wonderful imaginative work, *A Strange Story*, describing the preparation of the Elixir of Life in the heart of the Australian Bush, were all founded on actual experience, with the notable reservation that all the recorded attempts made to produce this magic fluid had failed from their very start. He had in his younger days joined a society of Rosicrucians, by which I do not mean the Masonic Order of that name, but persons who sought to penetrate into the Forbidden Domain. Some forty years ago a very interesting series of articles appeared in *Vanity Fair* (the weekly newspaper, not Thackeray's masterpiece), under the title of "The Black Art." In one of these there was an account of a *séance* which took place at the Pantheon in Oxford Street, in either the "forties" or the "fifties." A number of people had hired the hall, and the Devil was invoked in due traditional form. Then *something* happened, and the entire assemblage rushed terror-stricken into Oxford Street, and nothing would induce a single one of them to re-enter the building. Sir Charles owned that he had been present at the *séance*, but he would never tell me what it was that frightened them all so ; he said that he preferred to forget the whole episode. Sir Charles had an idea that I was a "sensitive," so, after getting my leave to try his experiment, he poured into the palm of my hand a little pool of quicksilver, and placing me under a powerful shaded lamp, so that a ray of light caught the mercury pool, he told me to look at the bright spot for a quarter of an hour, remaining motionless meanwhile. Any one who has shared this experience with me, knows how the speck of light flashes and grows until that little pool of quicksilver seems to fill the entire horizon, darting out gleaming rays like an Aurora Borealis. I felt myself growing dazed and hypnotised, when Sir Charles emptied the mercury from my hand, and commenced making passes over me, looking, with his slender build and his white hair and beard, like a real mediæval magician. " Now you can neither speak nor move," he cried at length. " I think I can do both, Sir Charles," I answered, as I got out of the chair. He tried me on another occasion, and then gave me up. I was clearly not a " sensitive."

Sir Charles had quite a library of occult books, from which I endeavoured to glean a little knowledge, and great rubbish most of them were. Raymond Lully, Basil Valentine, Paracelsus, and Van Helmont; they were all there, in French, German, Latin, and English. The Alchemists had two obsessions : one was the discovery of the Elixir of Life, by the aid of which you could live for ever ; the other that of the Philosopher's Stone, which had the property of transmuting everything it touched into gold. Like practical men, they seemed to have concentrated their energies more especially on the latter, for a moment's consideration will show the exceedingly awkward predicament in which any one would be placed with only the first of these conveniences at his command. Should he by the aid of the Elixir of Life have managed to attain the age of, say, 300 years, he might find it excessively hard to obtain any remunerative employment at that time of life ; whereas with the Philosopher's Stone in his pocket, he would only have to touch the door-scraper outside his house to find it immediately transmuted into the purest gold. In case of pressing need, he could extend the process with like result to his area railings, which ought to be enough to keep the wolf from the door for some little while even at the present-day scale of prices.

Basil Valentine, the German Benedictine monk and alchemist, who wrote a book which he quaintly termed *The Triumphant Wagon*, in praise of the healing properties of antimony, actually thought that he had discovered the Elixir of Life in tartrate of antimony, more generally known as tartar emetic. He administered large doses of this turbulent remedy to some ailing monks of his community, who promptly all died of it.

The main characteristics of the Alchemists is their wonderful clarity. For instance, when they wish to refer to mercury, they call it "the green lion," and the "Pontic Sea," which makes it quite obvious to every one. They attached immense importance to the herb "Lunary," which no one as yet has ever been able to discover. Should any one happen to see during their daily walks "a herb

with a black root, and a red and violet stalk, whose
leaves wax and wane with the moon," they will at
once know that they have found a specimen of the
rare herb " Lunary." The juice of this plant, if
boiled with quicksilver, has only to be thrown over
one hundred ounces of copper, to change them
instantly into fine gold. Paracelsus' directions for
making the Philosopher's Stone are very simple :
" Take the rosy-coloured blood of the lion, and
gluten from the eagle. Mix them together, and
the Philosopher's Stone is thine. Seek the lion in
the west, and the eagle in the south." What could
be clearer ? Any child could make sufficient
Philosopher's Stones from this simple recipe to
pave a street with—a most useful asset, by the way,
to the Chancellor of the Exchequer at the present
time, for every bicycle, omnibus and motor-lorry
driving over the Philosopher Stone-paved street
would instantly be changed automatically into pure
gold, and the National Debt could be satisfactorily
liquidated in this fashion in no time.

Whenever I returned home on leave, whether
from Berlin, Petrograd, Lisbon, or Buenos Ayres,
I invariably spent a portion of my leave at Glamis
Castle. This venerable pile, " whose birth tradition
notes not," though the lower portions were undoubtedly standing in 1016, rears its forest of
conical turrets in the broad valley lying between
the Grampians and the Sidlaws, in the fertile
plains of Forfarshire. Apart from the prestige of
its immense age, Glamis is one of the most beautiful

buildings in the Three Kingdoms. The exquisitely weathered tints of grey-pink and orange that its ancient red sandstone walls have taken on with the centuries, its many gables and towers rising in summer-time out of a sea of greenery, the richness of its architectural details, make Glamis a thing apart. There is nothing else quite like it. No more charming family can possibly be imagined than that of the late Lord Strathmore, forty years ago. The seven sons and three daughters of the family were all born musicians. I have never heard such perfect and finished part-singing as that of the Lyon family, and they were always singing : on the way to a cricket-match ; on the road home from shooting ; in the middle of dinner, even, this irrepressible family could not help bursting into harmony, and such exquisite harmony, too ! Until their sisters grew up, the younger boys sang the treble and alto parts, but finally they were able to manage a male-voice quartet, a trio of ladies' voices, and a combined family octette. The dining-room at Glamis is a very lofty hall, oak-panelled, with a great Jacobean chimney-piece rising to the roof. After dinner it was the custom for the two family pipers to make the circuit of the table three times, and then to walk slowly off, still playing, through the tortuous stone passages of the ancient building until the last faint echoes of the music had died away. Then all the lights in the dining-room were extinguished except the candles on the table, and out came a tuning-fork, and one note was sounded—"Madrigal," "Spring is Come, third beat," said the conducting brother, and off they went, singing exquisitely; glees, madrigals, part-songs, anything and everything, the acoustic properties of the lofty room adding to the effect. All visitors to Glamis were charmed with this most finished singing—always, of course, without accompaniment. They sang equally well in the private chapel, giving admirable renderings of the most intricate "Services," and, from long practice together, their voices blended perfectly. This gifted family were equally good at acting. They had a permanent stage during the winter months at Glamis, and as every new Gilbert and Sullivan opera was produced in London, the concerted portions were all duly repeated at Glamis, and given most excellently. I have never heard the duet and minuet between "Sir Marmaduke" and "Lady Sangazure" from *The Sorcerer* better done than at Glamis, although Sir Marmaduke was only nineteen, and Lady Sangazure, under her white wig, was a boy of twelve. The same boy sang "Mabel" in the *Pirates of Penzance* most admirably.

In 1884 it was conveyed to Lord Strathmore that Mr. and Mrs. Gladstone, whom he did not know personally, were most anxious to see Glamis. Of course an invitation was at once dispatched, and in spite of the rigorously Tory atmosphere of the house, we were all quite charmed with Mr. Gladstone's personality. Lord Strathmore wished to stop the part-singing after dinner, but I felt sure that Mr. Gladstone would like it, so it took place as usual. The old gentleman was perfectly enchanted with it, and complimented this tuneful family enthusiastically on the perfect finish of their singing. Next evening Mr. Gladstone asked for a part-song in the middle of dinner, and as the singing was continued in the drawing-room afterwards, he went and, with a deferential courtesy charming to see in a man of his age and position, asked whether the young people would allow an old man to sing bass in the glees with them. Mr. Gladstone still had a very fine resonant bass, and he read quite admirably. It was curious to see the Prime Minister reading off the same copy as an Eton boy of sixteen, who was singing alto. Being Sunday night, they went on singing hymns and anthems till nearly midnight ; there was no getting Mr. Gladstone away. Mrs. Gladstone told me next day that he had not enjoyed himself so much for many months.

There was a blend of simplicity, dignity, and kindliness in Mrs. Gladstone's character that made her very attractive. My family were exceedingly fond of her, and though two of my brothers were always attacking Mr. Gladstone in the most violent terms, this never strained their friendly relations with Mrs. Gladstone herself. I always conjure up visions of Mrs. Gladstone in her sapphire-blue velvet, her invariable dress of ceremony. Though a little careless as to her appearance, she always looked a "great lady," and her tall figure, and the kindly old face with its crown of silvery hair, were always welcomed in the houses of those privileged to know her.

The Lyon family could do other things besides singing and acting. The sons were all excellent shots, and were very good at games. One brother was lawn-tennis champion of Scotland, whilst another, with his partner, won the Doubles Championship of England.

Glamis is the oldest inhabited house in Great Britain. As Shakespeare tells us in *Macbeth*:

> "This castle hath a pleasant seat; the air
> Nimbly and sweetly recommends itself
> Unto our gentle senses."

The vaulted crypt was built before 1016, and another ancient stone-flagged, stone-vaulted hall leading out of it is the traditional scene of the murder of Duncan by Macbeth, the "Thane of Glamis." In a room above it King Malcolm II. of Scotland was murdered in 1034. The castle positively teems with these agreeable traditions. The staircases and their passages are stone-walled, stone-roofed, and stone-floored, and their flags are worn into hollows by the feet which have trodden them for so many centuries. Unusual features are the secret winding staircases debouching in the most unexpected places, and a well in the front hall, which doubtless played a very useful part during the many sieges the castle sustained in the old days. The private chapel is a beautiful little place of worship, with eighty painted panels of Scriptural subjects by De Witt, the seventeenth-century Dutch artist, and admirable stained glass. The Castle, too, is full of interesting historical relics. It boasts the only remaining Fool's dress of motley in the kingdom; Prince Charlie's watch and clothes are still preserved there, for the Prince, surprised by the Hanoverian troops at Glamis, had only time to jump on a horse and escape, leaving all his belongings behind him. There is a wonderful collection of old family dresses of the seventeenth and eighteenth centuries, and above all there is the very ancient silver-gilt cup, " The Lion of Glamis," which holds an entire bottle of wine, and on great family occasions is still produced and used as a loving-cup, circulating from hand to hand round the table. Walter Scott in a note to *Waverley* states that it was the " Lion of Glamis " cup which gave him the idea of the " Blessed Bear of Bradwardine." In fact, there is no end to the objects of interest this wonderful old castle contains, and the Lyon family have inhabited it for six hundred years in direct line from father to son.

It is difficult for me to write impartially about Glamis, for it is as familiar to me as my own home. I have been so much there, and have received such kindness within its venerable walls, that it can never be to me quite as other places are. I can see vast swelling stretches of purple heather, with the dainty little harebells all a-quiver in the strong breeze sweeping over the grouse-butts, as a brown mass of whirling wings rushes past at the pace of an express train, causing one probably to reflect how well-nigh impossible it is to "allow" too much for driven grouse flying down-wind. I can picture equally vividly the curling-pond in winter-time, tuneful with the merry chirrup of the curling-stones as they skim over the ice, whilst cries of "Soop her up, man, soop! Soop!" from the anxious "skip" fill the keen air. I like best, though, to think of the Glamis of my young days, when the ancient stone-built passages and halls, that have seen so many generations pass through them and disappear, rang with perpetual youthful laughter, or echoed beautifully finished part-singing; when nimble young feet twinkled, and kilts whirled to the skirl of the pipes under the vaulted roof of the nine-hundred-year-old crypt; when the whole place was vibrant with joyous young life, and the stately, grey-bearded owner of the historic castle, and of many broad acres in Strathmore besides, found his greatest pleasure in seeing how happy his children and his guests could be under his roof.

CHAPTER IX

WHEN I was in Canada for the first time in
1884, the Canadian Pacific Railway was not completed, and there was no through railway connection
between the Maritime Provinces, " Upper " and
" Lower " Canada, and the Pacific Coast, though,
of course, in 1884 those old-fashioned terms for the
Provinces of Ontario and Quebec had been obsolete
for some time. Since the Federation of the
Dominion in 1867, the opening of the Trans-Continental railway has been the most potent factor in
the knitting together of Canada, and has developed
the resources of the Dominion to an extent which
even the most enthusiastic of the original promoters

of the C.P.R. never anticipated. When British Columbia threw in its lot with the Dominion in 1871, one of the terms upon which the Pacific Province insisted was a guarantee that the Trans-Continental railway should be completed in ten years—that is, in 1881. Two rival Companies received in 1872 charters for building the railway; the result was continual political intrigue, and very little construction work. British Columbia grew extremely restive under the continual delays, and threatened to retire from the Dominion. Lord Dufferin told me himself, when I was his Private Secretary in Petrograd, that on the occasion of his official visit to British Columbia (of course by sea), in either 1876 or 1877, as Governor-General, he was expected to drive under a triumphal arch which had been erected at Victoria, Vancouver Island. This arch was inscribed on both sides with the word "Separation." I remember perfectly Lord Dufferin's actual words in describing the incident: "I sent for the Mayor of Victoria, and told him that I must have a small—a very small—alteration made in the inscription, before I could consent to drive under it; an alteration of one letter only. The initial "S" must be replaced with an "R," and then I would pledge my word that I would do my best to see that "Reparation" was made to the Province." This is so eminently characteristic of Lord Dufferin's methods that it is worth recording. The suggested alteration in the inscription was duly made, and Lord Dufferin drove under the arch,

In spite of continued efforts the Governor-General was unable to expedite the construction of the railway under the Mackenzie Administration, and it needed all his consummate tact to quiet the ever-growing demand for separation from the Dominion on the part of British Columbia, owing to the non-fulfilment of the terms of union. It was not until 1881, under Sir John Macdonald's Premiership, that a contract was signed with a new Company to complete the Canadian Pacific within ten years, but so rapid was the progress made, that the last spike was actually driven on November 7, 1886, five years before the stipulated time. The names of three Scotsmen will always be associated with this gigantic undertaking: those of the late Donald Smith, afterwards Lord Strathcona; George Stephen, now Lord Mountstephen; and Mr. R. B. Angus of Montreal. At first, before the track became consolidated, the running of the trains over the western sections was rather irregular. I remember going to the C.P.R. station in Ottawa in February 1887, to meet a friend of mine who was arriving from Vancouver, and being advised to return next day about the same time, as the Trans-Continental train had left Winnipeg twenty-five hours late.

There are few finer views in the world than that from the terrace of the Citadel of Quebec over the mighty expanse of the St. Lawrence, with ocean-going steamers lying so close below that it would be possible to drop a stone from the Citadel on to their decks; and the view from the Dufferin Terrace, two hundred feet lower down, is just as fine. My brother-in-law Lord Lansdowne had been appointed Governor-General in 1883, and I well remember my first arrival in Quebec. We had been living for five weeks in the backwoods of the Cascapedia, the famous salmon-river, under the most primitive conditions imaginable. I had come there straight from the Argentine Republic on a tramp steamer, and we lived on the Cascapedia coatless and flannel-shirted, with our legs encased in "beef moc-casins" as a protection against the hordes of voracious flies that battened ravenously on us from morning to night. It was a considerable change from a tent on the banks of the rushing, foaming Cascapedia to the Citadel of Quebec, which was then appointed like a comfortable English country house, and gave one a thoroughly home-like feeling at once. After my prolonged stay in South America I was pleased, too, to recognise familiar pictures, furniture and china which I had last met in their English Wiltshire home, all of them with the stolid impassiveness of inanimate objects una-ware that they had been spirited across the Atlantic, three thousand miles from their accustomed abiding-place.

In September 1884, at a point immediately below the Falls, I swam Niagara with Mr. Cecil Baring, now a partner in Baring Brothers, then an Oxford undergraduate. We were standing at the foot of the American Falls, when we noticed a little board inscribed, "William Grenfell of Taplow Court, England" (the present Lord Desborough), "swam Niagara at this spot." I looked at Baring, Baring looked at me. "I don't see why we shouldn't do it too," he observed, to which I replied, "We might have a try," so we stripped, sent our clothes over to the Canadian side, and entered the water. It was a far longer swim than either of us had anticipated, the current was very strong, and the eddies bothered us. When we landed on the Canadian shore I was utterly exhausted, though Baring, being eight years younger than me, did not feel the effects of the exertion so much. I remember that the Falls, seen from only six inches above the surface of the water, looked like a splendid range of snow-clad hills tumbling about in mad confusion, and that the roar of waters was deafening. As we both lay panting and gasping, *puris naturalibus*, on the Canadian bank, I need hardly say, as we were on the American continent, that a reporter made his appearance from nowhere, armed with notebook and pencil. This young newspaper-man was not troubled with false delicacy. He asked us point-blank what we had made out of our swim. On learning that we had had no money on it, but had merely done it for the fun of the thing, he mentioned the name of a place of eternal punishment, shut up his notebook in disgust, and walked off: there was evidently no "story" to be made out of us. After some luncheon and a bottle of Burgundy, neither Baring nor I felt any the worse for our swim, nor were we the least tired during the remainder of the day. I have seen Niagara in summer, spring and in mid-winter, and each time the fascination of these vast masses of tumbling waters has grown on me. I have never, to my regret, seen the Victoria Falls of the Zambesi, as on two separate occasions when starting for them unforeseen circumstances detained me in Cape Town. The Victoria Falls are more than double the height of Niagara, Niagara falling 160 feet, and the Zambesi 330 feet, and the Falls are over one mile broad, but I fancy that except in March and April, the volume of water hurling itself over them into the great chasm below is smaller than at Niagara. I have heard that the width of the Victoria Falls is to within a few yards exactly the distance between the Marble Arch and Oxford Circus. When I was in the Argentine Republic, the great Falls of the River Iguazú, a tributary of the Parana, were absolutely inaccessible. To reach them vast tracts of dense primeval forest had to be traversed, where every inch of the track would have to be laboriously hacked through the jungle. Their very existence was questioned, for it depended on the testimony of wandering Indians, and of one solitary white man, a Jesuit missionary. Now, since the railway to Paraguay has been completed, the Iguazú Falls can be reached, though the journey is still a difficult one. The Falls are 200 feet high, and nearly a mile wide. In the very heart of the City of Ottawa there are the fine Chaudière Falls, where the entire River Ottawa drops fifty feet over a rocky ledge. The boiling whirl of angry waters has well earned its name of cauldron, or "Chaudière," but so much of the water has now been drawn off to supply electricity and power to the city, that the volume of the falls has become sensibly diminished. I know of no place in Europe where the irresistible might of falling waters is more fully brought home to one than at Trollhättan in Sweden. Here the Gotha River whirls itself down 120 feet in seven cataracts. They are rapids rather than falls, but it is the immense volume of water which makes them so impressive. Every year Trollhättan grows more and more disfigured by saw-mills, carbide of calcium works, and other industrial buildings sprouting up like unsightly mushrooms along the river-banks. The last time that I was there it was almost impossible to see the falls in their entirety from any point, owing to this congestion of squalid factories.

Rideau Hall, the Government House at Ottawa, stands about two miles out of the town, and is a long, low, unpretentious building, exceedingly comfortable as a dwelling-house, if somewhat inadequate as an official residence for the Governor-General of Canada. Lord Dufferin added a large and very handsome ball-room, fitted with a stage at one end of it, and a full-sized tennis-court. This tennis-court, by an ingenious arrangement, can be converted in a few hours into a splendid supper-room. A red and white tent is lowered bodily from the roof; a carpet is spread over the floor; great white-and-gold electric standards bearing the arms of the different Provinces are placed in position, and the thing is done. The intense dryness of the Canadian winter climate, especially in houses where furnace-heat intensifies the dryness, produces some unexpected results. My brother-in-law had brought out a number of old pieces of French inlaid furniture. The excessive dryness forced out some of the inlaid marqueterie of these pieces, and upon their return to Europe they had to undergo a long and expensive course of treatment. Some fine Romneys and Gainsboroughs also required the picture-restorer's attentions before they could return to their Wiltshire home after a five years' sojourn in the dry air of Canada. The ivory handles of razors shrink in the dry atmosphere; as the steel frame cannot shrink correspondingly the ivory splits in two. The thing most surprising to strangers was that it was possible in winter-time to light the gas with one's finger. All that was necessary was to shuffle over the carpet in thin shoes, and then on touching any metal object, an electric spark half an inch long would crack out of your finger. The size and power of the spark depended a great deal on the temperament of the experimenter. A high-strung person could produce quite a large spark; a stolid, bovine individual could not obtain a glimmer of one. The late Mr. Joseph Chamberlain, whilst staying at Government House, was told of this, but was inclined to be sceptical. My sister Lady

Lansdowne made him shuffle over the carpet, and then and there touch a gas-burner from which she had removed the globe. Mr. Chamberlain, with his nervous temperament, produced a spark an inch long out of himself, and of course the gas flared up immediately. I do not think that I had ever seen any one more surprised. This power of generating static electricity from their own bodies was naturally a source of immense delight to the Lansdowne children. They loved, after shuffling their feet on the carpet, to creep up to any adult relation and touch them lightly on the ear, a most sensitive spot. There would be a little spark, a little shock, and a little exclamation of surprise. Outside the children's schoolroom there was a lobby warmed by a stove, and the air there was peculiarly dry. The young people, with a dozen or so of their youthful friends, would join hands, taking, however, care not to complete the circle, and then shuffle their feet vigorously. On completing the circuit, they could produce a combined spark over two inches long, with a correspondingly sharp shock. In my bed-room at Ottawa there was an old-fashioned high brass fender. Had I put on slippers, and have attempted to warm myself at the fire previous to turning-in, I should be reminded, by a sharp discharge from my protesting calves into the metal fender, that I was in dry Canada. (At that date the dryness of Canada was atmospherical only.) Curiously enough, a spark leaving the body produces the same shock as one entering it, and no electricity whatever can be generated with bare feet. One of the footmen at Ottawa must have been an abnormally high-strung young man, for should one inadvertently touch the silver dinner-plate he handed one, a sharp electric shock resulted. The children delighted in one very pretty experiment. Many books for the young have their bindings plentifully adorned with gold, notably the French series, the "Bibliothèque Rose." Should one of these highly-gilt volumes be taken into a warm and dry place, and the lights extinguished, the *inner* side of the binding had only to be rubbed briskly with a fur cap for all the gilding to begin to sparkle and coruscate, and to send out little flashes of electricity. The children took the utmost pleasure in this example of the curious properties of electricity.

The Ottawa of the "eighties" was an attractive little place, and Ottawa Society was very pleasant. There was then a note of unaffected simplicity about everything that was most engaging, and the people were perfectly natural and free from pretence. The majority of them were Civil servants of limited means, and as everybody knew what their neighbours' incomes were, there was no occasion for make-believe. The same note of simplicity ran through all amusements and entertaining, and I think that it constituted the charm of the place. I called one afternoon on the very agreeable wife of a high official, and was told at the door that Lady R—— was not at home.

Recognising my voice, a cry came up from the kitchen-stairs. " Oh, yes! I am at home to you. Come right down into the kitchen," where I found my friend, with her sleeves rolled up, making with her own hands the sweets for the dinner-party she was giving that night, as she mistrusted her cook's capabilities. The Ottawa people had then that gift of being absolutely unaffected, which makes the majority of Australians so attractive. Now everything has changed; Ottawa has trebled in size since I first knew it, and on revisiting it twenty-five years later, I found that it had become very "smart" indeed, with elaborate houses and gorgeous raiment.

Rideau Hall had two open-air skating-rinks in its own grounds, two imposing toboggan-slides, and a covered curling-rink. The "roaring game" is played in Canada with very heavy straight-sided iron " stones," weighing from 50 to 60 lbs. As the ice in a covered rink can be constantly flooded, it can be kept in the most perfect order, and with the heavy stones far greater accuracy can be attained than with the granite stones used in Scotland. The game becomes a sort of billiards on ice. The Rideau Hall team consisted of Lord Lansdowne himself, General Sir Henry Streatfield, a nephew of mine, and one of the footmen, who seemed to have a natural gift as a curler. Our team were invincible in 1888. At a curling-match against Montreal in 1887, a long-distance telephone was used for the first time in Canada. Ottawa is

120 miles distant from Montreal, and a telephone was specially installed, and each " end " telephoned from Rideau Hall to Montreal, where the result was shown on a board, excitement over the match running high. Montreal proved the victors. On great occasions such as this, the ice of the curling-rink was elaborately decorated in colours. It was very easily done. Ready-prepared stencils, such as are used for wall-decoration, were laid on the ice, and various coloured inks mixed with water were poured through the stencil holes, and froze almost immediately on to the ice below. In this fashion complicated designs of roses, thistles and maple-leaves, all in their proper colours, could be made in a very short time, and most effective they were until destroyed by the first six " ends." When the Governor-General's time in Canada expired and he was transferred to India, the curlers of Canada presented him with a farewell address. Lord Lansdowne made, I thought, a very happy reply. Speaking of the regret he felt at leaving Ottawa, and at severing his many links of connection with Canada, he added that, bearing in view the climate of Bengal, he did not anticipate much curling in India, and that he would miss the " roaring game "; in fact, the only " roaring game " he was likely to come in contact with would probably take the unpleasant form of a Bengal tiger springing out at him. Lord Lansdowne went on to say, " Let us hope that it will not happen that your ex-Governor-General will be

found, not pursuing the roaring game, but being pursued by it."

From skating daily, most of the Government House party became very expert, and could perform every kind of trick upon skates. Lord and Lady Lansdowne and their two daughters, now Duchess of Devonshire and Lady Osborne Beauclerk, could execute the most complicated Quadrilles and Lancers on skates, and could do the most elaborate figures.

Once a week all Ottawa turned up at Rideau Hall to skate to the music of a good military band. Every year in December a so-called ice-palace was built for the band, of clear blocks of ice. Once given a design, ice-architecture is most fascinating and very easy. Instead of mortar, all that is required is a stream of water from a hose to freeze the ice-blocks together, and as ice can be easily chipped into any shape, the most fantastic pinnacles and ornaments can be contrived. Our ice-palace was usually built in what I may call a free adaptation of the Canado-Moresque style. A very necessary feature in the ice-palace was the large stove for thawing the brass instruments of the band. A moment's consideration will show that in the intense cold of a Canadian winter, the moisture that accumulates in a brass instrument would freeze solid, rendering the instrument useless. The bandsmen had always to handle the brass with woollen gloves on, to prevent getting burnt. How curious it is that the sensation of touching very hot or very cold metal is identical, and that it produces the same effect on the human skin! With thirty or more degrees of frost, great caution must be used in handling skate-blades with bare fingers if burns are to be avoided. The coldest day I have ever known was New Year's Day 1888, when the thermometer at Ottawa registered 41° below, or 73° of frost. The air was quite still, as it invariably is with great cold, but every breath taken gave one a sensation of being pinched on the nose, as the moisture in the nostrils froze together.

The weekly club-dances of the Ottawa Skating Club were a pretty sight. They were held in a covered public rink, gay with many flags, with garlands of artificial flowers and foliage, and blazing with sizzling arc-lights. These people, accustomed to skates from their earliest childhood, could dance as easily and as gracefully on them as on their feet, whilst fur-muffled mothers sat on benches round the rink, drinking tea and coffee as unconcernedly as though they were at a garden-party in mid-July instead of in a temperature of zero. An "Ottawa March" was a great institution. Couples formed up as though for a country dance, the band struck up some rollicking tune, the leader shouted his directions, and fifty couples whirled and twirled, and skated backwards or forwards as he ordered, going through the most complicated evolutions, in pairs or fours or singly, joining here, parting there, but all in perfect time.

Woe betide the leader should he lose his head! A hundred people would get tangled-up in hideous confusion, and there was nothing for it but to begin all over again.

It is curious that in countries like England and France, where from the climatic conditions skating must be a very occasional amusement, there is a special word for the pastime, and that in Germany and Russia, where every winter brings its skating as a matter of course, there should be no word for it. "Skate" in English, and *patiner* in French, mean propelling oneself on iron runners over ice, and nothing else; whereas in German there is only the clumsy compound-word *Schlittschuh-laufen*, which means "to run on sledge shoes," and in Russian it is called in equally roundabout fashion *Katatsa-na-konkach*, or literally "to roll on little horses," hardly a felicitous expression. As a rule people have no word for expressing a thing which does not come within their own range of experience; for instance, no one would expect that Arabs, or Somalis, or the inhabitants of the Sahara would have any equivalent for either skating or tobogganing, nor do I imagine that the Eskimo have any expression for "sunstroke" or "heat-apoplexy," but one would have thought that Russians and Germans might have evolved a word for skating.

Apropos of Eskimo, I once heard a missionary describe the extraordinary difficulty he had found in translating the Bible into Eskimo. It was useless to talk of corn or wine to a people who did not know even what they meant, so he had to use equivalents within their powers of comprehension. Thus in the Eskimo version of the Scriptures the miracle of Cana of Galilee is described as turning the water into *blubber;* the 8th verse of the 5th chapter of the First Epistle of St. Peter ran: " Your adversary the devil, as a roaring Polar *bear* walketh about, seeking whom he may devour." In the same way " A land flowing with milk and honey" became " A land flowing with whale's blubber," and throughout the New Testament the word "Lamb" had to be translated "little seal," as the nearest possible equivalent. The missionary added that his converts had the lowest opinion of Jonah for not having utilised his exceptional opportunities by killing and eating the whale.

Fired by the example of the builders of the ice-palace on the rink at Rideau Hall, I offered to build for the Lansdowne children an ice-hut for their very own, a chilly domicile which they had ardently longed for. As it is my solitary achievement as an architect, I must dwell rather lovingly on the building of this hut. The professional ice-cutters were bringing up daily a large supply of great gleaming transparent blocks from the river, both for the building of the band-house and for the summer supply of Rideau Hall, so there was no lack of material. On the American continent one is being told so constantly that this-and-that "will cut no ice," that it is satisfactory to be able to report that those French-Canadians cut ice in the most efficient fashion. My sole building implement was a kettle of boiling water. I placed ice-blocks in a circle, pouring boiling water between each two blocks to melt the points of contact, and in half an hour they had frozen into one solid lump. I and a friend proceeded like this till the ice-walls were about four feet high, spaces being left for the door and windows. As the blocks became too heavy to lift, we used great wads of snow in their stead, melting them with cold water and kneading them into shape with thick woollen gloves, and so the walls rose. I wanted a snow roof; had we been mediæval cathedral builders we might possibly have fashioned a groined and vaulted snow roof, with ice ribs, but being amateurs, our roof perpetually collapsed, so we finally roofed the hut with grooved-and-tongued boards, cutting a hole through them for the chimney. We then built a brick fire-place, with mantelpiece complete, ending in an iron chimney. The windows were our great triumph. I filled large japanned tea-trays two inches deep with water and left them out to freeze. Then we placed the trays in a hot bath and floated the sheets of ice off. They broke time and time again, but after about the twentieth try we succeeded in producing two great sheets of transparent ice which were fitted into the window-spaces, and firmly cemented in place with wet snow. Then the completed hut had to be furnished. A

carpenter in Ottawa made me a little dresser, a
little table, and little chairs of plain deal; I bought
some cooking utensils, some enamelled-iron tea-
things and plates, and found in Ottawa some crude
oleographs printed on oil-cloth and impervious to
damp. These were duly hung on the snow walls
of the hut, and the little girls worked some red
Turkey-twill curtains for the ice windows, and a
frill for the mantelpiece in orthodox south of
England cottage style. The boys made a winding
tunnel through the snow-drifts up to the door of
the hut, and Nature did the rest, burying the hut
in snow until its very existence was unsuspected
by strangers, though it may be unusual to see
clouds of wood-smoke issuing from an apparent
snow-drift. That little house stood for over three
months; it afforded the utmost joy to its youthful
occupiers, and I confess that I took a great paternal
pride in it myself. Really at night, with the red
curtains drawn over the ice windows, with the
pictures on its snow walls, a lamp alight and a
roaring log fire blazing on the brick hearth, it was
the most invitingly cosy little place. It is true
that with the heat the snow walls perspired freely,
and the roof was apt to drip like a fat man in
August, but it was considered tactful to ignore
these details. Here the children entertained their
friends at tea-parties, and made hideous juvenile
experiments in cookery; here, too, "Jerusalem the
Golden" was prepared. It was a simple operation;
milk and honey were thoroughly mixed in a bowl,

the bowl was put out to freeze, and the frozen
mass dipped into hot water to loosen it; "Jerusalem the Golden" was then broken up small,
and the toothsome chips eagerly devoured. Those
familiar with the hymn will at once understand
the allusion.

Sir John Macdonald, the Prime Minister, was
very often at Government House, and dined there
perpetually. When at the Petrograd Embassy, I
was constantly hearing of Sir John from my chief,
Lord Dufferin, who had an immense admiration
for him, and considered him the maker of the
Dominion, and a really great statesman. I was
naturally anxious to meet a man of whom I had
heard so much. "John A.," as he was universally
known in Canada, had a very engaging personality,
and conveyed an impression of having an enormous
reserve of latent force behind his genial manner.
Facially he was reminiscent of Lord Beacons-
field, but there was nothing very striking about
him as an orator: his style was direct and straight-
forward.

The Houses of Parliament at Ottawa are a
splendid pile of buildings, and though they may
owe a great deal to the wonderful site they
occupy on a semicircular wooded bluff projecting
into the river, I should consider them one of the
most successful group of buildings erected anywhere during the nineteenth century. All the
details might not bear close examination, but the
general effect was admirable, especially that of

the great circular library, with its conical roof. In addition to the Legislative Chambers proper, two flanking buildings in the same style housed various Administrative departments. Seen from Rideau Hall in dark silhouette against the sunset sky, the bold outline of the conical roof of the library and the three tall towers flanking it gave a sort of picturesque Nuremberg effect to the distant view of Ottawa. The Parliament buildings proper were destroyed by an incendiary during the war, but the library and wings escaped.

Everything in the House of Commons was modelled accurately on Westminster. The Canadian Parliament being bi-lingual, French members addressed the Speaker as " Monsieur l'Orateur," and the Usher of the Black Rod of the Senate became "l'Huissier de la Verge Noire." To my mind there was something intensely comical in addressing a man who seldom opened his mouth except to cry, " Order, order," as " Monsieur l'Orateur." A Frenchman from the Province of Quebec seems always to be chosen as Canadian Speaker. In my time he was a M. Ouimet, the *twenty-first* child of the same parents, so French Canadians are apparently not threatened with extinction. I heard in the House of Commons at Ottawa the most curious peroration I have ever listened to. It came from the late Nicholas Flood Davin, a member of Irish extraction who sat for a Far-Western constituency.

The House was debating a dull Bill relating to the lumber industry, when Davin, who may possibly have been under the influence of temporary excitement, insisted on speaking. He made a long and absolutely irrelevant speech in a voice of thunder, and finished with these words, every one of which I remember: "There are some who declare that Canada's trade is declining; there are some who maintain that the rich glow of health which at present mantles o'er Canada's virgin cheek will soon be replaced by the pallid hues of the corpse. To such pusillanimous propagandists of a preposterous pessimism, I answer, Mr. Speaker, with all confidence, never! never!" As a rhetorical effort this is striking, though there seems a lack of lucidity about it.

In the Canadian House of Commons there are a number of little pages who run errands for members, and fetch them books and papers. These boys sit on the steps of the Speaker's chair, and when the House adjourns for dinner the pages hold a "Pages' Parliament." One boy, elected by the others as Speaker, puts on a gown and seats himself in the Speaker's chair; the "Prime Minister" and the members of the Government sit on the Government benches, the Leader of the Opposition with his supporters take their places opposite, and the boys hold regular debates. Many of the members took great interest in the "Pages' Parliament," and coached the boys for their debates. I have seen Sir John

Macdonald giving the fourteen-year-old " Premier "
points for his speech that evening.

All-night sittings were far rarer at Ottawa than
with us, and constituted quite an event. Some
of us went into the gallery at 5 a.m. after a dance,
to see the end of a long and stormy sitting. The
House was very uproarious. Some member had
brought in a cricket-ball, and they were throwing
each other catches across the House. To the
credit of Canadian M.P.'s, I must say that we
never saw a single catch missed. When Sir John
rose to close the debate, there were loud cries of,
" You have talked enough, John A. Give us a
song instead." " All right," cried Sir John, " I
will give you 'God save the Queen.'" And he
forthwith started it in a lusty voice, all the
members joining in. The introduction of a
cricket-ball might brighten all-night sittings in
our own Parliament, though somehow I cannot
quite picture to myself Mr. Asquith throwing
catches to Sir Frederick Banbury across the floor
of the House of Commons.

I was once in the gallery of the South African
Parliament at Capetown, after the House had been
sitting continuously for twenty hours. The Speaker
had had a stool brought him to rest his legs on, and
was fast asleep in his chair, with his wig all awry.
Dutch farmer members from the Back-Veld were
stretched out at full length on the benches in the
lobbies, snoring loudly; in fact, the whole place
was a sort of Parliamentary Pullman Sleeping-car.

That splendid man, the late General Botha, told me that late hours in Parliament upset him terribly, as he had been used all his life to going early to bed. Though the exterior of the Capetown Parliament buildings is nothing very wonderful architecturally, the interior is very handsome, and quite surprisingly spacious.

The Governor-General gave two evening skating and tobogganing parties at Rideau Hall every winter. He termed these gatherings his "Arctic Cremornes," after the then recently defunct gardens in London, and the parties were wonderfully picturesque. In those days, though the fashion now has quite disappeared, all members of snow-shoe and tobogganing clubs, men and women alike, wore coloured blanket-suits consisting of knickerbockers and long coats, with bright-coloured stockings, sash, and knitted *toque* (invariably pronounced "tuke"). The club colours of course varied. Rideau Hall was white with purple stockings and "tuke," and red sash. Others were sky-blue, with scarlet stockings and "tuke," or crimson and black, or brown and green. A collection of three hundred people in blanket-suits gave the effect of a peripatetic rainbow against the white snow. For the "Arctic Cremorne" the rinks were all fringed with coloured fairy-lamps; the curling-rink and the tea-room above it were also outlined with innumerable coloured electric bulbs, and festoons of Japanese lanterns were stretched between the fir trees in all directions. At the top of the toboggan slides powerful arc-lamps blazed, and a stupendous bon-fire roared on a little eminence. The effect was indescribably pretty, and it was pleasant to reflect how man had triumphed over Nature in being able to give an outdoor evening party in mid-winter with the thermometer below zero. The gleaming crystals of snow reflecting the coloured lamps; the Bengal lights staining the white expanse crimson and green, and silhouetting the outlines of the fir trees in dead black against the burnished steel of the sky; the crowd of guests in their many-coloured blanket-suits, made a singularly attractive picture, with a note of absolute novelty in it; and the crash of the military band, the merry whirr of the skates, and the roar of the descending toboggans had something extraordinarily exhilarating about them in the keen, pure air. The supper-room always struck me as being pleasingly unconventional. Supper was served in the long, covered curling-rink, where the temperature was the same as that of the open air outside, so there was a long table elaborately set out with silver branched-candle-sticks and all the Governor-General's fine collection of plate, but the servants waited in heavy fur-coats and caps. Of course no flowers could be used in that temperature, so the silver vases held branches of spruce, hemlock, and other Canadian firs. The French cook had to be very careful as to what dishes he prepared, for anything

271

with moisture in it would freeze at once; *meringues*, for instance, would be frozen into uneatable cricket-balls, and tea, coffee, and soup had to simmer perpetually over lamps. One so seldom has a ball-supper with North Pole surroundings. We had a serious toboggan accident one night owing to the stupidity of an old Senator, who insisted on standing in the middle of the track, and the Aides-de-Camps' room was converted into an operating theatre, and reeked with the fumes of chloroform. The young man had bad concussion, and was obliged to remain a week at Rideau Hall, whilst the poor girl was disfigured for life.

Whilst on the subject of ball-suppers, there was a curious custom prevailing in Lisbon. Most Portuguese having very limited means, it was not usual to offer any refreshments whatever to guests at dances; but when it was done, it took the form of a " toothpick-supper " (*souper aux cure-dents*). Small pieces of chicken, tongue, or beef were piled on plates, each piece skewered with a wooden toothpick. The guests picked these off the plate by the toothpick, and nibbled the meat away from it, eating it with slices of bread. This obviated the use of plates, knives and forks, most Portuguese families having neither sufficient silver table-plate for an entertainment nor the means to hire any. There was another reason for this quaint custom. Some Portuguese are —how shall we put it?—inveterate souvenir-hunters. The Duke of Palmella, one of the few rich men in Portugal, gave a ball whilst I was in Lisbon at which the supper was served in the ordinary fashion, with plates, spoons, knives and forks. It was a matter of common knowledge in Lisbon that 50 per cent. of the ducal silver spoons and forks had left the house in the pockets of his Grace's guests, who doubtless wished to preserve a slight memento of so pleasant an evening.

In a certan Balkan State which I will refrain from naming, the inhabitants are also confirmed souvenir-hunters, At a dinner-party at the British Legation in this nameless State, one of the Diplomatic ladies was wearing a very fine necklace of pearls and enamel. A native of the State admired this necklace immensely, and begged for permission to examine it closer. The Diplomat's wife very unwisely unfastened her pearl necklace, and it was passed round from hand to hand, amidst loud expressions of admiration at its beautiful workmanship. At the end of dinner the Diplomatic lady requested that her necklace might be returned to her, but it was not forthcoming; no one knew anything about it. The British Minister, who thought that he understood the people of the country, rose to the occasion. Getting up from his chair, he said with a smile, " We have just witnessed a very clever and very amusing piece of legerdemain. Now we are going to see another little piece of conjuring." The Minister walked quietly to both doors of the room, locked them, and put the keys in his pocket. He then placed a small silver bowl from the sideboard in the centre of the dinner-table, and continued : " I am now going to switch off all the lights, and to count ten slowly. When I have reached ten, I shall turn on the lights again, and hey presto ! Madame de ——'s necklace will be found lying in that silver bowl ! " The room became plunged in darkness, and the Minister counted slowly up to ten. The electric light blazed out again, there was no necklace, but the silver bowl had vanished !

I have enjoyed the exceptional experience of having inspected many convents in Canada, even those of the most strictly cloistered Orders. By long-established custom, the Governor-General's wife has the right to inspect any convent in Canada on giving twenty-four hours' notice, and she may take with her any two persons she chooses, of either sex. My sister was fond of visiting convents, and she often took me with her as I could speak French. We have thus been in convents of Ursulines, Poor Clares, Grey Sisters, and in some of those of the more strictly cloistered Orders. The procedure was always the same. We were ushered into a beautifully clean, bare, whitewashed *parloir*, with a highly polished floor redolent of beeswax. There would be hard benches running round the *parloir*, raised on a platform, much after the fashion of raised benches in a billiard-room. In the centre would be a chair for the Reverend Mother. We then made polite conversation for a few minutes, after which coffee (usually compounded of scorched beans, with no relation whatever to " Coffea Arabica ") was handed to us, and we went over the convent. It was extremely difficult for two Protestants to find any subject of conversation which could interest a Mother Superior who knew nothing of the world outside her convent walls, nor was it easy to find any common ground on which to meet her, all religious topics being necessarily excluded. I had noticed that the nuns made frequent allusions to a certain Marie Alacoque. Misled by the similarity of the sound in French, I, in my ignorance, thought that this referred to a method of cooking eggs. I learnt later that Marie Alacoque was a French nun who lived in the seventeenth century, and I discovered why her memory was so revered by her co-religionists. It was easy to get a book from the Ottawa Library and to read her up, and after that conversation became less difficult, for a few remarks about Marie Alacoque were always appreciated in conventual circles. The convents were invariably neat and clean, but I was perpetually struck by the wax-like pallor of the inmates. The elder nuns in the strictly cloistered Orders were as excited as children over this unexpected irruption into their convent of two strangers from the world outside, which they had left for so long. They struck me as most excellent, earnest women, and they delighted in exhibiting all their treasures, including the ecclesiastical vestments and their Church plate. They always made a point of showing us, as an object of great interest, the flat candlestick or *bougie* that the Cardinal-Archbishop had used when he had last celebrated Pontifical High Mass in their chapel. In one strictly cloistered convent there was a high wooden trellis across the chapel, so that though the nuns could see the priest at the altar through the trellis-work, he was unable to see them. In the Convent of the Grey Sisters at Ottawa we found an old English nun who, in spite of having spent thirty-five years in a French-Canadian convent, still retained the strong Cockney accent of her native London. She was a cheery old soul, and, with another old English nun, had charge of the wardrobe, which they insisted on showing me. I was gazing at piles of clothing neatly arranged on shelves, when the old Cockney nun clapped her hands. "We will dress you up as a Sister," she cried, and they promptly proceeded to do so. They put me on a habit (largest size) over my other clothes, chuckling with glee meanwhile, and I was duly draped in the *guimpe*, the piece of linen which covers a nun's head and shoulders and frames her face, called, I believe, in English a "wimple," and my toilet was complete except for my veil, when, by a piece of real bad luck, the Reverend Mother and my sister came into the room. We had no time to hide, so we were caught. Having no moustache, I flattered myself that I made rather a saintly-looking novice,

276

and I hid my hands in the orthodox way in my sleeves, but the Mother Superior was evidently very much put out. The clothes that had come in contact with my heretical person were ordered to be placed on one side, I presume to be morally disinfected, and I can only trust that the two old nuns did not get into serious trouble over their little joke. I am sorry that my toilet was not completed; I should like to have felt that just for once in my life I had taken the veil, if for five minutes only.

In the "eighties" the city of Montreal spent large sums over their Winter Carnival. It attracted crowds of strangers, principally from the United States, and it certainly stimulated the retail trade of the city. The Governor-General was in the habit of taking a house in Montreal for the Carnival, and my brother-in-law was lent the home of a hospitable sugar magnate. The dining-room of this house, in which its owner had allowed full play to his Oriental imagination and love of colour, was so singular that it merits a few words of description. The room was square, with a domed ceiling. It was panelled in polished satin-wood to a height of about five feet. Above the panelling were placed twelve owls in carved and silvered wood, each one about two feet high, supporting gas-standards. Rose-coloured silk was stretched from the panelling up to the heavy frieze, consisting of "swags" of fruit and foliage modelled in high relief, and brilliantly coloured in their natural hues. The domed ceiling was painted sky-blue, covered with golden stars, gold and silver suns and moons, and the signs of the Zodiac. I may add that the effect of this curious apartment was not such as to warrant any one trying to reproduce it. The house also contained a white marble swimming bath; an unnecessary adjunct, I should have thought, to a dwelling built for winter occupation in Montreal.

The Ice-Castle erected by the Municipality was really a joy to the eye. It was rather larger than, say, the Westminster Guildhall, and had a tower eighty feet high. It was an admirable reproduction of a Gothic castle, designed and built by a competent architect, with barbican, battlements, and machicolations all complete, the whole of gleaming, transparent ice-blocks, a genuine thing of beauty. One of the principal events of the Carnival was the storming of the Ice-Castle by the snow-shoe clubs of Montreal. Hundreds of snow-shoers, in their rainbow-hued blanket suits, advanced in line on the castle and fired thousands of Roman candles at their objective, which returned the fire with rockets innumerable, and an elaborate display of fireworks, burning continually Bengal lights of various colours within its translucent walls, and spouting gold and silver rain on its assailants. It really was a gorgeous feast of colour for the eye, a most entrancing spectacle, with all this polychrome glow seen against the dead-white field of snow which covered Dominion Square, in the crystal

278

clearness of a Canadian winter night, with the thermometer down anywhere.

Another annual feature of the Carnival was the great fancy-dress skating *fête* in the covered rink. The Victoria Rink at Montreal is a huge building, and was profusely decorated for the occasion with the usual flags, wreaths of artificial foliage, and coloured lamps. An American sculptor had modelled six colossal groups of statuary out of wet snow, and these were ranged down either side of the rink. As they froze, they took on the appearance and texture of white marble, and were very effective. Round a cluster of arc-lights in the roof there was a sort of revolving cage of different coloured panes of glass; these threw variegated beams of light over the brilliant kaleidoscopic crowd below. Previous Governors-General had, in opening the *fête*, shuffled shamefacedly down the centre of the rink in overshoes and fur coats to the dais, but Lord and Lady Lansdowne, being both expert skaters, determined to do the thing in proper Carnival style, and arrived in fancy dress, he in black as a Duke of Brunswick, she as Mary Queen of Scots, attended by her two boys, then twelve and fourteen years old, as pages, resplendent in crimson tights and crimson velvet. The band struck up "God Save the Queen," and down the cleared space in the centre skimmed, hand-in-hand, the Duke of Brunswick and Mary Queen of Scots, with the two pages carrying her train, all four executing a "Dutch roll" in the most workmanlike manner. It was really a very effective entrance, and was immensely appreciated by the crowd of skaters present. I represented a Shakespearean character, and had occasion to note what very inadequate protection is afforded by blue silk tights, with nothing under them, against the cold of a Canadian February. One of the Aides-de-Camp had arrayed himself in white silk as Romeo; being only just out from England, he was anything but firm on his skates. Some malicious young Montrealers of tender age, noticing this, deliberately bumped into him again and again, sending his conspicuous white figure spinning each time. Poor Romeo's experiences were no more fortunate on the rink than in the tragedy associated with his name; by the end of the evening, after his many tumbles, his draggled white silk dress suggested irresistibly the plumage of a soiled dove.

A hill (locally known as "The Mountain") rises immediately behind Montreal, the original Mont Réal, or Mount Royal, from which the city derives its name. This naturally lends itself to the formation of toboggan slides, and one of them, the "Montreal Club Slide," was really terrifically steep. The start was precipitous enough, in all conscience, but soon came a steep drop of sixty feet, at which point all the working parts of one's anatomy seemed to leave one, to replace themselves at the finish only. The pace was so tremendous that it was difficult to breathe, but it was immensely exciting. The Montreal slide was just one-third of a mile long, and the time occupied in the descent on good ice was about twenty seconds, working out at sixty miles an hour. Every precaution was taken against accidents; there was a telephone from the far end, and no toboggan was allowed to start until "track clear" had been signalled. Everything in this world is relative. We had thought our Ottawa slides very fast, though the greatest speed we ever attained was about thirty miles an hour, whilst at home we had been delighted if we could coax fifteen miles an hour out of our rough machines. The Lansdowne boys were very expert on toboggans, and could go down the Ottawa slides standing erect, a thing no adult could possibly manage. They had fitted their machines with gong-bells and red and green lanterns, and the "Ottawa River Express" would come whizzing down at night with bells clanging and lights gleaming.

I can claim to be the absolute pioneer of ski on the American continent, for in January 1887 I brought my Russian ski to Ottawa, the very first pair that had ever been seen in the New World. I coasted down hills on them amidst universal jeers; every one declared that they were quite unsuited to Canadian conditions. The old-fashioned *raquettes* had their advantages, for one could walk over the softest snow in them. Here, again, I fancy that it was the sense of man triumphant over Nature that made snow-shoeing so attractive. The Canadian snow-shoe brings certain unaccustomed muscles into play, and these muscles show their resentment by aching furiously. The French *habitants* term this pain *mal de raquettes*. In my time snow-shoe tramps at night, across-country into the woods, were one of the standard winter amusements of Ottawa, and the girls showed great dexterity in vaulting fences with their snow-shoes on.

A Canadian winter is bathed in sunshine. In the dry, crisp atmosphere distant objects are as clear-cut and hard as though they were carved out of wood; the air is like wine, and with every breath human beings seem to enter on a new lease of life.

It is not so in the lower world. There is not a bird to be seen, for no bird could secure a living with three feet of snow on the ground. Nature is very dead, and I understood the glee with which the children used to announce the return of the crows, for these wise birds are the unfailing harbingers of Spring. With us Spring is undecided, fickle, and coy. She is not sure of herself, and after making timid, tentative advances, retreats again, uncertain as to her ability to cope with grim Winter. In Canada, Spring comes with an all-conquering rush. In one short fortnight she clothes the trees in green, and carpets the ground with blue and white hepaticas. She is also, unfortunately, accompanied by myriads of self-appointed officious maids-of-honour in the shape of mosquitoes, anxious to make up for their long winter fast. As the fierce suns of April melt the surface snow, the water percolates through to the ground, where it freezes again, forming a sheet of what Canadians term " glare-ice." I have seen at Rideau Hall this ice split in all directions over the flower-beds by the first tender shoots of the crocuses. How these fragile little spears of green have the power to penetrate an inch of ice is one of the mysteries of Nature.

Would space admit of it, and were paper not such an unreasonably expensive commodity just now, I would like to speak of the glories of a Canadian wood in May, with the ground flecked with red and white trilliums ; of the fields in British Columbia, gorgeous in spring-time with blue lilies and drifts of rose-coloured cyclamens ; of the autumn woods in their sumptuous dress of scarlet, crimson, orange, and yellow, the sugar-maples blazing like torches against the dark firs ; of the marvels of the three ranges of the Rockies, Selkirks, and Cascades, and of the other wonders of the great Dominion.

As boys, I and my youngest brother knew " Hiawatha's Fishing" almost by heart, so I had an intense desire to see " Gitche Gumee, the Big-Sea Water," which we more prosaically call Lake Superior, the home of the sturgeon " Nahma," of " Ugudwash " the sun-fish, of the pike the " Maske-nozha," and the actual scene of Hiawatha's fishing. To others, without this sentimental interest, the Great Lakes might appear vast but uninteresting expanses of water, chiefly remarkable for the hideous form of vessel which has been evolved to navigate their clear depths.

One thing I can say with confidence. No one who makes a winter journey to that land of sunshine and snow, with its energetic, pleasant, and hospitable inhabitants, will ever regret it, and the wayfarer will return home with the consciousness of having been in contact with an intensely virile race, only now beginning to realise its own strength.

CHAPTER X

LORD LANSDOWNE had in 1888 been transferred
from Canada to India, and in May of that year he
left Ottawa for Calcutta, taking on the way a
three months' well-earned holiday in England.
Two of his staff accompanied him from the
vigorous young West to the immemorially old East.

He succeeded as Viceroy Lord Dufferin, who
had also held the appointment of Governor-General
of Canada up to 1878, after which he had served
as British Ambassador both at Petrograd and at
Constantinople, before proceeding to India in 1884.

Lord Minto, too, in later years filled both
positions, serving in Canada from 1898 to 1904,
and in India from 1905 to 1910.

Whether in 1690 Job Charnock made a wise
selection in fixing his trading-station where Calcutta now stands, may be open to doubt. He

285

certainly had the broad Hooghly at his doors, affording plenty of water not only for trading-vessels, but also for men-of-war in cases of emergency. Still, from the swampy nature of the soil, and its proximity to the great marshes of the Sunderbunds, Calcutta could never be a really healthy place. An arrival by water up the Hooghly unquestionably gives the most favourable impression of the Indian ex-capital, though the river banks are flat and uninteresting. The Hooghly is one of the most difficult rivers in the world to navigate, for the shoals and sand-banks change almost daily with the strong tides, and the white Hooghly pilots are men at the very top of their profession, and earn some £2000 a year apiece. They are tremendous swells, and are perfectly conscious of the fact, coming on board with their native servants and their white "cub" or pupil. There is one shoal in particular, known as the "James and Mary," on which a ship, touching ever so lightly, is as good as lost. Calcutta, since I first knew it, has become a great manufacturing centre. Lines of factories stand for over twenty miles thick on the left bank of the river; the great pall of black smoke hanging over the city is visible for miles, and the atmosphere is beginning to rival that of Manchester. Long use has accustomed us to the smoke-blackened elms and limes of London, but there is something peculiarly pathetic in the sight of a grimy, sooty palm tree.

The outward aspect of the stately Government House at Calcutta is familiar to most people. It is a huge and imposing edifice, but when I first knew it, its interior was very plain, and rather bare. Lady Minto changed all this during her husband's Viceroyalty, and, with her wonderful taste, transformed it into a sort of Italian palace at a very small cost. She bought in Europe a few fine specimens of old Italian gilt furniture, and had them copied in Calcutta by native workmen. In the East, the Oriental point of view must be studied, and Easterns attach immense importance to external splendour. The throne-room at Calcutta, under Lady Minto's skilful treatment, became gorgeous enough for the most exacting Asiatic, with its black marble floor, its rose-coloured silk walls where great silver sconces alternated with full-length portraits of British sovereigns, its white "chunam" columns and its gilt Italian furniture. "Chunam" has been used in India from time immemorial for decorative purposes. It is as white as snow and harder than any stone, and is, I believe, made from calcined shells. Let us suppose a Durbar held in this renovated throne-room for the official reception of a native Indian Prince. The particular occasion I have in mind was long after Lord Lansdowne's time, when a certain Rajah, notoriously ill-disposed towards the British Raj, had been given the strongest of hints that unless he mended his ways, he might find another ruler placed on the throne of his State. He was also recommended to come to Calcutta and to pay his respects to the Viceroy there, when, of course, he would be received with the number of guns to which he was entitled. The Indian Princes attach the utmost importance to the number of guns they are given as a salute, a number which varies from twenty-one in the case of the Nizam of Hyderabad, who alone ranks as a Sovereign, to nine for the smaller princes. Should the British Government wish to mark its strong displeasure with any native ruler, it sometimes does so by reducing the number of guns of his salute, and correspondingly, to have the number increased is a high honour. Sulkily and unwillingly the Rajah of whom I am thinking journeyed to Calcutta, and sulkily and unwillingly did he attend the Durbar. On occasions such as these, visiting native Princes are the guests of the Government of India at Hastings House (Warren Hastings' old country house in the suburbs of Calcutta, specially renovated and fitted up for the purpose), and the Viceroy's state carriages are sent to convey them to Government House. Everything in the way of ceremonial in India is done strictly by rule. The precise number of steps the Viceroy will advance to greet visiting Rajahs is all laid down in a little book. The Nizam of Hyderabad is met by the Viceroy with all his staff at the state entrance of Government House, and he is accompanied through all the rooms, both on his arrival and on his departure; but, as I said before, the Nizam ranks as a Sovereign. In the case of lesser lights the Viceroy advances anything from three to twenty steps. These points may appear very trivial to Europeans, but to Orientals they assume great importance, and, after all, India is a part of Asia. At right angles to the Calcutta throne-room is the fine Marble Hall, with marble floor and columns and an entirely gilt ceiling ; empty except for six colossal busts of Roman Emperors, which, together with a number of splendid cut-glass chandeliers of the best French Louis XV. period, and a full-length portrait of Louis XV. himself, fell into our hands through the fortunes of war at a time when our relations with our present firm ally, France, were possibly less cordial than at present. For a Durbar a long line of red carpet was laid from the throne-room, through the Marble Hall and the White Hall beyond it, right down the great flight of exterior steps, at the foot of which a white Guard of Honour of one hundred men from a British regiment was drawn up. Aligned through the outer hall, the Marble Hall and the throne-room were one hundred men of the Viceroy's Bodyguard, splendid fellows chosen for their height and appearance, and all from Northern India. They wore the white leather breeches and jack-boots of our own Life Guards, with scarlet tunics and huge turbans of blue and gold, standing with their lances as motionless as so many bronze statues. For a Durbar, many precious things were unearthed from the " Tosha-

Khana," or Treasury: the Viceroy's silver-gilt
throne; an arm-chair of solid silver for the visiting
Rajah; great silver-gilt maces bearing a crown and
"V.R.I."; and, above all, the beautiful Durbar
carpets of woven gold wire. The making of these
carpets is, I believe, a hereditary trade in a Benares
family; they are woven of real gold wire, heavily
embroidered in gold afterwards, and are immensely
expensive. The visiting Rajah announces before-
hand the number of the suite he is bringing with
him, and the Viceroy has a precisely similar number,
so two corresponding rows of cane arm-chairs are
placed opposite each other, at right angles to the
throne. Behind the chairs twelve resplendent
red-and-gold-coated servants with blue-and-silver
turbans, hold the gilt maces aloft, whilst behind
the throne eight more gorgeously apparelled natives
hold two long-handled fans of peacock's feathers,
two silver-mounted yak's tails, and two massive
sheaves of peacock's feathers, all these being the
Eastern emblems of sovereignty.

We will suppose this particular Rajah to be
a "nine-gun" and a "three-step" man. Bang go
the cannon from Fort William nine times, and the
Viceroy, in full uniform with decorations, duly
advances three steps on the gold carpet to greet
his visitor. The Viceroy seats himself on his silver-
gilt throne at the top of the three steps, the visiting
Rajah in his silver chair being one step lower. The
two suites seat themselves facing each other in
dead silence; we Europeans assuming an absolutely

Oriental impassivity of countenance. The ill-conditioned Rajah, though he spoke English perfectly, had insisted on bringing his own inter-preter with him. A long pause in conformity with Oriental etiquette follows, then the Viceroy puts the first invariable question : " I trust that your Highness is in the enjoyment of good health," which is duly repeated in Urdu by the official white interpreter. The sulky Rajah grunts some-thing that sounds like " Bhirrr Whirrr," which the native interpreter renders, in clipped staccato English, as " His Highness declares that by your Excellency's favour his health is excellent. Lately, owing to attack of fever, it was with His Highness what Immortal Bard has termed a case of 'to be or not to be ! ' Now, danger happily averted, His Highness has seldom reposed under the canopy of a sounder brain than at present." Another long pause, and the second invariable question : " I trust that your Highness' Army is in its usual efficient state." The surly Rajah, " Khirrr Virrr." The native interpreter, " Without doubt His Highness' Army has never yet been so efficient. Should troubles arise, or a pretty kettle of fish unfortunately occur, His Highness places his entire Army at your Excellency's disposal ; as Swan of Avon says, ' Come the three corners of the world in arms, and we shall shock them.' " A third question, " I trust that the crops in your High-ness' dominion are satisfactory." The Rajah, " Ghirrr Firrr." The interpreter, " Stimulated

without doubt by your Excellency's auspicious
visit to neighbouring State, the soil in His Highness' dominions has determined to beat record and
to go regular mucker. Crops tenfold ordinary
capacity are springing from the ground everywhere." One has seen a conjurer produce half a
roomful of paper flowers from a hat, or even from
an even less promising receptacle, but no conjurer
was in it with that interpreter, who from two sulky
monosyllabic grunts evolved a perfect garland of
choice Oriental flowers of speech. It reminded
me of the process known in newspaper offices as
"expanding" a telegram. When the customary
number of formal questions have been put, the
Viceroy makes a sign to his Military Secretary,
who brings him a gold tray on which stand a little
gold flask and a small box; the traditional "Attar
and pan." The Viceroy sprinkles a few drops of
attar of roses on the Rajah's clothing from the
gold flask, and hands him a piece of betel-nut
wrapped in gold paper, known as "pan." This is
the courteous Eastern fashion of saying "Now I
bid you good-bye." The Military Secretary per-
forms a like office to the members of the Rajah's
suite, who, however, have to content themselves
with attar sprinkled from a silver bottle and "pan"
wrapped in silver paper. Then all the traditional
requirements of Oriental politeness have been
fulfilled, and the Rajah takes his leave with the
same ceremonies as attended his arrival. At the
beginning of a Durbar "tribute" is presented—that

is to say that a folded napkin supposed to contain one thousand gold mohurs is handed to the
Viceroy, who "touches it and remits it." I have
often wondered what that folded napkin really
contained.

When I first knew Calcutta, most of the grain,
jute, hemp and indigo exported was carried to its
various destinations in sailing-ships, and there
were rows and rows of splendid full-rigged ships
and barques lying moored in the Hooghly along
the whole length of the Maidan. The line must
have extended for two miles, and I never tired
of looking at these beautiful vessels with their
graceful lines and huge spars, all clean and spick
and span with green and white paint, the ubiquitous Calcutta crows perched in serried ranks
on their yards. To my mind a full-rigged ship is
the most beautiful object man has ever devised,
and when the dusk was falling, with every spar
and rope outlined in black against the vivid
crimson of the short-lived Indian sunset, the long
line of shipping made a glorious picture. Nineteen
years later every sailing-ship had disappeared from
the Hooghly, and in their place were rows of
unsightly, rusty-sided iron tanks, with squat pole-
masts and ugly funnels vomiting black smoke.
A tramp-steamer has its uses, no doubt, but it is
hardly a thing of beauty. Ichabod! Ichabod!

Calcutta is fortunate in having so fine a lung as
the great stretch of the Maidan. It has been
admirably planted and laid out, with every palm

or tree of aggressively Indian appearance carefully excluded from its green expanse, so it wears a curiously home-like appearance. The Maidan is very reminiscent of Hyde Park, though almost double its size. There is one spot, where the Gothic spire of the cathedral emerges from a mass of greenery, with a large sheet of water in the foreground, which recalls exactly the view over Bayswater from the bridge spanning the Serpentine.

Considering that Calcutta Cathedral was built in 1840; that it was designed by an Engineer officer, and not by an architect; that its "Gothic" is composed of cast-iron and stucco instead of stone, it is really not such a bad building. The great size of its interior gives it a certain dignity, and owing to the generosity of the European community, it is most lavishly adorned with marbles, mosaics, and stained glass. It possesses the finest organ in Asia, and a really excellent choir, the men Europeans, the boys being Eurasians. These small half-castes have very sweet voices, with a curious and not unpleasing metallic *timbre* about them. At evening service in the cathedral, should one ignore such details as the rows of electric punkahs, the temperature, and the dingy complexions of the choir-boys, it was almost impossible to realise that one was not in England. I had been used to singing in a church choir, and it was pleasant to hear such familiar cathedral services as Garrett in D, Smart in F, Walmisley in D minor, and Hopkins in F, so perfectly rendered seven thousand miles away from home, thanks to that excellent musician, Dr. Slater, the cathedral organist.

St. Andrew's Scottish Presbyterian Church stands in its own wooded grounds in which there are two large ponds, or, as Anglo-Indians would put it, it stands in a compound with large tanks. The church is consequently infested with mosquitoes. The last time that I was in Calcutta, the Gordon Highlanders had just relieved an English regiment in the fort, and on the first Sunday after their arrival, four hundred Gordons were marched to a parade service at St. Andrew's. The most optimistic mosquito had never in his wildest dreams imagined such a succulent banquet as that afforded by four hundred bare-kneed, kilted Highlanders, and the mosquitoes made the fullest use of their unique opportunity. Soon the church resounded with the vigorous slapping of hands on bare knees and thighs, as the men endeavoured to kill a few of their little tormentors. The minister, hearing the loud clapping, but entirely misapprehending its purport, paused in his sermon, and said, " My brethren, it is varra gratifying to a minister of the Word to learn that his remarks meet with the approbation of his hearers, but I'd have you remember that all applause is strictly oot of place in the Hoose of God."

The Gordon Highlanders were originally raised by my great-grandfather, the fourth Duke of Gordon, in 1794, or perhaps more accurately, by my great-grandmother, Jean, the beautiful Duchess of Gordon. Duchess Jean, then in the height of her beauty, attended every market in the towns round Gordon Castle, and kissed every recruit who took the guinea she offered. The French Republic had declared war on Great Britain in 1793, and the Government had made an urgent appeal for fresh levies of troops. Duchess Jean, by her novel osculatory methods, raised the Gordons in four months. My father and mother were married at Gordon Castle in 1832, and the wedding guests grew so excessively convivial that they carried everything on the tables at the wedding breakfast, silver plate, glass, china, and all, down to the bridge at Fochabers, and threw them into the Spey. We may congratulate ourselves on the fact that it is no longer incumbent on wedding guests to drink the health of the newly married couple so fervently, and that a proportional saving in table fittings can thus be effected.

Barrackpore, the Viceroy's country place, is unquestionably a pleasant spot, with its fine park and famous gardens. Like the Maidan in Calcutta, Barrackpore is a very fairly successful attempt at reproducing England in Asia. With a little make-believe and a determined attempt to ignore the grotesque outlines of a Hindoo temple standing on the confines of the park, and the large humps on the backs of the grazing cattle like the steam domes on railway engines, it might be possible to imagine oneself at home, until the illusion is shattered in quite another fashion. There is an excellent eighteen-hole golf course in Barrackpore park, but when you hear people talking of the second " brown " there can be no doubt but that you are in Asia. A " green " would be a palpable misnomer for the parched grass of an Indian dry season, still a " brown " comes as a shock at first. The gardens merit their reputation. There are innumerable ponds, or " tanks," of lotus and water-lilies of every hue : scarlet, crimson, white, and pure sky-blue, the latter an importation from Australia. When these are in flower they are a lovely sight, and perhaps compensate for the myriads of mosquitoes who find in these ponds an ideal breeding-place, and assert their presence day and night most successfully. There are great drifts of Eucharis lilies growing under the protecting shadows of the trees along shady walks, and the blaze of colour in the formal garden surrounding the white marble fountain in front of the house is positively dazzling. The house was built especially as a hot-weather residence, and as such is not particularly successful, for it is one of the hottest buildings in the whole of India. The dining-room is in the centre of the house, and has no windows whatever; an arrangement which, though it may shut out the sun, also excludes all fresh air as well. The bedrooms extend up through two storeys, and are so extremely lofty that one has the sensation of sleeping in a lift-shaft. Apart from its heat, the house has a dignified old-world air about it, with vague hints of Adam decoration in its details.

The establishment of Government House consisted of five hundred and twenty servants, all natives, so it could not be termed short-handed. With so many men, the apparently impossible could be undertaken. Lord Lansdowne left Calcutta for Barrackpore every Saturday afternoon. As soon as we had gone into luncheon at Calcutta on the Saturday, perfect armies of men descended on the private part of the house and packed up all the little things about the rooms into big cases. An hour later they were on their way up the river by steamer, and when we arrived at Barrackpore for tea, the house looked as though it had been lived in for weeks, with every object reposing on the tables in precisely the same position it had occupied earlier in the day in Calcutta. Late on Sunday night this process was reversed for the return journey at seven on Monday morning. The Viceroy had a completely fitted-up office in his smart little white-and-gold yacht, and was able to get through a great deal of work on his voyage down the Hooghly before breakfast on Monday mornings. A conscientious Viceroy of India is one of the hardest-worked men in the world, for he frequently has ten hours of office work in the day, irrespective of his other duties.

An enormous banyan tree stands on the lawn at Barrackpore. I should be afraid to say how much ground it covers; perhaps nearly an acre, for these

.trees throw down aerial suckers which form into fresh trunks, and so spread indefinitely. Lady Lansdowne thought she would have a bamboo house built in this great banyan tree for her little daughter, the same little girl for whom I had built the snow-hut at Ottawa, for she happens to be my god-daughter. It was to be a sort of "Swiss Family Robinson" tree-house, infinitely superior to the house on the tree-tops of Kensington Gardens, which Wendy destined for Peter Pan. The house was duly built, with bamboo staircases, and little fenced-off bamboo platforms fitted with seats and tables, at different levels up the tree. The Swiss Family Robinson would have gone mad with jealousy at seeing such a desirable aerial abode, so immeasurably preferable to their own, and even Wendy might have felt a mild pang of envy. When the house was completed, one of the Aides-de-Camp inspected it and found a snake hanging by its tail from a branch right over one of the little aerial platforms. He reported that the tree was full of snakes. The risk was too great to run, so prompt orders were given to demolish the house, and the little girl never enjoyed her tree-top playground.

The Viceroy's State elephants were all kept at Barrackpore, and the elephant-lines had a great attraction for children, especially for a small great-nephew of mine, now a Lieut.-Colonel, and the father of a family, then aged six. The child was very fearless, but the only elephant he was allowed to approach was a venerable tusker named "Warren Hastings," the very identical elephant on which Warren Hastings made his first entry into Calcutta. "Warren" was supposed to be nearly 200 years old, and his temper could be absolutely relied on. It is curious that natives, in speaking of a quiet, good-tempered animal, always speak of him as "poor" (*gharib*). The little boy was perpetually feeding Warren Hastings with oranges and bananas, and the two became great friends. It was a pretty sight seeing the fearless small boy in his white suit, bare legs, and little sun-helmet, standing in front of the great beast who could have crushed him to a wafer in one second, and ordering him in the vernacular, with his shrill child's voice, to kneel. It was a more curious sight seeing the huge animal at once obey his little mentor, and, struggling with the infirmities and rheumatic joints of old age (to which, alas! others besides elephants are subject), lower himself painfully on to his knees. "Salaam karo" ("Salute me"), piped the white child, and the great pachyderm instantly obeyed, lifting his trunk high in salute; which, if you think it out, may have a certain symbolism about it.

It was the same small boy who on returning to England at the age of seven, after five years in India, looked out of the windows of the carriage with immense interest, as they drove through London from Charing Cross station. "Mother," he piped at length, "this is a very odd country! All the natives seem to be white here."

My little great-nephew was immensely petted by the native servants, and as he could speak the vernacular with greater ease than English, he picked up from the servants the most appalling language, which he innocently repeated, entailing his frequent chastisement.

I can sympathise with the child there, for at the age of nine, in Dublin, I became seized with an intense but short-lived desire to enlist as a trumpeter in a Lancer regiment. Seeing one day a real live, if diminutive, Lancer trumpeter listening to the band playing in the Castle yard, I ran down and consulted him as to the best means of attaining my desire. The small trumpeter was not particularly intelligent, and was unable to help me. Though of tender years, he was regrettably lacking in refinement, for his conversation consisted chiefly of an endless repetition of three or four words, not one of which I had ever heard before. Carefully treasuring these up, as having a fine martial smack about them suitable to the military career I then proposed embracing, I, in all innocence, fired off one of the trumpeter's full-flavoured expressions at my horror-stricken family during luncheon, to be at once ordered out of the room, and severely punished afterwards. We all know that " what the soldier said" is not legal evidence; in this painful fashion I also learnt that "what the trumpeter said" is not held to be a valid excuse for the use of bad language by a small boy.

In the late autumn of 1890 Admiral Sir Edmund

Fremantle brought his flagship, the *Boadicea*, right up the Hooghly, and moored her alongside the Maidan. The ship remained there for six weeks, the Admiral taking up his quarters at Government House. My sister Lady Lansdowne had a mistaken weakness for midshipmen, whom she most inappropriately termed "those dear little fellows." At that time midshipmen went to sea at fifteen years of age, so they were much younger than at present. As these boys were constantly at Government House, four of us thought that we would lend the midshipmen our ponies for an early morning ride. The boys all started off at a gallop, and every one of them was bolted with as soon as he reached the Maidan. As they had no riding-breeches, their trousers soon rucked up, exhibiting ample expanses of bare legs; they had no notion of riding, but managed to stick on somehow by clinging to pommel and mane, banging here into a sedate Judge of the High Court, with an apologetic "Sorry, sir, but this swine of a pony won't steer;" barging there into a pompous Anglo-Indian official, as they yelled to their ponies, "Easy now, dogs-body, or you'll unship us both;" galloping as hard as their ponies could lay legs to the ground, cannoning into half the white inhabitants of Calcutta, but always with imperturbable good-humour. When their panting ponies tried to pull up to recover their wind a little, these rising hopes of the British Navy kicked them with their heels into a gallop again, shouting strange nautical oaths, and grinning from ear to ear with delight, until finally four ponies lathered in sweat, in the last stages of exhaustion, returned to Government House, and four dripping boys alighted, declaring that they had had the time of their lives in spite of a considerable loss of cuticle. It was the same at the dances at Government House. The smart young subalterns simply weren't in it; the midshipmen got all the best partners, and, to do them justice, they could dance very well. They started with the music and whirled their partners round the room at the top of their speed, in the furnace temperature of Calcutta, without drawing rein for one second until the band stopped, when a dishevelled and utterly exhausted damsel collapsed limply into a chair, whilst a deliquescent brass-buttoned youth, with a sodden wisp of white linen and black silk round his neck to indicate the spot where he had once possessed a collar and tie, endeavoured to fan his partner into some semblance of coolness again.

Lady Lansdowne having invited eight midshipmen to spend a Sunday at Barrackpore, they arrived there by launch with a drag-net, which the Viceroy had given them leave to use on the largest of the ponds. My sister at once set them down to play lawn-tennis, hoping to work off some of their superfluous energy in this way. In honour of the occasion, the midshipmen had extracted their best white flannels from their chests, and they proceeded to array themselves in these. The *Boadicea*, however, had been two years in commission, the flannels were two years old, and the lads were just at the age when they were growing most rapidly. They squeezed themselves with great difficulty into their shrunken garments, which looked more like tights than trousers, every button and seam obviously strained to the bursting point, and set to work playing tennis with their accustomed vigour. Soon there was a sound of rending cloth, and the senior midshipman, a portly youth of Teutonic amplitude of outline, lay down flat on his back on the lawn. A minute later there was a similar sound, and another boy laid down on his back and remained there, and a third lad quickly followed their example. A charming lady had noticed this from the verandah above, and ran down in some alarm, fearing that these young Nelsons had got sunstrokes. Somewhat confusedly they assured her that they were quite well, but might they, please, have three rugs brought them. Otherwise it was impossible for them to move. With some difficulty three rugs were procured, and, enveloped in them, they waddled off to their bungalow to assume more decent apparel. A few minutes later there were two more similar catastrophes (these garments all seemed to split in precisely the same spot), and the supply of rugs being exhausted, these boys had to retreat to their bungalow walking backwards like chamberlains at a Court function. After luncheon, in the burning heat of Bengal, most sensible people keep quiet in the shade, but the midshipmen went off to inspect the great tank, and to decide how they should drag it.

Soon we heard loud shoutings from the direction of the tank, and saw a long string of native servants carrying brown *chatties* of hot water towards the pond. We found that the courteous House-Baboo had informed the midshipmen that the holes in the banks of the tank were the winter resting-places of cobras. It then occurred to the boys that it would be capital fun to pour hot water down the holes, and to kill the cobras with sticks as they emerged from them. It was a horribly dangerous amusement, for, one bad shot, and the Royal Navy would unquestionably have had to mourn the loss of a promising midshipman in two hours' time. When we arrived the snake-killing was over, and the boys were all refreshing themselves with large cheroots purloined from the dining-room on their behalf by a friendly kitmutgar. The dragging of the tank was really a wonderful sight. As the net reached the far end it was one solid mass of great shining, blue-grey fish, of about thirty pounds weight each. The most imaginative artist in depicting the "Miraculous Draught of Fishes" never approached the reality of Barrackpore, or pictured such vast quantities of writhing, silvery finny creatures. They were a fish called *cattla* by the natives, a species of carp, with a few eels and smaller fish of a bright red colour thrown in amongst them. I could never have believed that one pond could have held such incredible quantities of fish. The Viceroy, an intrepid pioneer in gastronomic matters, had a great *cattla* boiled for his dinner. The first mouthful defeated him; he declared that the consistency of the fish was that of an old flannel shirt, and the taste a compound of mud and of the smell of a covered racquet-court. A lady insisted on presenting the midshipmen with two dozen bottles of a very good champagne for the Gun-room Mess. In the innocence of her heart she thought that the champagne would last them for a year, but on New Year's Eve the little lambs had a great celebration on board, and drank the whole two dozen at one sitting. As there were exactly eighteen of them, this made a fair allowance apiece; they all got exceedingly drunk, and the Admiral stopped their leave for two months, so we saw no more of them. They were quite good boys really, though, like all their kind, rather over-full of high spirits.

As is well known, Queen Victoria celebrated her seventieth birthday by commencing the study of Hindustani under the tuition of a skilled Moonshee. At the farewell audience the Queen gave my sister, Her Majesty, on learning that Lady Lansdowne intended to begin learning Hindustani as soon as she reached India, proposed that they should correspond occasionally in Urdu, to test the relative progress they were making. Every two months or so a letter from the Queen, beautifully written in Persian characters, reached Calcutta, to which my sister duly replied. In strict confidence, I may say that I strongly suspect that Lady Lansdowne's letters were written by her Moonshee, and that she merely copied the Persian characters, which she could do very neatly. The Arabic alphabet is used in writing Persian, with three or four extra letters added to express sounds which do not exist in Arabic; it is, of course, written from right to left. I had an hour and a half's daily lesson in Urdu from an efficient, if immensely pompous, Moonshee, but I never attempted to learn to read or write the Persian characters.

I do not think that any one who has not traversed the plains of Northern India can have any idea of their deadly monotony. Hour after hour of level, sun-baked wheat-fields, interspersed with arid tracts of desert, hardly conforms to the traditional idea of Indian scenery, nor when once Bengal is left behind is there any of that luxuriant vegetation which one instinctively associates with hot countries. In bars in the United States, any one wishing for whisky and water was (I advisedly use the past tense) accustomed to drain a small tumbler of neat whisky, and then to swallow a glass of water. In India everything is arranged on this principle; the whisky and the water are kept quite separate. The dead-flat expanse of the Northern plains is unbroken by the most insignificant of mounds; on the other hand, in the hills it is almost impossible to find ten yards of level ground. In the same way during the dry season you know with absolute certainty that there will be no rain; whilst during the rains you can predict, without the faintest shadow of doubt, that the downpour will continue day by day. Personally, I prefer whisky and water mixed.

In 1891 the Viceroy had selected the Kumaon district for his usual official spring tour, and all arrangements had been made for this. As my sister was feeling the heat of Calcutta a great deal, she and I preceded the Viceroy to Naini Tal in the Kumaon district, as it stands at an altitude of 6500 feet. The narrow-gauge railway ends at Kathgodam, fifteen miles from Naini Tal, and the last four miles to the hill-station have to be ridden up, I should imagine, the steepest road in the world. It is like the side of a house. People have before now slipped over their horses' tails going up that terrific ascent, and I cannot conceive how the horses' girths manage to hold. Naini Tal is a delightful spot, with bungalows peeping out of dense greenery that fringes a clear lake. As in most hill-stations, the narrow riding tracks are scooped out of the hill-sides with a perpendicular drop of, say, 500 feet on one side. These *khudd* paths, in addition to being very narrow, are so precipitous that it takes some while getting used to riding along them. A rather tiresome elderly spinster had come up to Naini Tal on a visit to a relative, and was continually bewailing the dangers of these *khudd* paths. She had hoped, she declared, to put on a little flesh in the hills, but her constant anxiety about the *khudds* was making her thinner than ever. A humorous subaltern, rather bored at these continual laments, observed to her : " At all events, Miss Smith, you'll have one consolation. If by any piece of bad luck you should fall over the *khudd*, you'll go over thin, but you'll fall down plump—a thousand feet."

The very evening that Lord Lansdowne arrived for his projected tour, the news of a serious outbreak in Manipur was telegraphed. The Viceroy at once decided to abandon his tour and to proceed straight to Simla, to which the Government offices had already moved, and where his presence would be urgently required. Lord William Beresford, the Military Secretary, a prince of organisers, at once took possession of the telegraph wires, and in two hours his arrangements were complete—or as an Anglo-Indian would put it, "he had made his bundobust." The Viceroy and my sister were to leave next morning at 6 a.m., and Lord William undertook to get them to Simla by special trains before midnight. He actually landed them there by 11 p.m.—quite a record journey, for Naini Tal is 407 miles from Simla, of which 75 miles have to be ridden or driven by road and 66 are by narrow-gauge railway, on which high speeds are impossible. There were 6500 feet to descend from Naini, and 6000 feet to ascend to Simla, but in India a good organiser can accomplish miracles.

The Viceroy's tour being abandoned, Colonel Erskine, the Commissioner for the Kumaon district, invited me to accompany him on his own official tour. It was through very difficult country where no wheeled traffic could pass, so we were to ride, with all our belongings carried by coolies. I bought two hill-ponies the size of Newfoundland dogs for myself and my "bearer," and we started. The little animals being used to carrying packs, have a disconcerting trick of keeping close to the very edge of the *khudd*, for experience has taught them that to bump their load against the rock wall on the inner side gives them an unpleasant jar. These little hill-ponies are wonderfully sure-footed, and can climb like cats over dry water-courses piled with rocks and great boulders, which a man on foot would find difficult to negotiate. The rhododendrons were then in full flower, and the hills were one blaze of colour. We were always going up and up, and as we ascended, the deep crimson rhododendron flowers of Naini Tal gradually faded to rose-colour, from rose-colour to pale pink, and from pink to pure white. It was a perfect education travelling with Colonel Erskine, for that shrewd and kindly old Scotsman had spent half his life in India, and knew the Oriental inside out. The French have an expression, " se fourrer dans la peau d'autrui, " to shove yourself into another person's skin," and therefore to be able to see things as they would present themselves to the mind of a man of a different race and of a different mentality, and from his point of view. All young diplomats are enjoined to cultivate this art, and some few succeed in doing so. Colonel Erskine had it to perfection. On arriving in a village he would call for a carpet, and a dirty cotton *dhuree* would be laid on the ground. He would then order a *charpoy*, or native bed, to be placed on the carpet, and he would seat himself on it, and call out in the vernacular, " Now, my children, what have you to tell me?" All this was strictly in accordance with immemorial Eastern custom. Then the long line of suppliants would approach, each one with a present of an orange, or a bunch of rhododendron flowers in his hand. This, again, from the very beginning of things has been the custom in the East (*cf.* 2 Kings, chap. viii., vers. 8, 9 : " And the King said unto Hazael, Take a present in thine hand, and go, meet the man of God. . . . So Hazael went to meet him, and took a present with him.") Colonel Erskine was a great stickler for these presents, and as they could be picked off the nearest rhododendron bush, they cost the donor nothing.

The outpouring of grievances and complaints then began, each applicant always ending with the two-thousand-year-old cry of India, " Dohai, Huzoor!" ("Justice, my lord!"). The old Commissioner meanwhile listened intently, dictating copious notes to his Brahmin clerk, and at the conclusion of the audience he would cry, " Go, my children. Justice shall be done to all of you," and we moved on to another village. It was very pleasant seeing the patriarchal relations between the Commissioner and the villagers. He understood them and their customs thoroughly ; they trusted him and loved him as their official father,

I fancy that this type of Indian Civil servant, knowing the people he has to deal with down to the very marrow of their bones, has become rarer of late years. The Brahmin clerk was a very intelligent man, and spoke English admirably, but I took a great dislike to him, noting the abject way in which the natives fawned on him. Colonel Erskine had to discharge him soon afterwards, as he found that he had been exploiting the villagers mercilessly for years, taking bribes right and left. From much experience Colonel Erskine was an adept at travelling with what he termed "a light camp." He took with him a portable office-desk, a bookcase with a small reference library, and two portable arm-chairs. All these were carried in addition to our baggage and bedding on coolies' heads, for our sleeping-places were seldom more than fifteen miles apart.

The Commissioner's old Khansama had very strict ideas as to how a "Sahib's" dinner should be served. He insisted on decorating the table with rhododendron flowers, and placing on it every night four dishes of Moradabad metal work containing respectively six figs, six French plums, six dates, and six biscuits, all reposing on the orthodox lace-paper mats, and the moment dinner was over he carefully replaced these in pickle-jars for use next evening. We would have broken his heart had we spoiled the symmetry of his dishes by eating any of these. It takes a little practice to master bills-of-fare written in "Kitmutgar English," and for

" Irishishtew" and " Anchoto " to be resolved into Irish-stew and Anchovy-toast. Once when a Viceroy was on tour there was a roast gosling for dinner. This duly appeared on the bill-of-fare as " Roasted goose's pup." In justice, however, we must own that we would make far greater blunders in trying to write a menu in Urdu.

The Kumaon district is beautiful, not unlike an enlarged Scotland, with deep ravines scooped out by clear, rushing rivers, their precipitous sides clothed with dense growths of deodaras. In the early morning the view of the long range of the snowy pinnacles of the Himalayas was splendid. I learnt a great deal from wise old Colonel Erskine with his intimate knowledge of the workings of the native mind, and of the psychology of the Oriental.

There is something very touching in the fidelity of Indian native servants to their employers. Lady Lansdowne returned to India eighteen years after leaving it, for the marriage of her son (who was killed in the first three months of the war) to Lord Minto's daughter, and I accompanied her. One afternoon all the pensioned Government House servants who had been in Lord Lansdowne's employment arrived in a body to offer their " salaams" to my sister. They presented a very different appearance to the resplendent beings in scarlet and gold whom I had formerly known, for on taking their pension they had ceased troubling to dye their beards, and they were merely dressed in plain white cotton. These grey-bearded, tooth-less old men with their high, aquiline features (they were nearly all Mahomedans), flowing white garments and turbans, might have stepped bodily out of stained-glass windows. They had brought with them all the little presents (principally watches) which my sister had given them ; they remembered all the berths she had secured for their sons, and the letters she had written on their behalf. An Oriental has a very long memory for a kindness as well as for an injury done him. Lady Lansdowne, whose Hindustani had become rather rusty, began feverishly turning over the pages of a dictionary in an endeavour to express her feelings and the pleasure she experienced in seeing these faithful retainers again : she wept, and the old men wept, and we all agreed, as elderly people will, that in former days the sun was brighter and life altogether rosier than in these degenerate times. Before leaving, the old servants simultaneously lifted their arms in the Mahomedan gesture of blessing, with all the innate dignity of the Oriental ; it was really a very touching sight, nor do I think that the very substantial memento of their visit which each of them received had anything to do with their attitude : they only wished to show that they were " faithful to their salt."

It is difficult to determine the age of a native, as wrinkles and lines do not show on a dark skin. Dark skins have other advantages. One of the European Examiners of Calcutta University told me that there had been great trouble about the examination-papers. By some means the native students always managed to obtain what we may term "advance" copies of these papers. My informant devised a scheme to stop this leakage. Instead of having the papers printed in the usual fashion, he called in the services of a single white printer on whom he could absolutely rely. The white printer had the papers handed to him early on the morning of the examination day, and he duly set them up on a hand-press in the building itself. The printer had one assistant, a coolie clad only in loin-cloth and turban, and every time the coolie left the room he was made to remove both his loin-cloth and turban, so that by no possibility could he have any papers concealed about him. In spite of these precautions, it was clear from internal evidence that some of the students had had a previous knowledge of the questions. How had it been managed? It eventually appeared that the coolie, taking advantage of the momentary absence of the white printer, had whipped off his loin-cloth, *sat down on the "form,"* and then replaced his solitary garment. When made to strip on going out, the printing-ink did not show on his dark skin: he had only to sit down elsewhere on a large sheet of white paper for the questions to be printed off on it, and they could then easily be read in a mirror. The Oriental mind is very subtle.

This is no place to speak of the marvels of Mogul architecture in Agra and Delhi. I do not believe that there exists in the world a more exquisitely beautiful hall than the Diwan-i-Khas in Delhi palace. This hall, open on one side to a garden, is entirely built of transparent white marble inlaid with precious stones, and with its intricate gilded ceilings, and wonderful pierced-marble screens it justifies the famous Persian inscription that runs round it :

> " If heaven can be on the face of the earth,
> It is this, it is this, it is this."

I always regret that Shah Jehan did not carry out his original intention of erecting a second Taj of black marble for himself at Agra, opposite the wonderful tomb he built for his beloved Muntaz-i-Mahal ; probably the money ran out. Few people take in that the dome of the Taj, that great airy white soap-bubble, is actually higher than the dome of St. Paul's. The play of fancy and invention of Shah Jehan's architects seems inexhaustible. All the exquisite white marble pavilions of Agra palace differ absolutely both in design and decoration, and Akbar's massive red sandstone buildings make the most perfect foil to them that could be conceived.

Lucknow is one of the pleasantest stations in India, with its ring of encircling parks, and the broad, tree-shaded roads of its cantonments, but the pretentious monuments with which the city is studded will not bear examination after the wonders of Agra and Delhi. The King of Oude wished to surpass the Mogul Emperors by the magnificence of his buildings, but he wished, too, to do it on the cheap. So in Lucknow stucco, with very debased details, replaces the stately red sandstone and marble of the older cities.

In 1890 after a long day's sight-seeing in Lucknow, in the course of which we ascended the long exterior flight of steps of the Great Imambarah on an elephant (who proved himself as nimble as a German waiter in going upstairs), Lady Lansdowne and I were taken to the Husainabad just as the short-lived Indian twilight was falling. On passing through its great gateway I thought that I had never in my life seen anything so beautiful. At the end of a long white marble-paved court, a stately black-and-white marble tomb with a gilded dome rose from a flight of steps. Down the centre of the court ran a long pool of clear water, surrounded by a gilded railing. On either side of the court stood great clumps of flowering shrubs, also enclosed in gilded railings. At the far end, a group of palms were outlined in jet black against that vivid lemon-coloured afterglow only seen in hot countries; peacocks, perched on the walls of the court, stood out duskily purple against the glowing expanse of saffron sky, and the sleeping waters of the long pool reflected the golden glory of the flaming vault above them.

In the hush of the evening, and the half-light, the scene was lovely beyond description, and for eighteen years I treasured in my mind the memory of the Husainabad at sunset as the vision of my life.

On returning to Lucknow in 1906, I insisted on
going at once to revisit the Husainabad, though
I was warned that there was nothing to see there.
Alas! in broad daylight and in the glare of the
fierce sun the whole place looked abominably
tawdry. What I had taken for black-and-white
marble was only painted stucco, and coarsely daubed
at that; the details of the decoration were deplor-
able, and the Husainabad was just a piece of showy,
meretricious tinsel. The gathering dusk and the
golden expanse of the Indian sunset sky had by
some subtle wizardry thrown a veil of glamour
over this poor travesty of the marvels of Delhi and
Agra. So a long-cherished ideal was hopelessly
shattered, which is always a melancholy thing.

We are all slaves to the economic conditions
under which we live, and the present exorbitant
price of paper is a very potent factor in the making
of books. I am warned by my heartless publishers
that I have already exceeded my limits. There
are many things in India of which I would speak:
of big-game hunts in Assam; of near views of the
mighty snows of the Himalayas; of jugglers and
their tricks, and of certain unfamiliar aspects of
native life. The telling of these must be reserved
for another occasion, for it is impossible in the brief
compass of a single chapter to do more than touch
the surface of things in the vast Empire, the origin
of whose history is lost in the mists of time.

CHAPTER XI

I HAD hoped to tell of reef-fishing in the West
Indies; of surf-riding on planks at Muizenberg in
South Africa; of the extreme inconvenience to
which the inhabitants of Southern China are subjected owing to the inconsiderate habits of their
local devils; of sapphire seas where coco-nut
palms toss their fronds in the Trade wind over
gleaming-white coral beaches; of vast frozen tracts
in the Far North where all animate life seems
suspended; of Japanese villages clinging to green
hill-sides where boiling springs gush out of the
cliffs in clouds of steam, and of many other things
besides, for it has been my good fortune to have
seen most of the surface of this globe. But all
these must wait until the present preposterous
price of paper has descended to more normal levels.

I consider myself exceptionally fortunate in
having lived at a time when modern conveniences
of transport were already in existence, but had not
yet produced their inevitable results. It is quite

sufficiently obvious that national customs and national peculiarities are being smoothed out of existence by facilities of travel. My father and mother, early in their married life, drove from London to Naples in their own carriage, the journey occupying over a month. They left their own front door in London, had their carriage placed on the deck of the Channel steamer, sat in it during the passage (what a singularly uncomfortable resting-place it must have been should they have encountered bad weather!), and continued their journey on the other side. During their leisurely progress through France and Italy, they must have enjoyed opportunities of studying the real life of these countries which are denied the passengers in a *rapide*, jammed in amongst a cosmopolitan crew in the prosaic atmosphere of dining and sleeping cars, and scarcely bestowing a passing glance on the country through which they are being whirled. Even in my time I have seen marked changes, and have witnessed the gradual disappearance of national costumes, and of national types of architecture. Every capital in Europe seems to adopt in its modern buildings a standardised type of architecture. No sojourner in any of the big modern hotels, which bear such a wearisome family likeness to each other, could tell in which particular country he might happen to find himself, were it not for the scraps of conversation which reach his ears, for the externals all look alike, and even the cooking has, with a greater or less degree of success, been standardised to the requisite note of monotony. Travellers may be divided into two categories: those who wish to find on foreign soil the identical conditions to which they have been accustomed at home, and those searching for novelty of outlook and novelty of surroundings. The former will welcome the process of planing down national idiosyncrasies into one dead level of uniformity of type, the latter will deplore it; but this, like many other things, is a matter of individual taste.

The ousting of the splendid full-rigged ships by stumpy, unlovely tramp-steamers in the Hooghly River, to which I have already referred, is only one example of the universal disappearance of the picturesque. In twenty-five years' time, every one will be living in a drab-coloured, utilitarian world, from which most of the beauty and every scrap of local colour will have been successfully eliminated. I am lucky in having seen some of it.

I have also witnessed great changes in social habits. I do not refer so much to the removal of the rigid lines of demarcation formerly prevailing in English Society, as to the disappearance of certain accepted standards. For instance, in my young days the possibility of appearing in Piccadilly in anything but a high hat and a tail coat was unthinkable, as was the idea of sitting down to dinner in anything but a white tie. Modern usage has common sense distinctly on its side. Again, in my youth the old drinking customs lingered, especially at the Universities. Though personally

I have never been able to extract the faintest gratification from the undue consumption of alcohol, my friends do not seem to have invariably shared my tastes. I am certain of one thing : it is to the cigarette that the temperate habits of the twentieth century are due. Nicotine knocked port and claret out in the second round. The acclimatisation of the cigarette in England only dates from the "seventies." As a child I remember that the only form of tobacco indulged in by the people that I knew was the cigar. A cigarette was considered an effeminate foreign importation ; a pipe was unspeakably vulgar.

In my mother's young days before her marriage, the old hard-drinking habits of the Regency and of the eighteenth century still persisted. At Woburn Abbey it was the custom for the trusted old family butler to make his nightly report to my grandmother in the drawing-room. "The gentlemen have had a good deal to-night ; it might be as well for the young ladies to retire," or "The gentlemen have had very little to-night," was announced according to circumstances by this faithful family retainer. Should the young girls be packed off upstairs, they liked standing on an upper gallery of the staircase to watch the shouting, riotous crowd issuing from the dining-room. My father very rarely touched wine, and I believe that it was the fact that he, then an Oxford undergraduate, was the only sober young man amongst the rowdy troop of roysterers that first drew my mother to him, though he had already proposed marriage to her at a children's party given by the Prince Regent at Carlton House, when they were respectively seven and six years old. My father had succeeded to the title at the age of six, and they were married as soon as he came of age. They lived to celebrate their golden wedding, which two of my sisters, the late Duchess of Buccleuch and Lady Lansdowne, were also fortunate enough to do, and I can say with perfect truth that in all three instances my mother and her daughters celebrated fifty years of perfect happiness, unclouded save for the gaps which death had made amongst their children.

Students of Pepys' Diary must have gasped with amazement at learning of the prodigious quantities of food considered necessary in the seventeenth century for a dinner of a dozen people. Samuel Pepys gives us several accounts of his entertainments, varying, with a nice sense of discrimination, the epithet with which he labels his dinners. Here is one which he gave to ten people, in 1660, which he proudly terms "a very fine dinner." " A dish of marrow-bones; a leg of mutton; a loin of veal; a dish of fowl; three pullets, and two dozen of larks, all in a dish; a great tart; a neat's tongue; a dish of anchovies; a dish of prawns, and cheese." On another occasion, in 1662, Pepys having four guests only, merely gave them what he modestly describes as "a pretty dinner." "A brace of stewed carps; six roasted chickens; a jowl of salmon; a tanzy; two neats' tongues, and cheese." For six distinguished guests in 1663 he provided "a noble dinner." (I like this careful grading of epithets.) "Oysters ; a hash of rabbits ; a lamb, and a rare chine of beef. Next a great dish of roasted fowl cost me about thirty shillings ; a tart, fruit and cheese." Pepys anxiously hopes that this was enough ! One is pleased to learn that on all three occasions his guests enjoyed themselves, and that they were "very merry," but however did they manage to hold one quarter of this prodigious amount of food ?

The curious idea that hospitality entailed the proffering of four times the amount of food that an average person could assimilate, persisted throughout the eighteenth century and well into the "seventies" of the nineteenth century. I remember as a child, on the rare occasions when I was allowed to "sit up" for dinner, how interminable that repast seemed. That may have been due to the fact that my brother and I were forbidden to eat anything except a biscuit or two. The idea that human beings required perpetual nourishment was so deep-grounded that, to the end of my father's life, the "wine and water tray" was brought in nightly before the ladies went to bed. This tray contained port, sherry and claret, a silver kettle of hot water, sugar, lemons and nutmeg, as well as two large plates of sandwiches. All the ladies devoured wholly superfluous sandwiches, and took a glass of wine and hot water before retiring. I think people would be surprised to find how excellent a beverage the obsolete "negus" is. Let them try a glass of either port, sherry, or claret, with hot water, sugar, a squeeze of lemon, and a dusting of nutmeg, and I think that they will agree with me.

A custom, I believe, peculiar to our family, was the burning of church incense in the rooms after dinner. At the conclusion of dinner, the groom-of-the-chambers walked round the dining-room, solemnly swinging a large silver censer. This dignified thurifer then made the circuit of the other rooms, plying his censer. From the conscientious manner in which he fulfilled his task, I fear that an Ecclesiastical Court might have found that this came under the heading of "incense used ceremonially."

My father had one peculiarity; he never altered his manner of living, whether the house was full of visitors, or he were alone with my mother, after his children had married and left him. At Baron's Court, when quite by themselves, they used the large rooms, and had them all lighted up at night, exactly as though the house was full of guests. There was to my mind something very touching in seeing an aged couple, after more than fifty years of married life together, still preserving the affectionate relations of lovers with each other. They played their chess together nightly in a room ninety-eight feet long, and delighted in still singing together, in the quavering tones of old age, the simple little Italian duets that they had sung in the far-off days of their courtship. As his years increased, my father did not care to venture much beyond the circle of his own family, though as thirteen of his children had grown up, and he had seven married daughters, the two elder of whom had each thirteen children of her own, the number of his immediate descendants afforded him a fairly wide field of selection. In his old age he liked to have his five sons round him all the winter, together with their wives and children. Accordingly, every October my three married brothers arrived at Baron's Court with their entire families, and remained there till January, so that the house persistently rang with children's laughter. What with governesses, children, nurses and servants, this meant thirty-three extra people all through the winter, so it was fortunate that Baron's Court was a large house, and that there was plenty of room left for other visitors. It entailed no great hardship on the sons, for the autumn salmon-fishing in the turbulent Mourne is excellent, there was abundance of shooting, and M. Gouffé, the cook, was a noted artist.

Both my father and mother detested publicity, or anything in the nature of self-advertisement, which only shows how hopelessly out of touch they would have been with modern conditions.

My father was also old-fashioned enough to read family prayers every morning and every Sunday evening; he was very particular, too, about Sunday observance, now almost fallen into desuetude, so neither the thud of lawn-tennis racquets nor the click of billiard-balls were ever heard on that day, and no one would have dreamed of playing cards on a Sunday.

It would be difficult to convey any idea of the pleasant family life in that isolated spot tucked away amongst the Tyrone mountains; of the long tramps over the bogs after duck and snipe; of the struggles with big salmon; of the sailing-matches on the lakes; of the grouse and the woodcocks; of the theatrical performances, the fun and jollity, and all the varied incidents which make country life so fascinating to those brought up to it.

It was the custom at Baron's Court to have two annual dances in the barn to celebrate " Harvest Home " and Christmas, and to these dances my father, and my brother after him, invited every single person in their employ, and all the neighbouring farmers and their wives. Any one hoping to shine at a barn-dance required exceptionally sound muscles, for the dancing was quite a serious business. The so-called barn was really a long granary, elaborately decorated with wreaths of evergreens, flags, and mottoes. The proceedings invariably commenced with a dance (peculiar, I think, to the north of Ireland) known as " Haste to the Wedding." It is a country dance, but its peculiarity lies in the fact that instead of the couples standing motionless opposite to one another, they are expected to " set to each other," and to keep on doing steps without intermission; all this being, I imagine, typical of the intense eagerness every one was supposed to express to reach the scene of the wedding festivities as quickly as possible. Twenty minutes of "Haste to the Wedding" are warranted to exhaust the stoutest leg-muscles. My mother always led off with the farm-bailiff as partner, my father at the other end dancing with the bailiff's wife. Both my father, and my brother after him, were very careful always to wear their Garter as well as their other Orders on these occasions, in order to show respect to their guests. Scotch reels and Irish jigs alternated with "The Triumph," "Flowers of Edinburgh," and other country dances, until feet and legs refused their office ; and still the fiddles scraped, and feet, light or heavy, belaboured the floor till 6 a.m. The supper would hardly have come up to London standards, for instead of light airy nothings, huge joints of roast and boiled were aligned down the tables. Some of the stricter Presbyterians, though fond of a dance, experienced conscientious qualms about it. So they struck an ingenious compromise with their consciences by dancing vigorously whilst assuming an air of intense misery, as though they were undergoing some terrible penance. Every one present enjoyed these barn-dances enormously.

My father was an admirable speaker of the old-fashioned school, with calculated pauses, an unusual felicity in the choice of his epithets, and a considerable amount of gesticulation. The veteran Lord Chaplin is the last living exponent of this type of oratory. Although my father prepared his speeches very carefully indeed, he never made a single written note. He had a beautiful speaking voice and a prodigious memory; this memory, he knew from experience, would not fail him. An excellent shot himself both with gun and rifle, and a good fisherman, to the end of his life he maintained his interest in sport and in all the pursuits of the younger life around him, for he was very human.

It is difficult for a son to write impartially of his mother. My mother's character was a blend of extreme simplicity and great dignity, with a limitless gift of sympathy for others. I can say with perfect truth that, throughout her life, she succeeded in winning the deep love of all those who were brought into constant contact with her. Very early in life she fell under the influence of the Evangelical movement, which was then stirring England to its depths, and she throughout her days remained faithful to its tenets. It could be said of her that, though in the world, she was not of the world. Owing to force of circumstances, she had at times to take her position in the world, and no one could do it with greater dignity, or more winning grace; but the atmosphere of London, both physical and social, was distasteful to her. She had an idea that the smoke-laden London air affected her lungs, and, apart from the pleasure of seeing the survivors of the very intimate circle of friends of her young days,

London had few attractions for her; all her interests were centred in the country, in country people, and country things. Although deeply religious, her religion had no gloom about it, for her inextinguishable love of a joke, and irrepressible sense of fun, remained with her to the end of her life, and kept her young in spite of her ninety-three years. From the commencement of her married life, my mother had been in the habit of "visiting" in the village twice a week, and in every cottage she was welcomed as a friend, for in addition to her gift of sympathy, she had a memory almost as tenacious as my father's, and remembered the names of every one of the cottagers' children, knew where they were employed, and whom they had married. With the help of her maid, my mother used to compound a cordial, bottles of which she distributed amongst the cottagers, a cordial which gained an immense local reputation. The ingredients of this panacea were one part of strong iron-water to five parts of old whisky, to which sal-volatile, red lavender, cardamoms, ginger and other warming drugs were added. "Her Grace's bottle," as it was invariably termed, achieved astonishing popularity, and the most marvellous cures were ascribed to it. I have sometimes wondered whether its vogue would have been as great had the whisky been eliminated from its composition. In her home under the Sussex downs, amidst the broad stretches of heather-clad common, the beautiful Tudor stone-built old farm-houses, and the undulating woodlands of that most lovable and typically English county, she continued, to the end of her life, visiting amongst her less fortunate neighbours, and finding friends in every house. Her immense vitality and power of entering into the sorrows and enjoyments of others, led at times to developments very unexpected in the case of one so aged. For instance, a small great-nephew of mine had had a pair of stilts given him. The boy was clumsy at learning to use them, and my mother, who in her youth could perform every species of trick upon stilts, was discovered by her trained nurse mounted on stilts and perambulating the garden on them, in her eighty-sixth year, for the better instruction of her little great-grandson. Again, during a great rat-hunt we had organised, the nurse missed her ninety-year-old charge, to discover her later, in company with the stable-boy, behind a barn, both of them armed with sticks, intently watching a rat-hole into which the stable-boy had just inserted a ferret.

My mother travelled up to London on one occasion to consult a celebrated oculist, and confided to him that she was growing apprehensive about her eyesight, as she began to find it difficult to read small print by lamplight. The man of Harley Street, after a careful examination of his patient's eyes, asked whether he might inquire what her age was. On receiving the reply that she had been ninety on her last birthday, the specialist assured her that his experience led him to believe that cases of failing eyesight were by no means unusual at that age.

My mother had known all the great characters that had flitted across the European stage at the beginning of the nineteenth century: Talleyrand, Metternich, the great Duke of Wellington, and many others. With her wonderful memory, she was a treasure-house of anecdotes of these and other well-known personages, which she narrated with all the skill of the born *raconteuse*. She belonged, too, to an age in which letter-writing was cultivated as an art, and was regarded as an intellectual relaxation. At the time of her death she had one hundred and sixty nine direct living descendants: children, grandchildren, great-grand-children, and great-great-grandchildren, in addition to thirty-seven grandchildren and great-grand-children by marriage. She kept in touch with all her descendants by habitually corresponding with them, and the advice given by this shrewd, wise old counsellor, with her ninety years of experience, was invariably followed by its recipients. She made a point of travelling to London to attend the weddings of every one of her descendants, and even journeyed up to be present at the Coronation of King Edward in her ninetieth year. It is given to but few to see their *grandson's grandson ;* it is granted to fewer to live ninety-three years with the full use of every intellectual faculty, and the retention of but slightly impaired bodily powers; and seldom is it possible to live to so great an age with the powers of enjoyment and of unabated interest in the lives of others still retained.

She never returned to Ireland after her widowhood, but was able, up to the end of her life, to pay a yearly autumn visit to her beloved Scotland. And so, under the rolling Sussex downs, amidst familiar woodlands and villages, full of years, and surrounded by the love of all those who knew her, the long day closed.

I think that there is a passage in the thirty-first chapter of Proverbs which says: " Her children rise up and call her blessed."

I have reached my appointed limits, leaving unsaid one-half of the things I had wished to narrate. Reminiscences come crowding in unbidden, and, like the flickering lights of the Will-o'-the-wisp, they tend to lead the wayfarer far astray from the path he had originally traced out for himself. " Jack-o'-lanthorn " is proverbially a fickle guide to follow, and should I have succumbed to his lure, I can only proffer my excuses, and plead in extenuation that sixty years is such a long road to re-travel that an occasional deviation into a by-path by elderly feet may perhaps be forgiven.

Charles Kingsley, in the *Water-Babies*, has put some very touching lines into the mouth of the old school-dame in Vendale, lines which come home with pathetic force to persons of my time of life:—

THE DAYS BEFORE YESTERDAY

" When all the world is young, lad,
    And all the trees are green;
And every goose a swan, lad,
    And every lass a queen;
Then hey for boot and horse, lad,
    And round the world away;
Young blood must have its course, lad,
    And every dog his day.

" When all the world is old, lad,
    And all the trees are brown;
And all the sport is stale, lad,
    And all the wheels run down;
Creep home, and take your place there,
    The old and spent among :
God grant you find one face there
    You loved when all was young."

I protest indignantly against the idea that all the wheels are run down; nor are the trees yet brown, for kindly autumn, to soften us to the inevitable passing of summer, touches the trees with her magic wand, and forthwith they blaze with crimson and russet-gold, pale-gold, and flaming copper-red.

In the mellow golden sunshine of the still October days it is sometimes difficult to realise that the glory of the year has passed beyond recall, though the sunshine has no longer the genial warmth of July, and the more delicate flowers are already shrivelled by the first furtive touches of winter's finger-tips. Experience has taught us that the many-hued glory of autumn is short-lived; the faintest breeze brings the leaves fluttering to the ground in golden showers. Soon the few that remain will patter gently down to earth, their mother. Winter comes.

INDEX

A

B

INDEX

INDEX

D

Daudet, M., 126

David, M., post-master of Nyons, his voluminous official instructions, 152

Davin, Mr. Nicholas Flood, curious peroration of, in Ottawa House of Commons, 267–268

Delhi, 316

Des Cars, Duc, 48

Devonshire, Duchess of, 259; *see also* Manchester, Duchess of

De Witt, his paintings at Glamis Castle, 246

Disraeli, Mr., 16, 18, 210, 215, 266

Dublin Castle, drawing-rooms and entertainments at, 77 *et seq.*; the Chapel Royal, 80–81

Dublin Zoological Gardens, the, 68

Ducros, Mme., 124 *et seq.*

Ducros, Mlle. Louise, 133, 134

Ducros, M., 124 *et seq.*; 155

Dudley, Georgiana, Lady 194,

Dufferin, Lord, 249, 254, 266, 285

Duncan, Emily, 196

Dunn, Chief Inspector, 86

Durham, Lord, 1

E

Edward, King. *See* Prince of Wales

Eglinton Tournament, 1839, the, 45

Eighteenth - century prodigal hospitality, 324

Elphinstone, Lord, 52

Emperor of Austria at Schönbrunn, 41

Empress Eugénie, 44

Empress Marie Louise, 40, 41

English and German commercial travellers compared, 174

English Society, changes of custom in, 321

Erskine, Colonel, 309 *et seq.*

Erskine, Sir David, Serjeant-at-Arms of the House of Commons, 52, 56, 57

Examination papers, and a curious printing press, 315

F

Fairchild Family, The, orthodox Sunday reading, 33–34

Faning, Mr. Eaton, and Harrow school songs, 113

Farmer, John, and Harrow school songs, 111–114, 123

Farren, Nellie, 196

Fenian rebellion of 1866, 75, 86

Flahault, Comte de, 39, 40

Flahault, Comtesse de, 39

Forbes, Helen, Lady, 194

Forbes-Robertson, Sir Johnston, 160–161

Forêt d'Aiguebelle, the, Trappist Monastery at, 146

Four Hamilton brothers in 1885 Parliament, 210

Fremantle, Admiral Sir Edmund, 301

French, Lord, 80

French legal procedure, 134; a logical people, 145

G

Garrotting in the " sixties," 4

Gätke, Prof., at Heligoland, 190

George III., 31

George IV., 31

German beer, 177–178

German travellers representing English firms, 174

INDEX

INDEX

INDEX

INDEX

INDEX

PRINTED IN GREAT BRITAIN BY RICHARD CLAY & SONS, LIMITED, BRUNSWICK ST., STAMFORD ST., S.E. 1, AND BUNGAY, SUFFOLK.